Eisenhower and the
Anti-Communist Crusade

EISEN★HOWER

& the Anti-Communist Crusade

Jeff Broadwater

The University of North Carolina Press

Chapel Hill and London

The paper in this book meets the guidelines for permanence and durability of the Committee on Production Guidelines for Book Longevity of the Council on Library Resources.

96   95   94   93   92   5   4   3   2   1

Library of Congress Cataloging-in-Publication Data

Broadwater, Jeff.
    Eisenhower and the anti-communist crusade / by Jeff Broadwater.
        p.   cm.
    Includes bibliographical references and index.
    ISBN 0-8078-2015-6 (alk. paper)
    1. Eisenhower, Dwight D. (Dwight David), 1896–
1969.   2. Anti-communist movements—United States—
History—20th century.   3. Communism—United States—
1917–   4. United States—Politics and government—1953–
1961.   I. Title.
E836.B75   1992
973.921′092—dc20   91-32011
                                                 CIP

Portions of chapter 2 appeared earlier, in somewhat different form, in "Communism and the Great Crusade: Internal Security and the Presidential Election of 1952," *The Maryland Historian* 20 (Fall/Winter 1989): 40–53, and are reprinted here with permission of the journal. The John Foster Dulles Papers, the Emmet J. Hughes Papers, the Paul D. Tillet, Jr., Papers, the Allen W. Dulles Papers, and the John Foster Dulles Oral History Collection were used with the permission of the Princeton University Libraries.

For Dewey W. Grantham

Contents

Illustrations

Preface

Everyone who mattered in postwar America abhorred communism. In that, the era was not unique. What distinguished the late 1940s and early 1950s from other periods in twentieth-century American history was an especially pernicious brand of "anticommunism." More than an intellectual rejection of Soviet-style socialism, postwar anticommunism, as I have used the term, contained at least two essential elements. First, it embraced an exaggerated and unhealthy fear of Communist-inspired internal subversion. The political radical represented more than simply a nuisance; he or she posed a real threat to the American way of life, although it was sometimes unclear how or why. From such anxieties flowed the second, critical element of contemporary anticommunism—the conviction that the subversive threat was so real, and so malignant, that it justified trampling on traditional freedoms and individual rights in the interests of internal security. Many Americans had long held such notions; by the late 1940s, their views seemed to be more widely accepted, and more deeply felt, than ever before in the nation's history.

My definition makes no reference to the career of Joseph R. McCarthy—anticommunism represented much more than the reckless charges of one irresponsible politician. Unfortunately, McCarthyism, narrowly defined to focus on the antics of the Wisconsin Republican, has largely dominated thinking about the Communist controversy during the Eisenhower years. That tendency has usually not benefited Dwight Eisenhower's reputation. Beyond question, President Eisenhower's handling of McCarthy fails to inspire great admiration, but it could have been worse. By the spring of 1954, at least, the president had made his hostility to the senator clear. More disturbing was Eisenhower's record elsewhere in the security field—on the federal employee loyalty program, the purge of the Foreign Service, the uncontrolled excesses of J. Edgar Hoover and the Federal Bureau of Investigation. The president's performance on these, and other, issues helps explain why the White House did so little to curb McCarthy. Ike, for all his basic decency, shared with the McCarthyites much of their obsession with internal security and their unconcern for civil liberties.

This is my thesis, but it sketches only in broad outline the contours of the Communist controversy of the 1950s. I have seen, whether or not I have told, a complex story of rich detail and subtle paradox. To cite one example, GOP conservatives, usually McCarthy's staunchest defenders, sometimes stood up against anti-Communist excesses, while Democrats and anti-McCarthy Republicans frequently indulged them. Such apparent inconsistencies do not occur often enough to suggest any particular pattern, but they are common enough to indicate the political complexity of the Communist controversy.

Anyone who undertakes a substantial research project accumulates a number of debts along the way, and I am no exception. At the outset, I must give special thanks to Professors Dewey W. Grantham and Samuel T. McSeveney, who have guided and assisted this endeavor since its inception. Paul K. Conkin, Erwin C. Hargrove, Donald L. Winters, and Cecilia Stiles Cornell also offered their comments on the manuscript.

I am indebted to the individuals who provided the raw material on which this study rests—the staffs of the Dwight D. Eisenhower Library at Abilene, Kansas, of the Laguna Nigel, California, branch of the National Archives, of the Massachusetts Historical Society in Boston, of the Kansas State Historical Society in Topeka, of the Baker Library of Dartmouth College, of the Mudd Library of Princeton University, of the Jean and Alexander Heard Library of Vanderbilt University, of the Oppenheimer Library of the University of Arkansas at Little Rock, and of the Little Rock Public Library. David Haight of the Eisenhower Library and Fred Klose at Laguna Nigel deserve special mention for directing me through the vast collections of documents in their care.

Dani Beasley, who typed the first several drafts, was, to borrow Dwight Eisenhower's assessment of Robert Taft, "a model of cheerful and effective cooperation." Mary Jean Whitehead and Betsy Nash skillfully put the manuscript in final form. Karen Groce assisted with the index.

Essential and greatly appreciated financial assistance was provided by the

Eisenhower Institute for World Affairs through the Graduate School of Vanderbilt University.

Thanks are also due Lewis Bateman and the staff of the University of North Carolina Press, along with copy editor D. Teddy Diggs.

Finally, my wife, Rhonda, helped in many different ways, which no acknowledgment can hope to repay.

Eisenhower and the
Anti-Communist Crusade

★ ★ ★

Red Menace or Red Herring?

General Eisenhower, American Politics,

and the Cold War

When Dwight D. Eisenhower entered the White House in January 1953, he inherited a controversy over domestic subversion that had been brewing since the end of World War II. Ironically, public concern about domestic communism had reached its height at a time when Communist influence in American society was rapidly declining. No longer did American Communists enjoy the tolerance that they had been granted in the decade before 1945. With the apparent failure of capitalism during the Great Depression, Marxist ideas had won at least the temporary allegiance of many American intellectuals. After the Kremlin softened its appeals for world revolution in 1935 in order to form a Popular Front of liberals and leftist forces against fascism, American Communists commanded a newfound measure of respectability. Communists wielded considerable influence within the unions of the Congress of Industrial Organizations, including the powerful United Auto Workers (UAW). Communists organized cells within the State Department and other important government agencies. By the time of the signing of the German-Soviet Non-Aggression Pact of 1939, Communist party membership in the United States had risen to approximately eighty thousand. Nevertheless, with the return of prosperity in the early 1940s and the outbreak of the cold war at the end of World War II, American communism soon fell on hard times. The election of a militant anti-Communist, Walter P. Reuther, as president of the UAW in

Dwight David Eisenhower, Thirty-fourth President
of the United States. (Eisenhower Library)

1946 signaled a march away from communism by the mainstream of the American labor movement. In his two terms as president, Harry S. Truman oversaw the dismissal from government employment of hundreds of suspected Communists, fellow travelers, and "loyalty risks." By 1954, Wisconsin Senator Joseph R. McCarthy, never one to minimize the extent of the Red menace to America, estimated the number of Communists in the United States at no more than roughly twenty-five thousand. In retrospect, the government's existing counterintelligence apparatus seems to have been perfectly capable of protecting American national interests against domestic subversion.[1]

If, however, the Communist controversy had become much ado about very little when Dwight Eisenhower took office, it remained a political reality that his administration could hardly be expected to ignore. Fully to appreciate the nature of the issue that confronted the incoming president requires at least a cursory review of the Red Scare as it unfolded in the years preceding General Eisenhower's election. Moreover, Eisenhower's reaction, as a general and as a college president, to the early stages of the anti-Communist crusade suggests the dilemma that the Communist controversy would pose for him once he entered the political arena. To these themes, we must now turn.

Given the country's traditional hostility toward radical political ideologies of foreign origins, as manifested by the Alien and Sedition Acts of the 1790s and A. Mitchell Palmer's raids after World War I, the United States never offered a particularly fertile field for a proletarian revolution.[2] Indeed, the reforms of Franklin D. Roosevelt's New Deal, now so widely accepted as a part of American life, were in their day attacked from the right as a menace to traditional American values like democracy and free enterprise. Conservative critics of the Roosevelt administration often drew little distinction between liberalism, socialism, and communism. The attempt to link New Deal liberalism with foreign radicalism became a favorite ploy of Republican politicians, but they never wholly monopolized the theme of Communist subversion of American institutions. In fact, what might be called the modern era of congressional red-baiting began under the leadership of a southern Democrat, Martin Dies of Texas, who in 1938 became the chairman of the newly created House Committee on Un-American Activities (HCUA).[3]

America's wartime alliance with the Soviet Union muted, but did not erase, the nation's historical antipathy to the socialism, atheism, and centralization of political power that Americans associated with the Soviet system. The popularity of William L. White's anti-Soviet *Report on the Russians* (1945), for example, attested to the survival of a latent American hostility to political radicalism throughout the war years. Among conservative intellectuals, the hierarchy of the Roman Catholic church, and Americans of East European descent, a virulent anticommunism persisted.[4]

Increasing tensions between the United States and the Soviet Union after the defeat of Nazi Germany created a political climate conducive to a surge of anti-Communist hysteria. The public had cause for a reasonable concern about America's internal security. Even before the end of the war, in February 1945, the Federal Bureau of Investigation (FBI) arrested six individuals, including the veteran diplomat John Stewart Service, when it discovered that classified documents had been leaked to a left-wing magazine, *Amerasia*. Service was no spy, and the *Amerasia* case proved to be a minor breach of American security, but it obviously suggested weaknesses in the State Department's security system. More ominously, the Canadian government announced early in 1946 that Igor Gouzenko, a clerk in the Soviet Embassy in Ottawa, had revealed the existence of a widespread Russian spy network in that country. Its Canadian agents had apparently supplied the Soviet Union with secret information critical to the development of radar and, more important, atomic weapons. In one of the biggest spy cases of the century, Gouzenko's revelations triggered a chain of investigations that eventually led to the arrests of Klaus Fuchs in England and Harry Gold and Julius and Ethel Rosenberg in the United States.[5]

Yet at the core of the postwar Red Scare was not a fear of Russian espionage but the specter of Communist influence at the policy-making levels of American government. During the tense years of the early cold war, Americans seemed to fear communism as an ideology, and its acceptance within the institutions of American society, more than they feared Soviet sabotage of their country's military defenses.[6] To the most fervid anti-Communists, for example, the agreements reached between Franklin Roosevelt and Soviet Premier Joseph Stalin at the Yalta Conference near the end of World War II far overshadowed the *Amerasia* affair or the Canadian spy case as a betrayal of the interests of the "free world." Many believed that, in the Yalta accords, a feckless FDR had cravenly acquiesced to Soviet expansion in Eastern Europe and the Far East. To those who advocated an "Asia first" foreign policy, the Far Eastern accords reached at Yalta quickly became anathema. This "China Lobby" consisted mainly of midwestern Republicans who had long seen China as a land of virtually unlimited opportunity for American businessmen and missionaries. They balked at any diplomatic move that might undermine the pro-Western Kuomintang government of Nationalist strongman Chiang Kai-shek. The fall of Chiang's regime to Mao Tse-tung's Communists in 1949 convinced many Americans of the almost treasonable failure of American diplomacy. *America's Retreat from Victory* (1951), a well-known polemic issued under the name of Senator McCarthy, ignored the *Amerasia* case and Igor Gouzenko but devoted an entire chapter to "the Yalta sellout."[7]

President Truman's failure to disclose the terms of the Far Eastern accords until January 1946, apparently because of his reluctance to implement them, damaged the new administration's credibility and made the Yalta Conference seem all the more sinister. But revisionist historians go too far in arguing that Truman virtually orchestrated the controversy over domestic communism in order to win support for foreign policy initiatives such as the Truman Doctrine and the Marshall Plan. Athan Theoharis is probably correct in arguing that Truman's warnings about the need to assist American allies in resisting Communist infiltration "heightened popular fears about internal subversion by implying that a numerically small minority could actually rule a hostile majority."[8] Yet it is another matter to suggest that Truman's cold war rhetoric was a primary cause of the widespread and exaggerated concern for internal security that characterized cold war politics. It also seems doubtful that the administration saw domestic communism primarily as a device to stifle opposition to its foreign policy.[9] Such arguments exaggerate the impact of presidential rhetoric and unduly minimize the existence of an anti-Communist consensus that long predated Truman's efforts to rally support for aid to Greece and Turkey.[10]

The Soviet occupation of Eastern Europe proved pivotal in turning public opinion against America's wartime ally.[11] Poland seemed particularly to engage the American consciousness as the cold war mentality developed.[12] Unlike Bulgaria and Romania, Poland had been an early victim, not an accomplice, of Nazi aggression. In May 1945, President Truman dispatched Harry L. Hopkins to Moscow in an attempt to persuade Stalin to permit the inclusion in the pro-Soviet Lublin government then controlling Poland of at least some members of the London-based, pro-American Polish Provisional Government. Stalin was widely believed to have agreed at Yalta to such an arrangement, and Hopkins presented the American case as a public relations problem. Hopkins told Stalin that "two months ago there had been over- whelming support among the American people for the Soviet Union." In the interim, he warned, public sentiment had so markedly changed, largely be- cause of the perception that Stalin had refused to abide by the Yalta agree- ment, as to jeopardize President Truman's ability to continue Franklin D. Roosevelt's conciliatory policies. Hopkins failed to convince Stalin, but there is no evidence that Hopkins's protestations were insincere.[13]

Indeed, Hopkins's representations to Stalin contained more than a germ of truth. Rather than seeking to incite anti-Communist sentiment, as the revi- sionists suggest, the Truman administration soon came under siege for being "soft on communism" both at home and abroad. At the 1946 London Foreign Ministers Conference, Senator Arthur Vandenberg of Michigan, the ranking Republican on the Foreign Relations Committee, expressed his fears that Secretary of State James F. Byrnes was "loitering around Munich" in an effort to appease the Soviets. In March of the same year, Andrew Jackson May of Kentucky, the Democratic chairman of the House Committee on Military Affairs, charged that a number of employees with "strong Soviet leanings" had been forced out of the War Department only to be hired at State. Truman's nomination of David E. Lilienthal, then chairman of the Tennessee Valley Authority (TVA), to be chairman of the Atomic Energy Commission encoun- tered stiff opposition, in large part because Lilienthal was alleged to have tolerated Communist cells at the utility agency.[14]

As Hopkins had suggested to Stalin, the anti-Communist consensus was taking hold among the general public as well as among politicians and jour- nalists. According to the Gallup poll, the percentage of Americans who be- lieved the Soviets could be trusted to cooperate with the United States in the postwar world fell from 54 percent in September 1945 to 35 percent in March 1946. Increasing hostility toward the Soviet Union meant diminishing tolerance for American Communists; a majority of respondents expressing an opinion on the issue believed that domestic Communists owed their principal loyalty to the Kremlin. By the summer of 1946, 56 percent of those surveyed believed American Communists should be executed, imprisoned, or otherwise rendered inactive. Along with the problems of converting the American economy to a peacetime footing, concern about Soviet aggression and domestic subversion aided the Republicans in gaining control of Congress for the first time in a generation. In fact, the 1946 congressional elections marked the first appearance on the national stage of two of America's best-known anti-Communists, California Congressman Richard M. Nixon and Wisconsin Senator Joseph R. McCarthy.[15]

On March 12, 1947, President Truman went before Congress and announced, "It must be the policy of the United States to support free peoples who are resisting attempted subjugation by armed minorities or by outside pressure." Many Americans could agree with Arthur Vandenberg that the Truman Doctrine was "a long-delayed statement" that the nation must support if there was to be "any hope of ever impressing Moscow with the necessity of paying any sort of peaceful attention to [the United States] whatever."[16] Major organs of the American press, along with former President Herbert C. Hoover, had taken up the case of aid to Greece even before Truman's speech.[17] In step with the mood of the country, Truman saw his job approval rating rise from 48 percent before the speech to 60 percent by the end of March. Calling it "a logical development of United States diplomacy," *Time* magazine reported a generally favorable reaction to the speech; "very few seemed shocked, or even particularly surprised" by the president's remarks.[18]

Truman won broad bipartisan support for his efforts to contain communism in Western Europe and the Middle East, but he enjoyed less success in silencing criticism of his ability to combat internal subversion, especially Communist infiltration of the executive branch of the federal government. Pressure had been mounting since Roosevelt's second term to crack down on suspected subversives on the federal payroll. The 1939 Hatch Act had prohibited federal employees from belonging to political parties that advocated "the overthrow of our constitutional form of government." In 1942, as fears about internal security grew after American entry into the Second World War, Attorney

General Francis Biddle created a four-member advisory committee on employee loyalty. Then, on February 5, 1943, President Roosevelt issued Executive Order No. 9300, creating a formal Interdepartmental Committee on Employee Investigations. By March 1947, approximately thirteen hundred individuals had been ruled ineligible for government employment for reasons of questionable loyalty. Shortly after becoming secretary of state in 1945, James F. Byrnes began his own informal, and extralegal, purge. His victims consisted of those employees transferred from other government agencies to the State Department at the end of the war "whose loyalty was doubtful but against whom there was no positive evidence." An amendment to a State Department appropriations bill eventually gave the secretary of state the power to dismiss subordinates summarily.[19] Despite the successive efforts of the Roosevelt and Truman administrations, however, the 1946 congressional elections seemed to demonstrate a growing popular concern about the reliability of the federal work force.

Acting on the heels of the election, Truman, on November 25, 1946, established a Temporary Commission on Loyalty consisting of several high-ranking officials from the Civil Service Commission and the departments of Justice, State, Treasury, War, and Navy. The Temporary Commission's hasty investigation produced little evidence supporting a change in security procedures. Unable to determine just "how far-reaching" the threat of subversion was, the commission embraced the idea that any disloyal employee was a threat to national security, a notion that was neither realistic nor reassuring. Ignoring the advice of Herbert Gaston, who had headed the wartime committee on internal security, that the government concentrate on traditional counterintelligence activities, the commission recommended the creation of a new, more comprehensive loyalty program. The commission's final report, in the words of journalist Robert J. Donovan, laid the groundwork "for some deplorable results for a constitutional democracy."[20]

To forestall more extreme congressional action and perhaps to allay his own concerns about internal security, Truman, on March 21, 1947, issued Executive Order No. 9835, which adopted most of the recommendations of the Temporary Commission.[21] The order mandated the investigation of the loyalty of applicants for government jobs and made department and agency heads "personally responsible" for the loyalty of their employees. It also sought to guard against obvious problems such as espionage and treason as well as against such vague menaces as the "sympathetic association" of federal employees with a wide assortment of "subversive" groups. The program was to be administered by a central Loyalty Review Board (LRB), which would supervise lower-level boards. Attempting to appease his GOP critics, Truman later in the year named Seth Richardson, a popular Republican conservative, to chair the LRB. Originally, a job could be denied to anyone about whom "reasonable grounds" existed to suspect his or her loyalty. In 1951, a subsequent presidential order lowered the government's burden of proof to require a showing only of a "reasonable doubt" about an individual's loyalty. By that time, the government had begun investigating charges of such personal characteristics as alcoholism and homosexuality as well as positive disloyalty.[22]

Attorney and educator Eleanor Bontecou, in a careful study of the Truman program, found no evidence that it ever uncovered a single case of treason, sedition, espionage, sabotage, or even advocacy of the violent overthrow of the U.S. government. Most of the cases she studied involved charges of "sympathetic association" with alleged subversives or with members of organizations identified by the attorney general as subversive. Procedures varied widely from agency to agency, but employees were routinely given little notice of the charges against them, denied the right to face their accusers, who were often paid informants of dubious credibility, and questioned about matters that had little to do with their loyalty—their tastes in music or their views on racial equality, for example. About half the cases appealed from boards were reversed, a fairly high reversal rate for a quasi-judicial body. By March 1952, approximately 380 employees had been dismissed under Executive Order No. 9835, and some 2,500 had resigned under suspicion. Perhaps an additional 200 employees were dismissed under separate programs operated by individual organizations, such as the armed forces, which had their own unique security needs.[23]

Truman's efforts to appear diligent in the battle for internal security went beyond the employee loyalty program. The administration soon began expediting the deportation of foreign radicals and the prosecution of contempt citations against individuals who refused to cooperate with congressional investigating committees. Under Attorney General Tom C. Clark, the Justice Department began publishing a sometimes arbitrarily compiled list of alleged subversive organizations, a kind of de facto government blacklist. Clark also persuaded Truman to allow increased use of electronic surveillance of suspected security risks. To rally popular support for the administration, Clark's successor, J. Howard McGrath, embarked on a national speaking tour to warn Americans of the subversive threat to American security. In 1948, the administration decided to prosecute eleven Communist party leaders for conspiring to overthrow the U.S. government in violation of the 1940 Smith Act. The government won convictions and saw them upheld by the Supreme Court in *Dennis et al.* v. *United States*, over the bitter dissents of Justices Hugo L. Black and William O. Douglas.[24]

Despite a sincere concern for both civil liberties and national security, Truman has received almost uniformly bad marks for his handling of the controversy over domestic subversion, and especially for his employee loyalty program. During Truman's presidency, conservatives attacked the loyalty program as inadequate while civil libertarians like former Attorney General Francis Biddle criticized its lack of procedural safeguards for the imposition of sanctions—the denial of employment and a stigma of disloyalty— comparable to those of the criminal justice system in their severity. More recent observers have echoed earlier complaints about the administration's disregard of fundamental constitutional standards such as the rights to free speech and due process of law. Ironically, many believe the administration's security initiatives served only to increase public apprehension.[25]

Sensitive to the complaints of civil libertarians, President Truman spoke out against McCarthyism and never seemed himself to be caught up in an anti-Communist hysteria. He opposed, for example, special loyalty oaths for schoolteachers. Recognizing that government personnel files often contained unsubstantiated derogatory information, Truman managed, as best he could, to protect the reputation of innocent employees by withholding their records from congressional investigators. When Congress passed the Internal Security Act of 1950, better known as the McCarran Act, requiring the registration of Communists, generally restricting their freedom, and creating a Subversive

Activities Control Board, Truman responded with a stirring veto message that "must rank among the most libertarian presidential documents in American history." After Congress overrode his veto, the president received a measure of vindication when the Supreme Court overturned parts of the act.[26] Plagued, however, by labor unrest, rising prices, and a series of minor scandals, as well as a deteriorating international environment, Truman lacked the political prestige to allay public concern about Communist subversion. It was one area in which he would leave the next president an unfortunate legacy.

The historian Eric F. Goldman has aptly described 1949 as "a year of shock."[27] As 1948 came to a close, Truman appeared to have an opportunity to put to rest the controversy over domestic communism. Thomas E. Dewey, the Republican nominee for president that year, had not exploited the controversy in the fall campaign, suggesting that Republicans might be tiring of the issue. In fact, Truman's victory could be interpreted as a popular endorsement of his handling of the subversive menace.[28] Then a series of events during the first year of Truman's second term revived concerns about American security and provided new ammunition for critics of the administration. First, in January 1949, Chinese Communists finally drove Chiang Kai-shek's decrepit Kuomintang government off the Chinese mainland and onto the island stronghold of Formosa. The "loss" of China came after the United States had spent two billion dollars in aid and credits and over one billion dollars in military equipment, much of it abandoned on the battlefield or sold on the black market. Next, on March 4, the FBI arrested a Justice Department employee, Judith Coplon, for passing FBI files to her boyfriend, the Soviet agent Valentin Gubitchev. Then, on September 23, 1949, President Truman announced that the Soviet Union had exploded its first atomic bomb. With a single explosion, the United States lost it nuclear monopoly, the cornerstone of its cold war defenses.[29]

The nation's woes mounted as spy cases dominated the headlines throughout the first months of 1950. In February, Great Britain announced the arrest of noted scientist Klaus Fuchs for giving atomic secrets to the Russians. Fuchs had worked on the Manhattan Project, and shortly after his arrest, Harry Gold, David Greenglass, and Julius and Ethel Rosenberg were also arrested as atomic spies.[30] More important politically, however, was a less damaging breach of American security—the case of Alger Hiss.

Years later Truman's secretary of state, Dean Acheson, recalled the Hiss case as "something approaching a national disaster, lending, as it did, support to a widespread attack throughout the country upon confidence in government itself."[31] Viewing the outcome of the case differently, Hiss's principal prosecutor, Richard M. Nixon, then a member of the House Committee on Un-American Activities (HCUA), nevertheless also attested to the significance of the Hiss affair. "It was the Hiss case," Nixon has written, "that completely changed the public's perception of domestic communism. People were now alerted to a serious threat to our liberties."[32] And it was the Hiss case that first brought Nixon to national prominence.

In 1948, Whittaker Chambers, an ex-Communist working for *Time* magazine, appeared before HCUA to accuse three former Roosevelt administration officials—Laughlin Currie, Harry Dexter White, and Alger Hiss—of having belonged to the Communist party in the 1930s. Chambers's allegations seemed perfectly specious—Truman denounced them as a "red herring"—until, sometime after Chambers's initial appearance before HCUA, he produced secret State Department documents and microfilm that Hiss had allegedly given him. Hiss vehemently denied Chambers's allegations. Because the statute of limitations on espionage had expired, Hiss was indicted for perjury. After his first trial ended in a hung jury, Hiss was found guilty in January 1950.[33] For conservative critics of the administration, Allen J. Matusow has observed, "it was almost too good to be true." Many Republicans had long charged that the New Deal was communistic; now they could link it to actual subversion.[34]

If one believes the newspaper headlines, the nation seemed to be in a state of near hysteria in February 1950, as a hitherto undistinguished Republican senator, Joseph R. McCarthy, traveled to Wheeling, West Virginia, for a Lincoln Day address to a group of Republican women.[35] At Wheeling, on February 9, the postwar Red Scare gained a new name, McCarthyism, and sank to a new low as the Wisconsin senator told a tale of massive Communist

Congressman Richard M. Nixon reviews a press account of Alger Hiss's conviction
in early 1950. "The Hiss case," Nixon later wrote, "completely changed
the public perception of domestic communism." (UPI/Bettmann Archive)

infiltration of the State Department. "I have in my hand," he is supposed to
have said, "205 cases of individuals who would appear to be either card
carrying members or certainly loyal to the Communist Party, but who nevertheless are still helping to shape our foreign policy." In reality, McCarthy
had no list but simply some outdated information on some possible security
risks. The assumption of guilt by association, the confusing of nonconformity
with disloyalty, and the exploitation of public fears for partisan purposes were
becoming established features of the anti-Communist crusade by the time of
McCarthy's Wheeling speech. Still, he added to it a penchant for wild, spectacular, and almost wholly unsubstantiated charges. Nixon, by contrast, had

made his reputation by meticulously building a case against a single suspect, Alger Hiss.[36]

McCarthyism thrived in the crisis atmosphere of the early cold war. It received a boost in June 1950, when the North Koreans invaded South Korea. For the next two years, McCarthy tormented the Truman administration, the Democratic party, and American liberals with his charges of Communist infiltration of the U.S. government. No one was too obscure or too great to be a target of McCarthy. In June 1951, McCarthy sought to implicate General George C. Marshall, the secretary of defense, in "a conspiracy so immense and an infamy so black as to dwarf any previous such venture in the history of man." McCarthy's attacks probably hastened Marshall's departure from the administration. A less celebrated McCarthy victim was the U.S. minister to Switzerland, John Carter Vincent, one of the State Department's old "China hands." Pressure from McCarthy blocked Vincent's appointment as ambassador to Costa Rica, forced him into virtual exile in the American mission in Tangier, and led to his suspension in December 1952. Although cleared by Secretary of State John Foster Dulles after a series of investigations, Vincent was eventually forced to resign from the foreign service.[37]

On the other hand, the impact of McCarthyism on American politics ought not to be exaggerated. At the height of his influence, Senator McCarthy encountered formidable opposition from the *New York Times*, the *Washington Post*, and the largest newspaper in his home state—the *Milwaukee Journal*. Prominent journalists like Edward R. Murrow, Walter Lippmann, and Drew Pearson emerged as outspoken critics of the excesses of the Wisconsin senator. The prestigious Washington law firm of Arnold and Porter stepped forward to represent China expert Owen Lattimore, a perennial right-wing target. The majority report of the Senate committee appointed to investigate the charges made in McCarthy's Wheeling speech denounced them as "a fraud and a hoax." In 1951, Connecticut Senator William Benton introduced a resolution calling for McCarthy's expulsion from the Senate. Dean Acheson, who considered McCarthy to be "essentially a lazy, small-town bully, without sustaining purpose," later wrote that McCarthy had little real influence on American diplomacy during the Truman years.[38] The White House most often surrendered to McCarthy when it had little reason, other than common decency, to oppose him. These were usually cases involving individuals like John Carter Vincent, who could be sacrificed to appease the McCarthyites. The cumulative effect of such cases inhibited public debate, distracted policymakers from more significant issues, and represented a considerable injustice, but it did not silence all the anti-McCarthyites or constitute a nationwide reign of terror.

Scholars have struggled since the 1950s to understand the source of McCarthy's appeal to seemingly millions of Americans as well as to explain the origins of the broader phenomenon he symbolized. Recent historians have tended to explain McCarthyism within the normal framework of American politics. McCarthyism, they argue, emerged as part of a Republican effort to defeat a Democratic administration and survived after the Republican victory of 1952 only among the GOP's extreme right wing.[39] In particular, the surprising defeat of the moderate Dewey in 1948 encouraged many Republicans to attempt to exploit the Communist controversy. According to Massachusetts Congressman Joseph W. Martin, the Republican leader in the House, Dewey's defeat after sixteen years of Democratic rule reduced the GOP to "dark frustration," discredited party moderates, and paved the way for the rise of McCarthy. Even the normally circumspect Robert A. Taft of Ohio seems to have concluded by 1950 that any tactic was acceptable to dislodge the Democrats from power. As Taft said of McCarthy in March of that year, he "should keep talking and if one case doesn't work out he should proceed with another."[40]

To explain the motives of the anti-Communists is not, however, to explain their apparent success in exploiting the issue of domestic communism. Several factors, in addition to a rash of spy cases and the emerging cold war, contributed to the public receptivity to a crusade against alleged subversives in American society. First, domestic communism presented an almost perfect political issue. As Bertrand Russell once noted, McCarthyism reconciled the two principal fears of the average American, taxes and communism. By stressing the enemy within over the danger from abroad, McCarthyites offered many Americans a cheap and painless way to battle godless communism. At the same time, the theme of Communist infiltration of the executive branch of the federal government offered an explanation for American reverses—among them, the fall of China and the loss of the nation's atomic monopoly—an

explanation that conformed to the prevailing postwar myth of American omnipotence. The McCarthyites, in their preoccupation with internal security
and their hostility toward the Democratic party's foreign policy, could also
draw on the nation's long-standing isolationist tradition, a sentiment especially popular among German- and Irish-Americans who had opposed entry into
two world wars on the side of Great Britain and against Germany.[41] Finally,
the press played an unwitting role in promoting the Red Scare. A naive
objectivity that led it to report without qualification exactly what McCarthy
said, abetted by a desire to sell newspapers, led much of the press to give full
coverage to McCarthy's charges, no matter how preposterous they were.
Always willing to oblige an inquiring reporter with a new allegation, McCarthy shrewdly manipulated the press and took full advantage of the common
assumption that no one, especially not a U.S. senator, would make such
sweeping accusations without some evidence to support them.[42]

Nevertheless, systematic studies of public opinion indicate that McCarthy
appealed to only a minority of the American people. According to a Gallup
survey in the summer of 1951, 63 percent of those polled either had no
opinion about McCarthy or could not identify him. Among those expressing
an opinion, unfavorable evaluations of the senator exceeded positive ratings
22 percent to 15 percent. A 1952 Roper poll reported that no more than 13
percent of those interviewed named communism as one of the two or three
most important issues then facing the United States. Indeed, political scientist
Michael Paul Rogin goes so far as to minimize the electoral significance of
domestic communism because, according to his interpretation, only voters
already committed to the Republican party were concerned about it.[43]

The influence of McCarthy and other congressional red-baiters rested less
on their ability to rally mass support to the anti-Communist crusade than on
their ability to intimidate other public officials.[44] The defeat in 1950 of two of
McCarthy's leading Senate critics, Maryland's Millard E. Tydings and Illinois's Scott W. Lucas, although the product of a variety of factors, understandably stifled opposition to McCarthy from his colleagues. Yet most important in explaining the McCarthy phenomenon was a widespread lack of
concern about the protection of civil liberties in the United States. According
to one survey, less than 1 percent of the American public placed either domes-

tic subversion or the McCarthyite threat to individual rights among the issues that most concerned them; and among that small group, more people worried about subversion than about civil liberties. At the same time, some two-thirds of those surveyed opposed even allowing a Communist to speak in a public place. With poll data demonstrating antilibertarian attitudes among the general public, along with a pervasive, if tepid, anticommunism, the average politician had little incentive to incur the wrath of the McCarthyites in the defense of free speech or due process of law. McCarthy gained power in Washington not at the head of a popular mass movement but in the face of widespread indifference toward the consequences of the cold war on civil liberties in the United States.[45]

Little in Dwight Eisenhower's background had prepared him to deal with the delicate philosophical and constitutional issues that the Communist controversy presented. Growing up in the conservative small town of Abilene, Kansas, Ike was sure to learn a great deal about decency and honesty but was far less likely to develop a tolerance of political dissenters or a recognition of the value of intellectual debate. Quoting a line from Sinclair Lewis's *Main Street*, one Eisenhower biographer described Abilene, perhaps unfairly, as a town where people were "ironed into glossy mediocrity."[46] Reared in a series of austere fundamentalist sects, Eisenhower lived an especially sheltered life, even by midwestern standards. He later wrote that until he went to West Point, he had never known anyone from a divorced family or anyone who did not go to church.[47]

By Ike's own account, education in Abilene was intended to produce reasonably well-informed citizens, but "beyond that, schools served to prepare the student for little more than the ordinary round of jobs."[48] As a boy, Eisenhower enjoyed history, especially military history. Yet reading history represented an end in itself, "not . . . a source of lessons to guide us in the present or to prepare me for the future."[49] The future president's lowest grade on his West Point entrance examination, a mediocre 73, came in American history, which suggests an early lack of interest in the broad political issues that the test emphasized. As a cadet, Eisenhower manifested little interest in anything other than sports. It was just as well. While he was there, instruction at the military academy, particularly in history, stressed indoctrination into an accepted body of facts, hardly an education calculated to encourage a subtlety of mind. Instead, West Point strove to produce an apolitical officer corps prepared, Douglas MacArthur once remarked, for the War of 1812.[50]

Neither were the long years Eisenhower spent in the narrow world of the peacetime army likely to expand his intellectual horizons. Martin Merson, who worked at the International Information Agency during Senator McCarthy's siege of the IIA, came to "wonder whether Eisenhower . . . fully understood the delicacy of the mechanism of government entrusted to his care." As Merson, a graduate of the Naval Academy and Harvard Law School, observed, "Concepts of civil liberties are quite alien in a militarily ordered life where discipline is so basic to an attitude of unquestioning obedience to command."[51]

In short, Dwight Eisenhower brought to the presidency a distinct anti-intellectualism that boded ill for efforts to protect freedom of thought in the United States from the McCarthyites. Intellectual giants, Ike once confided to a friend, "are usually uncomfortable characters to have around."[52] After Eisenhower became president, his attitude revealed itself in his hostility toward the most common embodiment of the American intellectual—the professor. While searching for a new director for the IIA, President Eisenhower made his preferences clear. He wanted a businessman for the position, not a "long-haired professor." And complaining to his diary about government conflict of interest laws, Ike fumed, "Sooner or later we will be unable to get anybody to take jobs in Washington but business failures, college professors, and New Deal lawyers."[53]

Eisenhower recognized a genuine threat to individual freedom in twentieth-century America, but he did not believe that it would come in the form of government repression of political nonconformists. He feared instead government paternalism—the growing reliance of the citizen, to a point of virtual helplessness, on the modern welfare state. As president, Ike hoped to unite a fractious Republican party on one fundamental principle, opposition to "the trend toward centralization of responsibility in the federal government, with its consequent increasing dependence of every citizen."[54] To Ike, the New Deal symbolized the hated welfare state. He used the term itself as anathema. He hoped, for example, to nominate relatively young men to the Supreme Court so that his appointees would not soon be replaced by "a New Deal President" and "the left-wingers."[55] Writing late in life, the former president even suggested that his place in history would ultimately depend on the eventual rejection of the New Deal by the American people. Otherwise, "the growth of paternalism to the point of virtual regimentation would so condition the attitude of future historians" as to blind them to his accomplishments.[56]

Psychohistorians might be tempted to explain Ike's dread of paternalism in terms of his strained relationship with a cold and unforgiving father. Whatever his motives, Eisenhower's warnings about the welfare state have a hollow ring. He spent the better part of his adult life in two of the most protective cocoons available to an American citizen—the peacetime army and the White House. As a general and as president, the simple boy from Kansas did not dress himself, drive himself, or manage his own finances. In fact, he never carried money. He did not know how to use a telephone or adjust a television set. He rarely shopped; his suits were given to him by New York clothiers.[57] Perhaps, in a perverse way, Eisenhower's virtual obsession with the dangers of the welfare state stemmed from his own elegant dependency. More important, from the early 1940s until his death in 1969, Eisenhower—hero and statesman—lived in a rarefied atmosphere remote from the daily concerns of the ordinary individual.

Rejecting a liberal statism, Eisenhower embraced what Robert Griffith, a student of both McCarthyism and the Eisenhower presidency, has termed "the corporate commonwealth." The old soldier, Griffith suggests, envisioned a harmonious society in which Americans muted their ideological differences and in which business, labor, and government worked together for the good of all. Primarily through the medium of public relations, a managerial elite, Eisenhower hoped, could mediate social conflict along a political middle way. If Ike's vision could not accommodate the slashing politics of a Joe McCarthy, neither did it have room for the political deviants of the Left.[58]

While one set of beliefs limited Eisenhower's will to resist the anti-Communist crusade, another set limited his capacity. The corporate commonwealth—as well as Eisenhower's personality—lent itself to leadership by indirection, seeking consensus and forging coalitions. From such considerations has come the notion of a "hidden-hand presidency," political scientist Fred I. Greenstein's term for an Eisenhower who was far more energetic behind the scenes than he was in public.[59] Yet Eisenhower hardly invented covert political action; it is a ubiquitous political reality. By appearing so diffident so often, Eisenhower surrendered important elements of presidential power—moral suasion and the ability to mobilize public opinion. Added to this, Eisenhower held to a rigid, almost elementary view of the separation of powers. Content to manage the executive branch of the federal government, Eisenhower as president seemed loath to interfere in the affairs of Congress.[60]

At the same time, the genial general was not, by temperament, disposed to look very hard for Communist witches in America's closets. As the cold war worsened after 1945, Eisenhower probably feared Communist propaganda and internal subversion more than a direct Soviet attack on the West.[61] Nevertheless, from the end of World War II until his race for the presidency, Dwight Eisenhower—largely free from political pressure and direct responsibility for the nation's internal security—appeared quite moderate, if not downright liberal, on the Communist issue.

Kevin McCann, in his 1952 campaign biography of Dwight D. Eisenhower, *Man from Abilene*, tried to assure voters of his candidate's foresight in matters affecting national security. In the 1930s, as American isolationists watched Adolf Hitler and Joseph Stalin consolidate their power, Eisenhower, McCann wrote, "was hardly as sanguine about international politics as the majority of his countrymen." And in a bow to cold war tensions, McCann added, Eisenhower "was by nature not one to brush Communism off lightly."[62]

In reality, little evidence exists to suggest that Dwight Eisenhower, in his early years, possessed more than the typical American's antipathy toward communism. The standard account of the general's military career, Kenneth S. Davis's *Soldier of Democracy*, scarcely mentions the subject. At a Washington, D.C., cocktail party in the mid-1930s, Eisenhower is reported to have mildly rebuked a George Washington University undergraduate for merely taking a course on communism, a course taught by the eminently respectable economist Arthur E. Burns, who would later serve in the Eisenhower White House. For the most part, however, during the troubled years between the world wars, young Eisenhower was far "too sensible an officer to have gotten himself involved in any public squabble over bolshevism."[63]

As late as May 1945, General Eisenhower foresaw a continuation of America's wartime alliance with the Soviet Union. Comparing relations between the United States and Russia in 1945 with those between the United States and Great Britain at the beginning of the war, the American commander seemed to believe that the maintenance of a peaceful relationship was largely a matter of the two countries learning to cooperate and communicate. With the Yalta agreements coming under increasing criticism from conservatives, Eisenhower expressed the view in his 1949 memoirs, the best-selling *Crusade in Europe*, that the Western Allies should have attempted to occupy more of Germany than they did at the end of World War II. He chided "our political heads" for not insisting at Yalta on a division between East and West at the Elbe River. Yet he admitted that in January 1945 the forces under his command were still west of the Rhine River and the Siegfried Line. He also conceded that he had not pressed the issue of the postwar division of Europe with his superiors. In all likelihood, Ike's acceptance of the Yalta decision can be explained at least in part by his failure to anticipate the subsequent division of much of the world into two hostile blocs.[64]

In the political context of 1949, *Crusade in Europe* revealed Eisenhower's views on communism and international affairs as slightly to the left of center but well within the mainstream of American thought. The general's wartime memoirs acknowledged his friendship with Soviet Marshal Georgi K. Zhukov, even though at one time Zhukov's political adviser had been Andrei Vishinsky, the former prosecutor in the Russian purge trials of the mid-1930s. The sight of the ruthless Stalinist at the side of Eisenhower's friend could hardly have been comforting to American anti-Communists. Eisenhower's endorsement of "some form of limited, federated world government" with a unified, multinational military command but without the Great Power veto that existed in the

United Nations Security Council must have sent shudders through the Republican right wing. And although *Crusade in Europe* closed with an eloquent statement of the cold war consensus against communism, acknowledging the role of military power, Eisenhower emphasized the humanitarian side of the anti-Communist crusade: "Whenever popular discontent is founded on group oppression or mass poverty or the hunger of children, there communism may stage an offensive that arms cannot counter."[65]

In June 1948, Eisenhower embarked on a new, and unlikely, career when he became president of Columbia University, a post only recently vacated by the famed Nicholas Murray Butler. With its thirty thousand students crowded onto twenty-six acres in uptown New York City, Columbia exhibited financial woes and a "factory yard appearance" that concerned its new president more than did Communist infiltration of the university, but the latter was at least one of the many issues Eisenhower had to address. Indeed, Columbia was among a handful of elite schools rumored to have harbored Communist cells in the 1930s, although the number of campus Communists was small and their influence limited. Eisenhower was not there to weed out radicals and subversive influences. Early in his tenure, he defended the university's decision to permit Arnold Johnson, the legislative director of the Communist party, to speak to a student gathering. In a letter circulated among alumni, Eisenhower suggested that censorship of such activities might lead students to suspect that the alumni themselves feared "a real comparison between democracy and dictatorship." Eisenhower repeatedly expressed opposition to hiring Communists as faculty members, but he opposed special loyalty oaths for teachers. Dr. Gene Weltfish, a Columbia anthropologist since 1947 and vice president of the pro-Communist International Federation of Women, retained a position in the university until 1953, long after Eisenhower had left.[66]

Before Eisenhower became its president, the university had agreed to accept grants from the Polish and Czechoslovakian governments to establish two chairs for the study of Polish and Czech culture. Such collaboration with Eastern European governments drew bitter criticism from hard-line anti-Communists. William Randolph Hearst's *San Francisco Examiner* used the affair to announce its opposition to Eisenhower as a possible presidential candidate in 1948. At Columbia, Arthur P. Coleman, an assistant professor of

Polish grammar and literature, resigned in protest, and Sigmund J. Sluska, a representative of the Polish-American Congress and a former Columbia graduate student, sent the *New York Times* a memorandum alleging Cominform infiltration of the university. Asserting that he would resist interference with the university's academic freedom from any source, Eisenhower stood by its decision to establish the chairs.[67]

In an interview in Denver, Eisenhower angered Mississippi Democrat John Rankin of HCUA by minimizing the danger that Soviet secret agents posed to American security. In August 1948, Eisenhower learned HCUA planned to investigate the university. By November, it was rumored that he would be called to Washington to testify before the committee; Eisenhower confided to William H. Burnham, a New York City investment banker, that he was "perfectly willing to answer any question" about himself or Columbia "as fully and frankly" as he could. Nothing came of the investigation except a request from HCUA Chairman John Stephens Wood for a list of all books used in Columbia's social sciences courses. In June 1949, Eisenhower assured Columbia historian Henry Steele Commager, "All elements of crisis have been removed from this affair." The textbook inquiry itself received considerable criticism and was disowned by GOP committee members, including Richard M. Nixon. After consulting with officials at Harvard and Brown, who had received similar requests, Eisenhower decided on a response somewhere between open defiance and full cooperation. Informing Wood that the university kept no list of approved books, Ike sent him some reading lists and class schedules.[68]

It was probably McCarthyite attacks on various individuals that brought Eisenhower his most intimate contacts with the politics of the cold war. At an April 19, 1947, banquet of the American Society of Newspaper Editors, Eisenhower expressed support for the embattled nomination of David E. Lilienthal to the Atomic Energy Commission. A trustee of the Carnegie Endowment for International Peace, Eisenhower had even closer ties to Alger Hiss, who was serving as the organization's president when Whittaker Chambers accused him of spying for the Soviet Union. Slow to turn against Hiss, Eisenhower found it "incomprehensible" that "the reputation of a man" could "almost be destroyed merely on the basis of another's startling accusations."

When McCarthy unsuccessfully attempted to block the nomination of manpower specialist Anna M. Rosenberg, a friend of Eisenhower's, as assistant secretary of defense, the general stated in a letter of recommendation to the Senate Armed Forces Committee, "It has never crossed my mind to question her sincerity, integrity, or her devotion to our country."[69]

McCarthy's opposition to Philip S. Jessup as a delegate to the United Nations General Assembly also provoked a protest from Eisenhower. A veteran diplomat who had lectured on international law at Columbia, Jessup raised conservative ire for his role in the development of the Truman administration's China policy and for testifying as a character witness on behalf of Hiss. Eisenhower, who had tried to recruit Jessup to serve as Columbia provost, openly defended him and endorsed Henry L. Stimson's view, stated in a March 1950 letter to the *New York Times*, that Senate harassment of the State Department threatened to harm innocent people and to disrupt American foreign policy. Eisenhower agreed with Stimson that the security problem should be handled quietly through existing administrative channels. After the conservative Texas oil millionaire H. L. Hunt chastised Eisenhower for making remarks likely to prejudice jurors in a future spy trial, Eisenhower promised to be more circumspect in his comments.[70]

Eisenhower said surprisingly little about strident right-wing attacks on his mentor, General George C. Marshall, whom Indiana Senator William E. Jenner once called "a front man for traitors." Marshall had shepherded Eisenhower's rise from lieutenant colonel in March 1941 to five-star general in December 1944. Eisenhower understandably thought of Marshall "practically as a god or father."[71] His relative silence is attributable in part to his appointment as the supreme commander of the North Atlantic Treaty Organization (NATO) forces in late 1950, which removed him from some of the uglier aspects of cold war politics. Yet as NATO commander, the general continued to expose himself to conservative wrath. Hoping to reach an accommodation with an independent Communist regime, he favored bringing Yugoslavia into the Western alliance. And insisting that only individual liberties and free trade be protected, he dismissed right-wing objections to American aid to the British Labour government and other European Socialist regimes.[72]

Late in 1951, as Dwight Eisenhower contemplated entering the presidential campaign, he wrote his friend Swede Hazlett that he was drawing attacks from both left and right. In reality, on the issue of Communists in government, his record seemed to offer more ammunition for conservative critics than for civil libertarians. Although the journalist John Gunther could assert that "on civil liberties" Eisenhower's record was "good," to many Republicans, his record was a political liability. In Eisenhower's activities at Columbia and in his NATO command, he had shown a certain tolerance for Communists and Socialists. He had opposed the McCarran Act and the creation of the Subversive Activities Control Board as a threat to civil liberty and the separation of powers, as well as an unnecessary expansion of the federal government. Neither was his record reassuring with respect to communism abroad. He had helped shape, or at least execute, unpopular American policies in Europe. Eisenhower had apparently acquiesced in the administration's China policy through the late 1940s. Acknowledging reports by the columnist Drew Pearson, the general conceded, "McCarthy is digging up alleged dirt with which to smear me if I run for President." And he well knew that a Wichita editor had labeled him "the darling of Moscow."[73]

2

★ ★ ★

1952

The Tarnished Crusade

Shortly after the Minnesota presidential primary in March 1952, it became known that Dwight Eisenhower would soon relinquish his NATO command to seek the Republican nomination for president. For months, Massachusetts Senator Henry Cabot Lodge, former Marshall Plan administrator Paul G. Hoffman, and others had been organizing a movement to draft the general. Their efforts to capitalize politically on Eisenhower's popularity paid off handsomely. A presidential preference poll early in March showed Eisenhower running twenty-five points ahead of Tennessee Senator Estes Kefauver, then the likely Democratic nominee in the event that President Truman decided not to seek reelection. On March 11, candidates pledged to Eisenhower, with the support of Governor Sherman Adams, won all fourteen delegate slots in New Hampshire's GOP primary. Perhaps more impressive were the returns from Minnesota a week later. With only favorite son Harold E. Stassen on the ballot, Eisenhower received 108,692 write-in votes and trailed Stassen by fewer than 21,000. Nevertheless, after the Minnesota results apparently nudged Eisenhower off the fence, he still faced a bitter fight for his party's nomination. In one poll, respondents identifying themselves as Republicans placed Eisenhower in a dead heat with his principal challenger, Ohio Senator Robert A. Taft.[1]

The issue of domestic communism played an ambiguous role in the struggle between Taft and Eisenhower. A preliminary poll taken by Eisenhower supporters in New Hampshire late in 1951 suggested that inflation, not subversion, was the main concern of Republicans. Only 4 percent of those leaning toward Eisenhower, and only 1 percent of those favoring Taft, considered communism to be one of the major problems facing the United States. A later poll by the Eisenhower camp indicated that foreign policy and high taxes concerned Americans generally more than did any other issues. Charges of communism and corruption in government—Truman had been forced to fire some 250 employees in the Bureau of Internal Revenue, along with the assistant attorney general in charge of the Justice Department's Tax Division, for wrongdoing—might, the pollsters concluded, have aroused "the wrath of the nation's comfortable 10%," but apparently the average voter lumped "these issues together with farm subsidies as strictly subsidiary."[2] At the same time, the Communist controversy was one of several issues that occasioned savage attacks on Eisenhower from the extreme Right, that threatened to alienate him from many within the mainstream of the Republican party, and that served to distinguish him from Taft.

General Eisenhower's entry into the presidential race prompted what one pro-Eisenhower magazine called "a campaign of character assassination" on a level that the United States had not seen "since the 1928 campaign against Alfred E. Smith." Two themes usually permeated most of the right-wing attacks on the general. First, citing as purported evidence the 1915 West Point yearbook, in which young cadet Eisenhower was referred to as the "Swedish Jew" in a tasteless attempt at humor, political extremists like Gerald L. K. Smith tried to appeal to anti-Semitism by branding Eisenhower as Jewish. Second, reactionary pamphleteers and letter writers portrayed Eisenhower as a crypto-Socialist who had turned "the best part of Germany over to the Russians" and "the Polish Department at Columbia over to the Communists." Robert H. Williams of Santa Ana, California, the publisher of the *Williams Intelligence Summary*, publicized a cropped photograph of Eisenhower toasting Marshal Georgi K. Zhukov near the end of World War II and suggested that the Roosevelt administration had decided to "dig down in the barrel and haul up an unknown major and promote him rapidly to five-star general" because of Eisenhower's willingness to cooperate with the Communists. Anti-Semitism and rabid anticommunism were often virtually inseparable, as when C. Leon de Aryan of San Diego, the publisher of *The Broom*, complained that

Eisenhower was "a Jew and creature of the Jewish conspiracy to destroy this government," or as when Williams warned his readers that it was the Jews who were "behind the Communist world offensive."[3]

The political significance of such criticism is difficult to assess. On the eve of the Republican convention, Taft himself denounced appeals to racial and religious prejudice in the campaign against Eisenhower. *Time* reported, "The inkwells of bigotry are far removed from any responsible political headquarters." Yet Henry Zweifel, the pro-Taft GOP national committeeman from Texas, helped circulate Wichita editor Joseph R. Kamp's *Headlines*, which accused Eisenhower of "coddling" Communists at Columbia University. In South Dakota, Taft's supporters sponsored newspaper advertisements repeating Kamp's charges. Leaflets smearing Eisenhower appeared on the chairs at an Eisenhower rally in upstate New York and flooded the delegates at the GOP national convention. Hatred for Eisenhower did not equate with support for Taft; the Ohio senator trailed General Douglas MacArthur as the favorite candidate of the radical Right. The smear campaign may have benefited Eisenhower by generating a backlash of sympathy for him and by creating the impression that the essentially conservative general was in reality a political moderate, an image that would prove useful in a fall campaign for Democratic and independent votes. As Zweifel's activities suggest, however, more respectable conservatives than Gerald L. K. Smith also expressed doubts about Eisenhower's reliability as an anti-Communist. Marty Snyder, who had served on Eisenhower's household staff in World War II and become an early advocate of an Eisenhower draft, recalled that "the charge that Eisenhower was liberal to the point of being a radical had popped up across the country" during the preconvention campaign. When Snyder found himself stuck in Chicago traffic during the Republican convention, he began promoting Eisenhower over a loudspeaker mounted on an automobile, only to have the actor John Wayne leap from a nearby taxi and yell, "Why don't you get a red flag?"[4]

In a party dominated by conservatives, as the GOP was, the perception that Eisenhower was soft on communism might have proven fatal to his presidential ambitions. And the Republicans in 1952 were a conservative party, at least when judged by the philosophical leanings of the party leadership. Herbert S. Parmet estimates that of forty-six Republican senators in the Eighty-second Congress, only a dozen could have been considered liberals or moderates. The right wing monopolized the Senate leadership. Under Taft, who served as minority leader, conservatives like Eugene Millikin of Colorado, William F. Knowland of California, and Styles Bridges of New Hampshire were powerful forces within the party caucus. Anti-Communist crusaders constituted an important part of the congressional GOP; in addition to McCarthy, Jenner, and Nixon, there were Harry P. Cain of Washington, George W. Malone of Nevada, Karl E. Mundt of South Dakota, and others. Although some of these men supported Eisenhower, long-standing ties to Taft and a distrust of internationalism in foreign affairs help to explain the preference of the party hierarchy for Taft. Suspicion of Eisenhower on the Communist issue further undermined his position. Even though public opinion polls in the late spring and early summer of 1952 revealed Ike as the favorite of rank-and-file Republicans and as the strongest candidate the GOP could field in November, Republican county chairpeople were reported to favor Taft over the general 61 percent to 31 percent.[5]

Ironically, on many domestic issues Eisenhower stood to the right of Taft, who favored such liberal causes as federal aid to education and public housing.[6] It was the issue of communism at home and abroad, however, that provided the critical philosophical distinction between the two men. Indeed, Eisenhower's opposition to the senator's views on foreign policy constituted the single most important factor motivating him to run for president. Neither a simpleminded isolationist nor a rabid McCarthyite, Taft recognized the threat posed by the cold war to national solvency and personal liberties. Taft opposed entangling military alliances, especially NATO, and American involvement in any land war in Asia, although he believed the Far East should take priority over Europe in the shaping of American foreign policy. Fully subscribing to the "illusion of American omnipotence," he was quick to condemn the Truman administration for losing China, although he had few concrete suggestions on how the advance of communism could be stemmed. Taft compiled an equally mixed record on domestic subversion. Opposed to outlawing the Communist party and to government efforts to expel Communists from college faculties, Taft normally eschewed the overheated rhetoric of the McCarthys and the Jenners. Yet during the debate on the Lilienthal appointment to the Atomic Energy Commission, the Ohio senator criticized the former TVA director as "soft on communism." Taft repeatedly defended Senator McCarthy. When he entered the presidential race, Taft enlisted the aid of Tom Coleman, one of McCarthy's principal Wisconsin supporters, sought an endorsement from McCarthy, and attacked Eisenhower for his collaboration in the execution of Democratic foreign policy. Campaigning in Wisconsin, Taft praised McCarthy for doing "a great job" in fighting Communist influence in the State Department. Yet Taft refused to embrace all of McCarthy's charges, in particular his assault on General Marshall, and this, apparently, cost Taft the unqualified endorsement of the Wisconsin senator.[7] Taft also unsuccessfully sought the support of Richard Nixon, who, by his own account, felt that the Ohio senator did not fully understand the threat presented by "communist subversion supported by the international communist movement."[8]

Eisenhower possessed numerous advantages in his struggle with Taft. First, by 1952 Eisenhower had become the heir apparent to New York Governor Thomas E. Dewey as the leader of the pragmatic, internationally minded eastern wing of the Republican party.[9] Moreover, there was Eisenhower's enormous personal popularity; one survey ranked him second only to MacArthur as the most admired man in the United States. Although some concern initially existed as to whether his war record and infectious grin could be translated into votes, polls soon showed him running ahead of Taft among Republican voters and doing even better among the electorate at large when pitted against potential Democratic opponents. In the preconvention campaign, Eisenhower fared extremely well among independents, who seemed to prefer him to Taft by better than two to one. Eisenhower ran well among women and young people. According to a June survey, the general led Kefauver by twenty points while Taft trailed the Democratic front-runner 50 percent to 41 percent.[10] Eisenhower's electability, and what it would mean to the rest of the ticket, surely gave him a decided edge over Taft. Early in the campaign to draft the general, Washington Governor Arthur B. Langlie confided to Senator Lodge his "doubts whether the Republicans in Washington" could "be elected in November if Eisenhower" was not on the ticket. And as an Arizona Republican reflected on the Senate race in that state, "I don't think there is a chance of [Republican challenger Barry M.] Goldwater beating [Democratic incumbent Ernest W.] McFarland without Eisenhower at the head of the ticket."[11]

Finally, Eisenhower displayed a deft, if opportunistic, touch in handling the Communist issue. At the formal opening of his campaign in Abilene, Kansas, on June 4, the general gave a poor oratorical performance—an uninspiring speech in a drenching rain—but he nevertheless struck an effective ideological chord. Avoiding the open embrace of McCarthyism, which he would have found unpalatable and which might have cost him moderate and liberal votes, he instead assailed the Yalta accords and the "loss" of China. These issues, to the extent that they could be divorced from the matter of domestic subversion, troubled GOP conservatives even more than did Communists in government. When asked about McCarthy at a press conference the next day, Eisenhower responded with what would become his standard refrain in the next two years. He would not discuss personalities but pledged that in his administration, "any kind of Communistic, subversive, or pinkish influence would be uprooted from responsible places in our government." Later in the primary campaign, while speaking in Detroit, Eisenhower attempted to distance himself from the Yalta Conference, the Morgenthau Plan for a pastoral Germany, and the decision not to race the Russians to Berlin.[12] On June 26, in his last major speech before the convention, to a Denver Coliseum crowd of eleven thousand, he said little about Communists in government, but he did complain, "We have been too ready for too long to trust a godless dictatorship." In one of his most partisan speeches of the campaign, Eisenhower blamed this misplaced trust for the loss of China and Eastern Europe and added, "If we had been less trustful, if we had been less soft and weak, there might easily have been no war in Korea."[13] If this kind of rhetoric did not win over Republican conservatives to the general, his echoing of their visceral criticism of the Truman administration's foreign policy woes, minus specific Mc-

Carthyite allegations of subversion, helped minimize the political gulf between him and the right wing, without, apparently, offending many in the
political center.

When the Republican party's twenty-fifth presidential nominating convention
assembled in Chicago's International Amphitheater on July 7, 1952, Senator
Taft appeared to have a slight lead over Eisenhower in delegate support,
although neither candidate was certain of enough votes to win the nomination
on the first ballot. Harold Stassen, the former governor of Minnesota, and
California Governor Earl Warren, Dewey's 1948 running mate, each enjoyed
some support, mainly in their home states. General Douglas MacArthur,
scheduled to deliver the keynote address, hoped that a deadlocked convention
might turn to him. The closeness of the race helped make the convention an
extraordinarily bitter affair, as is suggested by the substance and tone of
Indiana Congressman Charles A. Halleck's later observation that because he
"wouldn't sign in blood for Bob Taft" the "damned fools . . . in Indiana
wouldn't let [him] be a delegate that year." A more spectacular example of
political fratricide occurred when Illinois Senator Everett M. Dirksen, a Taft
supporter, attacked Thomas Dewey during a floor fight over the report of the
credentials committee. Amid a chorus of boos and applause, Dirksen admonished the delegates, "Reexamine your hearts before you take this action in
support of the Minority Report." With eyes glaring and a finger pointed at the
New York governor, he went on, "We followed you before and you took us
down the path to defeat." In fact, the fight over contested delegations, mostly
ones from southern states where conservative Democrats–turned–Eisenhower
Republicans had swamped small, pro-Taft party organizations in local conventions and caucuses, proved to be the turning point of the convention. With
aid from Warren and Stassen, and Taft unable to hold all his delegates in
check, the Eisenhower forces won the credentials fight and made Eisenhower's nomination virtually inevitable. When the first ballot on the presidential nomination showed Eisenhower leading Taft 595 to 500, Stassen capitu-

lated. The twenty votes he had received were enough to put Eisenhower over the top. Stassen's withdrawal began a stampede to Ike, although the archconservative Texas delegate H. L. Hunt switched his vote from Taft to MacArthur. Denied the GOP nomination, MacArthur was drafted instead by Gerald L. K. Smith's Christian Nationalist party.[14]

Republican conservatives could not control the nominating process, but their dominance of the party machinery did give them control of the podium throughout most of the convention. As a result, a succession of conservative orators vehemently denounced Democratic foreign policy and, to a lesser extent, Democratic tolerance of subversives in government. A few resorted to the old tactic of trying to draw direct links between Democrats and Communists, between liberalism and communism. MacArthur, in the keynote address, and former President Herbert Hoover, in a speech on the second day of the convention, criticized the Democrats for doing too much in Europe and too little in Asia, although neither suggested that a militant foreign policy might call for sacrifice. MacArthur criticized the idea that the United States could "spend" itself "into a position of leadership abroad." Hoover promised that the GOP would not send American youth "into the overwhelming Communist quicksands." Decrying the "bureaucratic fascism" of the Democrats, the former president charged that "policies participated in by our Government and by Communists in the highest echelons of our Washington Administration" had helped place a "horde of eight hundred million people" under the Kremlin "whip." Lesser figures repeated the charges. Senator Styles Bridges claimed, "Communist sympathizers, fellow travelers, and their dupes in the Democratic Administration have multiplied rapidly." According to Patrick J. Hurley, the former ambassador to China, he himself had dismissed proCommunist members from the American mission only to see them rehired by the State Department. Missouri Senator James P. Kem pledged that the Republicans would "drive out the Communist rats" that had been and were still "undermining the foundation of our Government." Washington Senator Harry P. Cain and Minnesota Congressman Walter Judd went even further in seeking to exploit popular fears of communism for political purposes. On the growth of the federal government under the Democrats, Cain said, "In a grotesque and spineless way it parallels the growth of the Communist autocracy." The Democratic party, Judd declared, professed "to abhor communism" but pressed "for the same kind of centralization of power."[15]

In this context, the speech delivered on the third day of the convention by Senator McCarthy, who otherwise played a minor role in the proceedings, seemed a fairly conventional exercise in political oratory. McCarthy's appearance, to the strains of "The Halls of Montezuma," provoked a demonstration of sufficient ferocity to frighten to tears the wife of one moderate senator; but even though McCarthy gave more attention to the issue of subversion than had other speakers, his language was hardly more violent. Criticizing Truman's reluctance to supply Congress with the loyalty files of federal employees, McCarthy proclaimed that the nation could not "fight communists or communism in the Acheson-Lattimore fashion of hitting them with a perfumed silk handkerchief." Yet he did offer the Democrats something of an olive branch when he called on "America's two great parties" to join together so that "the rights of all men" could be saved.[16]

The platform reflected the emphasis and concerns of the speakers. The first and longest plank attacked the Democrats' foreign policy for swinging "erratically from timid appeasement to reckless bluster." The platform devoted a separate plank of four paragraphs to the issue of internal security. It condemned infiltration of the executive branch and the refusal of the White House to give loyalty files to Congress and proclaimed, "There are no Communists in the Republican Party." The platform promised that a Republican president would appoint "only persons of unquestioned loyalty," would "overhaul loyalty and security programs," and would cooperate with Congress in fighting subversion.[17]

In contrast to the platform and many of the speakers who had preceded him, Governor Theodore K. McKeldin of Maryland, delivering the principal nominating speech for Eisenhower, referred to the corruption and extravagance in the Truman administration but ignored the issue of subversion. Likewise, Eisenhower, in a restrained and dignified acceptance speech, stressed general, positive themes. Saying that he had been summoned to lead "a great crusade—for freedom in America and freedom in the world," Ike ignored the controversy over domestic communism except to praise his running mate,

Richard M. Nixon, as an individual with "a special talent and an ability to ferret out any kind of subversive influence."[18]

Indeed, Nixon's selection as the vice-presidential nominee constituted the single most important political consequence of the anti-Communist controversy up to that time, and perhaps thereafter. If, as Nixon later observed, his "major job" as Eisenhower's running mate was to heal the breach between the forces of Taft and Eisenhower, the California senator was not forced on Eisenhower in a desperate attempt to restore party unity. The Eisenhower camp wanted Nixon. Herbert Brownell, the influential Republican lawyer, later called the Eisenhower-Nixon combination "a natural" ticket meeting "all of the political requirements." As Brownell observed, Nixon brought youth, geographic balance, and congressional experience to the ticket. So too, it might be added, would have California's other senator, William F. Knowland, but Knowland lacked Nixon's reputation as an anti-Communist. According to Sherman Adams, "Realizing that in the campaign he was going to face the McCarthy issue of Communists in the federal government, Eisenhower wanted above all a vice-presidential nominee with a demonstrable record of anticommunism." Though recognizing the other assets he brought to the campaign, Nixon later acknowledged somewhat coyly, "Perhaps my anticommunist credentials from the Hiss case were what most tilted the decision to me."[19]

Eisenhower and then-Congressman Nixon had first met in the summer of 1950 at the Bohemian Grove, the annual summer retreat of San Francisco's Bohemian Club, where Eisenhower spoke to a group consisting mainly of wealthy conservatives, including Herbert Hoover. In the fall of that year, Nixon defeated Helen Gahagan Douglas in a bitter contest for a seat in the U.S. Senate. Eisenhower and the freshman senator met again in May 1951 when Nixon went to Europe to attend an international conference in Geneva. Eisenhower reportedly told Nixon then of his pleasure that Nixon "not only got Hiss, but . . . got him fairly," a point Eisenhower would repeat in later years.[20] Nixon, meanwhile, did more than rest on his laurels from the Hiss case. Never shy about acknowledging the political expediency of the anti-Communist crusade, Nixon, in a June 1951 speech to the National Young Republican Convention in Boston, articulated the GOP battle plan. The Democrats' "most vulnerable point" was "the failure of this administration to develop an effective program to meet the activities of the fifth column in the United States." The GOP, Nixon said, could "conduct a thorough house cleaning of communists and fellow travelers," because, he explained, "We have no fear of finding any Communist skeletons in our political closets."[21]

What Nixon called his "road to the ticket" began on May 8, 1952, when he spoke, at Dewey's invitation, to the annual fund-raising dinner of the New York State Republican party at the Waldorf-Astoria in New York City. In Dewey's suite after the dinner, the governor suggested that Nixon might be considered for vice president and introduced him to Brownell. The decision on Ike's running mate may, for all practical purposes, have been made then.[22]

The night before he was to be nominated, Eisenhower had dinner with Brownell, and they discussed the vice-presidential nomination. The two men agreed on a list of candidates, which included Nixon, to be submitted by Dewey and Brownell to a group of party leaders. How enthusiastic the general personally was about Nixon remains somewhat unclear. Sherman Adams thought Nixon stood at the top of Ike's list, but Brownell described Eisenhower as indicating simply that if the party leadership wanted Nixon, "he would take him." Several names were discussed the next day when Dewey and Brownell met with the leaders. After dismissing Taft as too conservative and disqualifying Dirksen because of his behavior in the credentials fight, the group seemed split between Nixon and Governor Alfred Driscoll of New Jersey. Once Dewey made clear his preference for the California senator, however, the group quickly agreed on Nixon.[23] If he had been the early choice of Eisenhower's supporters, Nixon believed, the Taft forces would nevertheless have recognized the political utility of his nomination. They knew that he "would hit hard against communism and corruption." According to Nixon, "They believed that it was essential to develop these issues if we were to pull in the candidates for the House and Senate who would assure us of majorities in Congress."[24]

Precisely which issues would bring victory in the fall, as well as how they would affect Republican strategy, had been one of the points dividing the

Eisenhower camp from conservative party regulars. Purportedly unconcerned about independent voters, among whom Robert Taft fared poorly, supporters of the Ohio senator emphasized the importance of winning over new voters and habitual nonvoters to the cause. Part rationale for their own weaknesses and part creditable analysis, the conservatives argued that the "stay-at-homes" could have elected Dewey in 1948 and could elect Taft despite his unpopularity among Democrats and independents. Arguing that "nothing could be more fallacious nor more destructive to the chances of Republican victory in 1952 than the attitude of the Taft campaigners," pollsters in the Eisenhower camp privately feared that the nonvoters the conservatives hoped to mobilize would, if they voted, favor the Democrats by a two-to-one margin. Such advice undoubtedly reinforced a preexisting intention to capitalize on Eisenhower's broad-based bipartisan support among the traditional voting population.[25]

Consistent with this strategy, Henry Cabot Lodge, warning Eisenhower that "abuse does not make votes," advised him to forgo attacks on corruption in the Truman administration and to minimize the economic issues that had long divided Democrats and Republicans. Nevertheless, Lodge believed that the Democrats could be profitably attacked for their failure to deal expeditiously with Communists in the State Department and for the department's role in the "loss" of China. If the Democrats counterattacked by trying to link Eisenhower to McCarthy and other GOP red-baiters, Eisenhower, Lodge believed, could respond effectively by asking the Democrats why they did not silence their own anti-Communist extremists. Indeed, regarding the potential manipulation of the Communist controversy, the Eisenhower camp, in the postconvention phase of the campaign, seemed mainly fearful of being associated with McCarthy and his allies. At a strategy meeting in mid-July, Brownell and Dewey apparently agreed with Lodge in urging Ike to hit the Democrats on the subversion issue, although Dewey, wary of anti-McCarthy sentiment, advised Eisenhower against endorsing all Republican candidates by name.[26]

As part of a larger effort to preserve its influence within the party, the Republican Old Guard was also pressuring Eisenhower to portray the Democrats as irresolute anti-Communists. On the evening of August 1, Eisenhower, Nixon, and most of the key Eisenhower strategists met with the national party's strategy committee at the Brown Palace Hotel in Denver, where the general had established a campaign headquarters. The committee's membership included Republican National Committee (RNC) Chairman Arthur Summerfield, RNC Executive Director Wayne J. Hood, RNC Public Relations Director Robert Humphreys, and Everett Dirksen from the party's Senate leadership. Conservatives dominated the committee. Dirksen and Hood had supported Taft during the primary campaign, and Hood, who also served as chairman of the Wisconsin GOP, was a close ally of Tom Coleman, a McCarthy loyalist. In a flip-chart presentation on behalf of the committee, Humphreys unveiled to Eisenhower a campaign strategy better suited to the ideologically pure Taft than to the more pragmatic general. Eisenhower's first task, Humphreys insisted, was to rally to his cause the twenty million voters who routinely supported the Republicans and then to build a winning coalition, not from the three to four million independents who normally voted in presidential elections but from the forty-five million Americans who usually stayed at home. A rejection of the "me too" Republicanism of which Dewey had been accused, the strategy committee's proposal made no suggestion that Eisenhower cater to independent voters by presenting a centrist image. Instead, Humphreys stressed the "stay-at-homes" as a potential protest vote. He added, "[They] usually vote only when discontent inspires them to do so." To rally the party faithful and to mobilize habitual nonvoters, the Republicans, Humphreys said, must "Attack! Attack! Attack!" Under the broad rubric of "Marxism," Humphreys proposed a line of attack that blurred the distinctions between liberalism, socialism, Communist subversion at home, and Soviet aggression abroad. The American people should be warned. "The trend toward a Socialist state is unmistakable as the Federal Government takes unto itself countless powers over the American people." And in a standard conservative refrain, Humphreys argued that the Democrats were vulnerable for both ignoring "the world-wide Communist conspiracy" and for wasting tax dollars on foreign aid and military hardware.[27]

Whatever the impact of the strategy committee's presentation, it indicates the pressure Eisenhower faced to join the anti-Communist crusade. Humphreys later could not recall that Eisenhower said "a single word during the evening once the presentation had been made," though he assumed that

Eisenhower accepted the plan. In Humphreys's opinion, it was "followed almost to the letter throughout the 1952 campaign." In reality, Eisenhower's silence may have indicated a polite lack of interest in the party organization's ideas, and in any event, the decision had already been made to attack the Democratic record on communism. Nevertheless, the position of the party establishment left the general with less room to maneuver and pushed him closer toward a hard line on the question of subversion. Summerfield, for example, persuaded Eisenhower to endorse all the party's candidates, including McCarthy and Jenner. And the Old Guard also influenced Eisenhower into making early campaign swings, as "a healing gesture," through Ohio, Indiana, and Wisconsin, the heartland of Republican conservatism and a hotbed of the anti-Communist crusade.[28]

Republican strategists apparently assumed that Communist subversion could be made an issue in the general election regardless of the identity of Eisenhower's Democratic opponent. Well before the Democratic convention assembled in Chicago on July 21, the early Democratic front-runner, Senator Estes Kefauver of Tennessee, had proved himself too liberal for his fellow southerners and too much of a maverick for the party leadership. Kefauver lost the nomination battle on the third ballot to a reluctant opponent, Governor Adlai E. Stevenson of Illinois. Fearful of the political consequences of a popular desire for change after twenty years of Democratic rule, Stevenson had hesitated in declaring his candidacy. An internationalist in foreign affairs, as well as a political realist, Stevenson seemed ready to challenge Taft, but much less willing to oppose Eisenhower. Stevenson believed that Eisenhower's nomination would neutralize any advantage the Democrats might have on foreign policy issues and probably doom their chances of retaining the White House. Under pressure months before the convention to enter the presidential race, Stevenson had expressed doubt at the idea that it was his "duty to save Western civilization from Ike Eisenhower." Richard Nixon, on the other hand, was one of the few people in public life whom Stevenson truly loathed. Convinced that Nixon's anti-Communist crusading had done much to make McCarthyism possible, Stevenson was reportedly appalled at the thought that Eisenhower's running mate could become president. Stevenson dismissed McCarthy as "a sick man."[29]

Ironically, despite his relatively conservative stance on most domestic political issues, Stevenson was vulnerable to Republican criticism on the matter of internal subversion. Stevenson did not support Truman's Fair Deal and disagreed with the president on federal aid for public housing and education. He failed to support Truman on the repeal of the Taft-Hartley Act, the Brannan Plan for agriculture, and national health insurance. Orthodox in economics, Stevenson fretted about the growth of the federal budget. The Democratic nominee favored the creation of state commissions on fair employment practices but showed little interest in civil rights initiatives on the federal level. Yet Stevenson had displayed liberal instincts in defending free speech and due process of law from abuse in the name of battling internal subversion. Admittedly, as the historian Charles C. Alexander has noted, Stevenson was a dutiful cold-warrior who acceded to the dismissals of Communist teachers and professors and defended Truman's employee loyalty program along with the administration's Smith Act prosecutions of Communist party leaders. At the same time, however, the Illinois governor spoke out against many of the worst excesses of McCarthyism with eloquence, courage, and common sense. "We are behaving . . . like nutty neurotics," he told the commencement audience at the University of Illinois in June 1950, "nervously looking for subversive enemies under the bed and behind the curtains." Stevenson won the admiration of liberals with his veto of the Broyles bill, which would have made it a felony in Illinois to belong to any alleged subversive organization and which would have required a loyalty oath for public employees and candidates for public office. Advised by FBI Director J. Edgar Hoover that such bills were a nuisance, sometimes leading state law enforcement officials to arrest undercover FBI agents, Stevenson asked in his veto message, "Does anyone seriously think that a real traitor will hesitate to sign a loyalty oath?" Warning of the danger such legislation posed to the Bill of Rights, Stevenson concluded, "We must not burn down the house to kill the rats." His famous acceptance speech at the 1952 convention, in which he promised to "talk sense to the American people," overshadowed his welcoming address of a few days earlier, but it was there that Stevenson said: "We want no shackles on the mind or the spirit, no rigid patterns of thought, no iron conformity. We want only the faith and conviction that triumph in free and fair contest."[30]

In the eyes of professional anti-Communists, Stevenson's ties to Alger Hiss were probably a more serious shortcoming than his Broyles bill veto or his liberal rhetoric. Stevenson had worked with Hiss in the Legal Division of the Agricultural Adjustment Administration in the 1930s and had seen him occasionally thereafter on State Department business, including the San Francisco Conference on the United Nations (UN), where Stevenson had been a member of the American delegation. When Hiss was brought to trial, he turned to Stevenson, as well as to other prominent public figures like Supreme Court Justices Felix Frankfurter and Stanley Reed, to testify as a character witness on his behalf. Stevenson did not appear at the trial, but in response to written interrogatories, he stated that, to the best of his knowledge, Hiss's reputation for loyalty was good.[31]

On August 4, Stevenson wrote Wilson Wyatt, his campaign manager, that he had learned from an informant in the Eisenhower camp that the Republican strategy would be to make foreign policy, especially toward Asia, the principal issue of the campaign. In addition, Nixon would "push hard on the Hiss business" while "every effort" would "be made to appease the Taft people" and to win the farm vote. Stevenson's source seems to have provided him with a fairly accurate account of the deliberations that had taken place in Denver. Indeed, Republican attacks on Stevenson's associations with Hiss began within days of his nomination.[32]

If it was obvious from the start of the campaign that the Republicans would attempt to exploit Stevenson's weak points on the internal security issue, it remained unclear just how far Eisenhower and Nixon would go in embracing the anti-Communist crusade. Republican party regulars pressed Eisenhower to support the party's entire electoral slate, but moderates like Paul Hoffman advised him that the "outright repudiation of McCarthyism and Jennerism would win millions of votes . . . among Independents and lose relatively few among the regular Republicans."[33] Hoffman's testimony, in a libel suit McCarthy had filed against William Benton, that McCarthy's charges against General Marshall were "fantastically false," and a spurious report in the *New*

York Times, fueled rumors that Eisenhower and Nixon would not support McCarthy in his bid for reelection. Such speculation forced them to address "the McCarthy problem," as it was coming to be called, but it did not force them off the fence. Nixon, for his part, issued a statement endorsing McCarthy's candidacy but specifically reserving judgment on the senator's record. In a remarkable, and unconvincing, assertion for one of the nation's leading anti-Communists, Nixon claimed that he had not examined McCarthy's allegations and added, "I don't intend to comment on his methods or charges until I know the facts."[34]

On August 22, Eisenhower gave a somewhat more plausible performance at his last Denver press conference before he left for New York City to prepare for his first round of active campaigning against Stevenson. The Republican nominee refused to give McCarthy "a blanket endorsement," but consistent with his agreement with Summerfield, Eisenhower said he would support the Wisconsin senator "as a member of the Republican organization." He would neither discuss any "proper name" in the campaign nor "support anything that smack[ed] . . . of un-Americanism," a thinly veiled jab at McCarthy. A question about McCarthy's attacks on Marshall brought Ike from behind his desk to the center of the room. Speaking quickly and emotionally, Eisenhower conceded that Marshall might have erred occasionally, but he asserted, "There was nothing of disloyalty in General Marshall's soul." At Hayward, Wisconsin, where he was convalescing after a hernia operation, McCarthy announced that he was "very happy" to learn that Eisenhower and Nixon would support him if he won his September 9 primary fight.[35]

Bernard M. Shanley, a young attorney serving on the general's staff, described September 9 as "an awful rough day" for the Eisenhower campaign. While Wisconsin voters were selecting their parties' nominees for the U.S. Senate, Eisenhower was campaigning in Indiana alongside William Jenner, who, like McCarthy, was running for reelection. Jenner not only had slandered Marshall but also had attacked Eisenhower, and that as recently as late July. One of the leading figures in Indiana politics, Eugene C. Pulliam, the publisher of the *Indianapolis Star and News*, described Jenner's criticism of the Republican nominee as an act of "political suicide" and confided to Henry Cabot Lodge that Jenner would "certainly . . . have to change his whole attitude" if he wanted to win. Eisenhower possessed little personal animosity toward McCarthy, but he considered Jenner "slimy." According to Shanley, Jenner agreed to support an Eisenhower administration in the event of a Republican victory, in exchange for "even a back-handed endorsement."[36]

Despite his contempt for Jenner, Eisenhower received in Indiana his warmest reception of the young campaign. At least one hundred thousand people lined the streets of Indianapolis to greet his motorcade, and perhaps fifty thousand attended a rally that night at Butler University. Attacking the Democrats on Korea, the "loss" of China, and the growth of the federal government, Eisenhower deleted from his prepared text an assertion that his administration would "not tolerate any trace of subversion or disloyalty in Government office." And he did not endorse Jenner by name. His concessions to the extreme Right were obvious, however, even to the general. Before asking "voters to support the entire Republican ticket from top to bottom," Ike allowed Jenner to introduce him, and the Indiana senator, at the end of Eisenhower's speech, seized the platform and grabbed Eisenhower's arm in a show of apparent unity. Near the end of the evening, Eisenhower told Shanley, "[If Jenner] puts his hand on me once again, I'm going to knock him right off that platform."[37] Saying he felt "dirty from the touch of the man," Eisenhower appeared "still almost purple with rage" when Gabriel Hague, a speechwriter, saw him in his room after the rally.[38]

Meanwhile, Senator McCarthy was coasting to victory in the Wisconsin primary with more votes than all the rest of the Senate candidates, in both parties, combined. Many observers believed that Democrats in large numbers had crossed over to support the incumbent senator and that Eisenhower might have to ride McCarthy's coattails to carry the state.[39] The Eisenhower camp may have nurtured some faint hopes that McCarthy would be denied renomination; a poll taken in January had shown him running far behind when pitted against Republican Governor Walter Kohler. Yet Kohler decided to run for reelection as governor, leaving McCarthy to defeat a less prominent opponent, Leonard F. Schmitt, by more than two to one. Disheartened by McCarthy's strong showing, Eisenhower's advisers now saw little chance of avoiding a trip to Wisconsin and a meeting with McCarthy.[40]

Whereas Stevenson was winning praise for his attack on McCarthyism in a speech to an American Legion gathering in New York City, Eisenhower's handling of the issue, according to his campaign research service, had thus far "pleased only his most uncritical supporters."[41] A few voices on the extreme Right, such as the archconservative Democrat George Creel and the reactionary Maryland publisher Talbot T. Speers, continued to urge Eisenhower to press the war on subversion, but more observers agreed with a *St. Louis Post-Dispatch* editorial that Eisenhower's failure to repudiate McCarthy and Jenner was hurting him among independent voters. Undoubtedly convinced that he would need the support of the Republican congressional leadership and national party organization to govern effectively, Eisenhower continued to defend his tolerance of anti-Communist extremists as a matter of party loyalty.[42] Nevertheless, if Americans, when they thought about domestic communism, were often prepared to take extreme steps to suppress it, they generally gave the issue scant attention. The campaign research service warned Sherman Adams in mid-September, "The theory of a 'Communist Plot' in the Government will elect no one but McCarthy, and there's doubt about that." Survey data suggested that the overwhelming concern of the public was ending the war in Korea, along with two traditional Republican issues—eliminating waste in the federal government and reducing the size of the federal bureaucracy. A poll taken by the campaign research service in four major cities indicated that those wanting Eisenhower actively to support McCarthy outnumbered respondents favoring an open repudiation 25 percent to 21 percent. Yet 40 percent expressed no opinion on the issue, while 14 percent believed Eisenhower should take a "middle of the road position."[43] That course, the one Eisenhower was trying to navigate, Stevenson had ridiculed as "the middle-of-the-gutter approach."[44]

In New York, Governor Dewey urged Eisenhower to resist pressure to visit Wisconsin, but Dewey's counsel was outweighed by that of other advisers and by Eisenhower's prior commitments to party conservatives. If he was going to be forced to campaign in McCarthy's backyard, however, Eisenhower would try to make the best of the situation. At a staff meeting at his Morningside Heights home, the candidate instructed speechwriter Emmet Hughes to insert a defense of Marshall into a speech to be delivered in Milwaukee at the climax of the Wisconsin trip. When he left for the Midwest, Eisenhower was apparently prepared to tell McCarthy publicly that the senator's attack on Marshall was "a sobering lesson of the way freedom must not defend itself."[45]

In all likelihood, someone on Eisenhower's staff who opposed a confrontation with McCarthy—perhaps Ike's close friend General Wilton B. "Jerry" Persons—leaked word of the general's intentions, because he was soon besieged by national party officials and Wisconsin politicians urging him to delete the reference to Marshall from his upcoming speech. As the campaign train moved through Michigan, Arthur Summerfield and Tom Coleman came aboard to warn Eisenhower of the dangers of offending McCarthy. On October 2, Governor Kohler, Senator McCarthy, and Henry Ringling, the Republican national committeeman from Wisconsin, flew by private plane from Madison to Peoria, Illinois, where Eisenhower's train had stopped for the night. Riding a freight elevator up to Summerfield's room at the Pere Marquette Hotel, they waited there until Eisenhower called for McCarthy. Presumably the two men argued then over the content of the Milwaukee speech; Kevin McCann, an Eisenhower speechwriter, later claimed he overheard Ike exploding at the Wisconsin senator. On the other hand, McCarthy told reporters he and the general had enjoyed a "very pleasant" visit. And Kohler, who saw Eisenhower immediately after the meeting, thought he appeared quite relaxed.[46]

On the train the next morning, Eisenhower met at least one more time with McCarthy. According to Adams, McCarthy told Eisenhower that if he did not change his speech, he would be "booed," to which Eisenhower reportedly replied, "I've been booed before, and being booed doesn't bother me."[47] As the train rolled into Wisconsin, Kohler asked Adams if he could see the controversial draft, and Adams let McCann review it with Kohler and his executive secretary, Phil Drothing. They expressed alarm at the possible effect that an affront to McCarthy could have on the state ticket, as well as the consequences for the presidential race. Mindful that President Truman had carried the state in 1948 and that Coleman had virtually "thrown in the sponge," Kohler warned Adams that the proposed speech would make it more difficult to rally Taft supporters to the general. Finally, Kohler presented Adams with a summary of remarks attributed to McCarthy in the *Congressional Record*, statements allegedly demonstrating that McCarthy had not, after all, meant to impugn Marshall's loyalty. Over the objections of Hague and Robert Cutler, a Boston banker also serving on the campaign staff, Adams at last decided to ask Eisenhower to drop the defense of Marshall. By some accounts Eisenhower readily agreed to the revision once Adams, a senior member of the campaign's inner circle, suggested it, but Hague recalled later that by the time Eisenhower agreed to the change, he was "glowering."[48]

The campaign train made several stops in Wisconsin on the way to Milwaukee. At Green Bay, McCarthy appeared briefly on the rear platform, greeted a crowd of some three thousand, and disappeared into the rear car with Kohler. Local Republican Congressman John Byrnes then introduced Eisenhower, who criticized McCarthy's tactics but said that he and the senator shared a desire to rid "this Government of the incompetents, the dishonest and above all the subversive and the disloyal." Out of sight of the crowd, McCarthy, Kohler recalled later, "kept shaking his head in disagreement and disapproval." Speculation abounded among the press corps and the campaign staff about how Eisenhower would handle the next stop, McCarthy's hometown of Appleton. Refusing to appear with McCarthy there could easily have been interpreted as a snub only slightly less offensive than the much-debated passage in the draft of Eisenhower's Milwaukee speech. According to the subsequent recollections of Kohler and Shanley, McCarthy did not introduce the general at Appleton, but one of McCarthy's biographers and press accounts of the incident disagree. According to the *New York Times*, it had been rumored that McCarthy would introduce Kohler, who would then present Ike, but instead "when the train came to a halt . . . it was Senator McCarthy who came bouncing out of the rear car onto the rear platform to introduce General Eisenhower." In his remarks, Eisenhower ignored McCarthy but told the crowd that to "clean up the mess" in Washington, the country needed "every single man . . . on the ticket here in Wisconsin from the Governor himself through the Senate and the House."[49] This is surely the most plausible account of the Appleton stop, since any other course of conduct by Eisenhower likely would have provoked a barrage of criticism from the McCarthy faithful.

Nevertheless, Eisenhower would not escape from Wisconsin unscathed. Unknown to Eisenhower and Adams, an aide, Fred Seaton, had apparently already told William Lawrence of the *New York Times* that Eisenhower was

General Eisenhower and Senator Joseph R. McCarthy (right) shake hands
after a GOP rally in Milwaukee in October 1952. The handshake
was as close as they ever came. (Eisenhower Library)

going to stand up to McCarthy at Milwaukee. In fact, Hague and Cutler had
been telling reporters all day, "Just wait till we get to Milwaukee, and you will
find out what the General thinks of Marshall."[50] The next day's headlines,
indicating that Eisenhower had abandoned a defense of his mentor in order to
placate McCarthy, constituted one of the most dramatic episodes of the campaign. Only the allegation that wealthy Nixon supporters had maintained a
secret fund for the California senator's personal use and Ike's later pledge to
"go to Korea" if elected overshadowed Eisenhower's refusal to defend Marshall at Milwaukee. *New York Times* publisher Arthur Hays Sulzberger, with
whom Eisenhower had discussed the speech before leaving New York, wired
Sherman Adams that he was "close to physically ill" about the affair. The
controversy about the missing paragraph, moreover, has since tended to obscure what Eisenhower did say in Milwaukee and to blur the extent to which
he had become caught up in the anti-Communist crusade.[51]

Choosing Milwaukee for his major campaign speech on communism was itself catering to McCarthy, and Eisenhower there seemed to embrace the paranoia on which McCarthyism thrived. At Milwaukee, Eisenhower claimed the idea that communism was not too different from American democracy had permeated schools, labor, and the press. "Most terrifying," it had reached "into Government itself." The Republican standard-bearer warned his listeners of the "contamination in some degree of virtually every department, every agency, every bureau, every section of our Government." Eisenhower asserted that the disloyal could not "be allowed to claim civil liberties as its [*sic*] privileged sanctuary from which to carry on subversion." Near the end of his speech, he added, "We have had enough, I believe, of those who have sneered at the warnings of men trying to drive Communists from high places but who have never had the sense or the stamina to take after the Communists themselves." Eisenhower's performance in Wisconsin satisfied the Old Guard, but it pained the general, perhaps for the rest of his life.[52]

"I have never before heard," the columnist Ernest K. Lindley wrote of Eisenhower in mid-October, "a Presidential candidate say quite so much which sounded so little like himself." Many surely agreed with Lindley's assessment. Despite the uncharacteristic rhetoric, some Republicans believed that Eisenhower was giving McCarthy too little support and encouraged him to renew his efforts to exploit public fears of domestic communism.[53] Most of the political pundits believed, however, that a growing perception that Eisenhower was being dominated by Taft, Jenner, and McCarthy, combined with the controversy over the Nixon fund, had produced a swing, at least among independents, toward Stevenson. The twelve-point lead Eisenhower had enjoyed over his Democratic opponent in the Gallup poll at the beginning of October had dwindled to a seven-point lead by the end of the month, and some pollsters, remembering the late shift to Truman in 1948, were saying that the race was too close to call.[54]

Nevertheless, Eisenhower and Nixon continued to hammer at the idea that the Democrats were weak on internal subversion. Perhaps the Nixon fund

"Off on a Strange Crusade"

Even many of Ike's admirers questioned his hesitancy in defending his mentor,
George C. Marshall, from attacks by McCarthy and William E. Jenner.
(Fitzpatrick, *St. Louis Post-Dispatch*, September 14, 1952)

controversy, by diluting the force of their assault on Democratic corruption,
encouraged them to emphasize the subversion issue. The campaign research
service concluded that the campaign should respond to attacks on Nixon's
hitherto secret fund as a Communist-assisted effort to discredit "one of the
nation's most out-spoken anti-Communists." Nixon later claimed that the
fund crisis simply allowed him to exploit the Hiss case more effectively by
drawing attention to his own vice-presidential candidacy. In any event, the
senator proclaimed that Stevenson in the White House would mean "more
Alger Hisses, more atomic spies, more crises."[55] At a campaign stop in
Billings, Montana, shortly after the Milwaukee speech, Eisenhower himself

promised that if he were elected, his administration would "find the pinks" in Washington. Traveling through New Jersey in late October, Eisenhower defended Marshall as one of the "great American patriots," and in a speech at Chicago Stadium he voiced concern "about methods to be used in routing communism out of our Government." Yet by never explaining the methods he thought were appropriate, he left unclear just how and where he differed with Jenner and McCarthy. His assertion in Philadelphia, during the final days of the campaign, that Americans needed "to destroy the reputation of no innocent man" in eliminating subversion was, like so much that had been said in the campaign, a mere platitude. By repeatedly claiming that communism in government was a serious problem, and that his political opponents could not be trusted to deal with it, Eisenhower had unwittingly accepted two of the basic tenets of McCarthyism.[56]

Part of the allure of the anti-Communist crusade, second to the need Eisenhower felt to cooperate with Republican conservatives, was a widespread perception that the issue could be used to woo Roman Catholics away from the Democratic party. Bernard Shanley, one of the few Catholics close to Eisenhower, repeatedly disputed the notion that McCarthy could deliver "the Catholic vote," but even Shanley thought that a strong stand by Eisenhower against communism would help him with Catholics. Stevenson's supposed unpopularity among Catholics probably encouraged the Republicans to try to reach out to that particular part of the electorate. Besides his divorce and liberal Protestant background, Stevenson compounded his difficulties with Catholics by neglecting to attend Cardinal Francis Spellman's annual Al Smith dinner in New York City, by announcing that he would not appoint an ambassador to the Vatican, and by failing to include more Catholics in key roles in his campaign. Moreover, even many of Stevenson's supporters feared that his association with Alger Hiss would hurt him among Catholics.[57]

Nowhere did the Catholic vote loom larger than in Massachusetts, where Henry Cabot Lodge faced a tough reelection battle against a popular Catholic congressman, John F. Kennedy. Lodge, as eager to take advantage of popular fears as anyone, urged Eisenhower early in the campaign to "hit communism hard" when he came to New England. By mid-October, state party officials were advising the Eisenhower campaign that communism was the number-one issue in Massachusetts and that, in light of the large Catholic population in Boston and surrounding areas, the issue had to be stressed in order to revive Eisenhower's and Lodge's flagging campaigns.[58] Late in the race, Senator Lodge asked McCarthy to come to Massachusetts to campaign against Kennedy, but because Lodge would not agree to endorse him publicly, McCarthy refused to come. In August, Lodge had warned Brownell of the political risks of Eisenhower's hesitancy in defending General Marshall. By October, however, Lodge was frantically seeking the support of John Fox, the McCarthyite editor of the *Boston Post*. He assured Fox, "I am of course endorsed by Eisenhower, Nixon, and McCarthy, and have endorsed them."[59]

During an October swing through New England, Eisenhower delivered a "hard-punching anti-Communist speech" before a huge crowd on Boston Commons. With a recent endorsement from the *Boston Post* in hand, Eisenhower warned his audience of the "terrible danger" presented to the West by "godless communism." Throughout New England, Eisenhower praised Lodge, who had been advocating the creation of a special commission to investigate internal subversion, as "a valiant fighter for his country against communism." Closing his campaign with an election-eve rally at Boston Garden, the general made a mild anti-Communist speech, omitting specific attacks on Democratic malfeasance but calling for a "devotion to the morality of freedom." At the end of the race, *Time* concluded, "In Massachusetts much depends on how much Eisenhower can cut into the Boston Irish vote on the softness-on-Communism issue."[60]

On election day, the controversy over domestic communism seemed to matter very little to most voters. All the major pollsters ultimately agreed that Communist soldiers in Korea concerned Americans far more than did Communist dupes in Washington. Louis Harris, the well-known pollster, later called domestic communism "a trailer issue" in 1952; no more than 11 percent of the American people, he found, had ever considered it one of the nation's most important problems. Eisenhower's tolerance of Senators McCarthy and Jenner probably helped him among German, Irish, and Catholic voters, but it may have hurt him among voters under age twenty-five. Harris calculated that, with 55.8 percent of the vote, Eisenhower ran ahead of twelve of the thirteen Senate candidates who could be associated with the Republican Old

Guard, and he concluded that Ike's coattails probably reelected Jenner.[61] Barry Goldwater, soon to replace Taft as the idol of the Republican Right, readily admitted that Eisenhower's popularity enabled him to triumph in his Arizona Senate contest. A subsequent study by the Republican National Committee found that Eisenhower ran ahead of GOP Senate candidates in twenty-three out of thirty contested races. As in the presidential race, communism in government played only a limited role in the congressional elections; no more than half of the successful Republican candidates had emphasized the issue in their campaigns.[62] In Wisconsin, McCarthy easily won reelection, but in the Republican sweep he received the smallest percentage of the two-party vote of all of the eleven Republicans on the statewide ticket. He ran seven points behind Eisenhower and twelve points behind an avowed anti-McCarthy Republican, Secretary of State Fred Zimmerman. And McCarthy lost every major city in the state.[63]

It also mattered very little in the end whether Eisenhower ran a campaign designed to appeal to independents by presenting a moderate image or conducted a strident, anti-Communist crusade designed to mobilize "the stay-at-homes." With 63.3 percent of eligible voters participating, the highest turnout since 1908, Eisenhower received 53 percent of the vote among those who voted in 1952 but who had stayed at home in 1948. Yet the "stay-at-homes" were not the key to the GOP victory; they voted about the same as did the rest of the electorate. To be sure, Eisenhower lost a few small constituencies, in part perhaps because of his treatment of McCarthy. The political reporters who covered the campaign and who watched the candidates more closely than anyone else preferred Stevenson over Eisenhower, according to a preelection report, better than two to one. And Eisenhower did not fare well among the nation's intellectual elite. According to *Time*'s postmortem on the campaign, Eisenhower's victory disclosed "an alarming fact, long suspected." There was "a wide and unhealthy gap between the American intellectuals and the people."[64]

Eisenhower's popularity and the lack of an appealing issue, not Stevenson's ties to Alger Hiss, doomed the Illinois governor from the start. Before the presidential conventions, 83 percent of those surveyed by the Gallup poll correctly identified Dwight Eisenhower; only 34 percent could identify Adlai

Stevenson. In March, the Gallup organization asked Democratic and Republican county chairpeople to list the five best reasons for supporting their respective parties. The five arguments most frequently occurring among the two groups were then submitted to a sample of independent voters. On three of the five "best" GOP arguments, including the claim that Democrats were soft on internal subversion, a majority of the independents found the Republican arguments convincing. More significant, on none of the five "best" Democratic issues did even a plurality of the independents find the Democratic position persuasive.[65]

If domestic communism ultimately emerged as less than an overriding issue in the 1952 election, General Eisenhower's handling of the controversy on the campaign trail did foreshadow, to some extent, his treatment of the issue as president. Far too sensible to embrace wholeheartedly the anti-Communist crusade, he nevertheless displayed a tenuous attachment to the moderately libertarian positions he had taken as a general and a college president. Although he was a political novice heavily dependent on the advice of others, Eisenhower in 1952 was less a "captive hero" than a candidate struggling to build, out of the divided factions of a minority party, a coalition capable of governing the nation. This objective, which seemed to require compromise with McCarthyite extremists, took precedence over the defense of civil liberties. In handling the Republican right wing and the Communist controversy, however, Eisenhower and his advisers made two miscalculations. They underestimated Eisenhower's advantages; the McCarthys and Jenners needed him far more than he needed them. And they underestimated the degree of cooperation the right wing would extend to Eisenhower in exchange for his endorsement.[66]

3

★ ★ ★

The General Takes Command

Delivering his first State of the Union Address on February 2, 1953, President Dwight D. Eisenhower sought to reassure Congress and the nation that his administration would tolerate neither subversives nor witch-hunters. Eisenhower told his listeners that he had already ordered department and agency heads to begin implementing a new employee security system under the direction of Attorney General Herbert Brownell, Jr. Nevertheless, Eisenhower implied that the new administration would proceed judiciously. Second only to security itself, the president's professed objective was "to clear the air of that unreasoned suspicion that accepts rumor and gossip as substitutes for evidence." Eisenhower's firm, yet restrained, tone was a clear attempt to preserve presidential control over government personnel policy from interference by Senator McCarthy and other congressional red-baiters. As Eisenhower told his audience, "The primary responsibility for keeping out the disloyal and the dangerous rests squarely upon the executive branch."[1]

For the moment, the State of the Union Address seemed to have the desired effect. The *Christian Science Monitor* reported that the president had won "a virtual pledge from Congress to allow him to establish a new and vigorous start to the whole loyalty question."[2] Arthur Krock of the *New York Times* agreed that Eisenhower had seized the initiative.[3] Many journalists and politicians believed that with the Democrats out of the White House, McCarthy would drop his complaints about Communists in government. Indeed, even before Eisenhower's victory, the columnist Ernest K. Lindley had sanguinely remarked that regardless who won the election, it would "become evident that

the federal government" had already been "thoroughly cleansed of Communists and fellow travelers." After the election, Senate Republicans, led by
Robert A. Taft, took steps to limit the amount of damage McCarthy might be
able to inflict on the incoming Republican regime. The less aggressive and
somewhat more manageable William E. Jenner was made chairman of the
Senate's internal security subcommittee and given supposedly exclusive jurisdiction over the issue of government subversion. The GOP hierarchy rele-
gated McCarthy to the chairmanship of the now allegedly innocuous Committee on Government Operations. New guidelines required all investigations to
be approved by the party's Senate leadership. Such changes reportedly led
Taft to coo, "We've got McCarthy where he can't do any harm."[4]

Senator McCarthy, of course, refused to cooperate. On January 22,
Eisenhower's second full day in office, McCarthy and his conservative allies
stalled the confirmation of General Walter Bedell Smith, Eisenhower's wartime chief of staff, as undersecretary of state. Smith, who had recently served
as ambassador to the Soviet Union and as director of the Central Intelligence
Agency (CIA), had crossed the McCarthyites by defending the veteran diplomat John Paton Davies. One of the State Department's old "China Hands,"
Davies was a favorite target of McCarthy's. On the same day that Eisenhower
delivered his State of the Union Address, McCarthy sent him a letter objecting
to the nomination of James Bryant Conant, the president of Harvard University, as U.S. high commissioner to Germany. Conant, McCarthy claimed, had
opposed the investigation of Communist infiltration in American colleges and
universities. In part as a result of Vice President Nixon's influence—and in
the case of Conant's nomination, after a personal telephone call from the
president to the Wisconsin senator—McCarthy dropped his opposition to
Smith and Conant. Both men were ultimately confirmed.[5] Nevertheless, Mc-
Carthy's hostility toward two relatively routine appointments demonstrated
what many in the administration would only reluctantly come to recognize:
McCarthy possessed no particular desire to support his party's president.
Eventually, the conflict between McCarthy and the administration seemed, in
much of the contemporary public mind and subsequent historical consciousness, to constitute the essence of the Communist issue during the Eisenhower
presidency. As we shall see, however, the confrontation between the senator

and the president represented only one facet of the administration's response to the Red Scare. The extent to which the controversy over McCarthy's behavior served as a substitute for a public debate on McCarthyism, and on the legitimacy of widespread fears about national security, was one of the real tragedies of the era.[6]

At the start of 1953, the administration's main goals seem to have been to establish its own supremacy in the search for security and to avoid unnecessary political risks. With regard to Senator McCarthy, Eisenhower believed that the GOP maverick ought simply to be ignored by the administration while it pursued its own tough anti-Communist policies. That strategy gave rise to charges that the White House was trying to appease McCarthy and to the later revisionist argument that Eisenhower, beyond the public's view, skillfully employed a subtle strategy to destroy the Wisconsin senator by preempting him. In reality, Eisenhower, early in his presidency, probably misjudged the Republican Right's commitment to McCarthy as a vehicle for the promotion of its own conservative agenda. Despite the president's desire to avoid a confrontation with McCarthy and despite a year of anti-Communist posturing by the White House, at the end of 1953 the senator, as shall soon be apparent, had reached the peak of his popularity as an outspoken critic of the administration.[7]

Dwight Eisenhower, regardless of his personal charm and electoral mandate, found himself poorly situated to deal with McCarthy. The optimism prevalent in the first weeks of 1953 and the assistance Eisenhower was receiving from Taft partially disguised certain weaknesses in the position of the administration. Homer H. Gruenther, one of the White House aides responsible for congressional relations, may have exaggerated when he recalled years later that during Eisenhower's first two years in office, Ike "was just learning the game, just learning how the pins were set up."[8] Undoubtedly, however, the politics of campaigning in 1952 had failed to prepare the general fully for the politics of governing in 1953. To complicate matters for the political newcomer in the White House, the McCarthy problem divided the administration into what might be identified as three separate camps.

First, many high-ranking administration officials, for a variety of reasons, manifested no reluctance in trying to appease McCarthy. This group included Old Guard conservatives like Postmaster General Arthur Summerfield, who had been drawn to Eisenhower, in the words of one student of the Republican Right, by "cold logic alone"—the conviction that the general was the strongest GOP candidate available in 1952.[9] A former Republican national committeeman from Michigan, Summerfield had commended McCarthy for his attack on General Marshall, had recruited the senator as a speaker at local party functions, and had funneled party funds to him, allegedly to assist McCarthy in investigating Communists in the State Department. Something of a red-baiter himself, Summerfield in 1952 called for public hearings in Michigan to expose, he said, Communist infiltration of organized labor, the professions, and the state government. As noted previously, he struggled as Republican national chairman to prevent a breach between Eisenhower and McCarthy during the presidential campaign.[10] Similarly, Secretary of Commerce Sinclair Weeks, a prominent New England Republican, had also supported McCarthy before joining the administration. Resisting suggestions that he speak out against McCarthy, Weeks had earlier defended the senator as a gallant ex-Marine who had "fought his way from one foxhole to another all the way from Honolulu to Okinawa" and who understandably did not want to see any more of the Pacific territory that he had liberated fall to communism. Former New York Congressman Leonard W. Hall, whom Eisenhower made GOP national chairman over the objections of Dewey and Taft, defended McCarthy even after the senator's differences with the administration had become public. McCarthy, Hall said in a nationally broadcast interview as late as May 1953, had been "smeared" by "the so-called liberal left wing group."[11]

This cooperationist faction also included men of unquestionable loyalty to the president, such as Secretary of State John Foster Dulles, about whom more will be said later.[12] In addition to Dulles, the administration's chief lobbyist, General Wilton B. "Jerry" Persons, with whom Ike golfed and played bridge, single-mindedly strove to deliver McCarthy's votes and those of at least three or four of his allies. Fearful of offending McCarthy, Persons would later try to keep the White House out of the army-McCarthy hearings. Persons's staff included Gerald D. Morgan, the former counsel to HCUA. Like Persons, Morgan, at least through the first months of the Eisenhower presidency, urged "getting along" with McCarthy.[13]

Secretary of the Treasury George M. Humphrey should probably be lumped among the cooperationists. The former Ohio industrialist cannot easily be ignored; his influence within the administration was immense. Recommended to Eisenhower by General Lucius Clay, Humphrey and the president from the very first "seemed to get along together famously." Preoccupied with matters of fiscal policy, however, Humphrey usually avoided direct involvement in the Communist controversy. A rock-ribbed conservative, Humphrey presumably represented a conciliatory force whenever the administration confronted the McCarthy question. Humphrey would later lobby against McCarthy's censure. Earlier in Eisenhower's tenure, Humphrey could hardly have toughened Ike's resolve to move decisively against McCarthyism. Dwight Eisenhower's frequent public diffidence toward McCarthy's outrages may well have mirrored Humphrey's own indifference.[14]

Among administration officials opposed to a confrontation with McCarthy, the closest to the senator was Vice President Richard M. Nixon. McCarthy and Nixon first met at a Stassen-for-President "cheese party" in 1947. Three years later, after the Tydings Committee had begun its investigation of McCarthy, Nixon loaned the senator his files on domestic subversion. In January 1951, after Nixon's election to the Senate, McCarthy, as the ranking Republican on the Committee on Expenditures in the Executive Departments, had Margaret Chase Smith of Maine removed from the panel to make room for Nixon; McCarthy then put him on the subcommittee on investigations. During the presidential campaign of 1952, McCarthy asserted that the election of his colleague would be "a body blow to the Communist conspiracy." Shortly after the election, Nixon, a staunch party loyalist, met with McCarthy and Persons at the home of incoming Deputy Attorney General William P. Rogers to urge McCarthy to cooperate with the administration. Nixon persisted in this conciliatory role for months. As he later said of McCarthy, "I never shared the disdain with which fashionable Washington treated him because of his lack of polished manners."[15]

At the opposite end of the spectrum from the cooperationists was a small but strategically located band of liberals who urged Eisenhower to repudiate McCarthy. Closest to the president among this group was his brother, Milton, then the president of Pennsylvania State University. In May 1953, Eisenhower wrote privately that Milton "is at this moment the most highly qualified man in the United States to be president. This most emphatically makes no exception of me." Milton Eisenhower had tried to keep his brother out of Wisconsin in 1952, and he thereafter continually urged the president to attack McCarthy publicly. Milton's outspokenness eventually led to a radio counterattack from the senator. Indeed, the president's brother believed that McCarthy tried to use him to provoke an open confrontation with the chief executive. Although Eisenhower failed to heed his brother's advice on the McCarthy problem, Milton Eisenhower's influence served to aggravate further the relationship between the Wisconsin Republican and the president.[16]

More intimately involved in the daily workings of the White House was another liberal Republican, General Robert Cutler, Eisenhower's first national security adviser. Phi Beta Kappa at Harvard, a published novelist, and the former president of the Old Colony Trust Company, Bobby Cutler had served during World War II as George Marshall's congressional liaison; Marshall called Cutler "a rose among cabbages." Repulsed by McCarthy, Cutler had urged Eisenhower to defend Marshall at Milwaukee and opposed efforts to conciliate the extreme Right. Cutler found allies on the White House staff in speechwriter Emmet Hughes, speechwriter and economist Gabriel Hague, and Press Secretary James C. Hagerty. And although Bryce N. Harlow, an assistant to Jerry Persons, seems initially to have supported Persons's efforts to work with McCarthy, Republican conservatives came to number Harlow among the group of "dangerous liberals" in the White House who were plotting against the Wisconsin senator.[17]

More influential than either the cooperationists or the liberals was a middle group of unabashed cold-warriors who nevertheless tried to distance the administration from McCarthy. This group included Henry Cabot Lodge,

Eisenhower's tactical expert on the politics of communism, and Herbert Brownell, Jr., who, as attorney general, was charged with implementing most of the administration's substantive antisubversive policies. The president ranked Lodge behind only Milton Eisenhower "in general all-round capability" for public service. Eisenhower believed, however, that Lodge, because of his long years in politics, was "apt to form judgments somewhat more colored by political considerations than would an individual whose background" was more "like Milton's." Defeated by John F. Kennedy in his bid for reelection to the Senate in 1952, Lodge became ambassador to the United Nations, where he soon made good use of his talent for anti-Communist invective. Advising Eisenhower against an open confrontation with congressional extremists, Lodge instead served, in the words of diplomatic historian Henry W. Brands, as "the administration's answer to . . . McCarthy, with the principal difference that Lodge went after real Communists."[18] With what *Time* magazine called "the unassuming air of a side-aisle usher in a big-city church," Herbert Brownell was designated by Eisenhower to oversee the administration's war on domestic subversion.[19] Doubts surfaced at his confirmation hearing about Brownell's commitment to the anti-Communist crusade, but the new attorney general soon disarmed his conservative critics. Yet even Brownell considered McCarthy to be "a very serious handicap."[20]

Among the lower echelons of the anti-McCarthyite cold-warriors, C. D. Jackson and Bernard Shanley deserve mention, in part because of what their careers suggest about McCarthy's brand of anticommunism and the administration's response to it. A journalist on loan from Henry Luce's fiercely anti-Communist *Time* magazine, Jackson served as Eisenhower's special assistant for psychological warfare. Before assuming that position, Jackson had headed the National Committee for a Free Europe, which broadcast American propaganda behind the Iron Curtain over Radio Free Europe. The CIA covertly funded the committee. Maintaining close ties to Eastern European émigrés in the United States, Jackson was an outspoken advocate of the "liberation" of the Soviet bloc countries. Despite, or perhaps because of, his impeccable anti-Communist credentials, Jackson advised against attempting to cooperate with Senator McCarthy even before Eisenhower's inauguration. And despite Jackson's credentials, McCarthy complained that Jackson was "unsympathetic toward 'strong patriotism' and Americanism." Roy M. Cohn, the chief counsel to McCarthy's committee, lumped Jackson together with Emmet Hughes and Bryce Harlow as one of the "dangerous liberals" infesting the White House. Jackson's career personified the difference between committed anticommunism and McCarthyism. So too, in a sense, did the career of White House counsel Bernard Shanley. Convinced by late February 1953 that Mc-Carthy "was completely and absolutely unpredictable," Shanley urged White House Chief of Staff Sherman Adams to adopt some plan to contain him. Once mail demanding executive action against the senator began flooding the White House, Shanley opposed any response that might be seen as offering McCarthy an olive branch. Moreover, Shanley's activities suggest that, contrary to some recent interpretations, the administration lacked a coherent strategy to undo the Wisconsin senator. Pushing Eisenhower and Brownell to support legislation to permit the deportation of native-born Communists and the revocation of their citizenship, Shanley repeatedly complained that the administration had abdicated the subversion issue to McCarthy. "If we had taken the issue from him," Shanley believed, "much of the fire would have been taken out of him and it would have been in our control where it belonged."[21]

The absence of a reliable Republican majority in Congress, as well as Eisenhower's political naïveté and disagreements within the administration, further limited the new president's ability to move decisively against McCarthy. When the Eighty-third Congress convened, Senate Republicans enjoyed a slim one-vote majority. Before the end of the term, Oregon's maverick Republican Wayne Morse defected to the opposition, and Robert Taft died, to be replaced by a Democrat. The Democrats could have reorganized the Senate before the 1954 elections had they so desired. On any given issue, McCarthy directly influenced only a handful of votes, but these could prove pivotal. Moreover, most congressional Republicans admired McCarthy, and most of them had opposed Eisenhower before the Chicago convention. The president almost immediately found Taft to be a "model of cheerful and effective cooperation," but Eisenhower's former rival lived only until June 1953. The rest of the Senate leadership offered Eisenhower scant encouragement. A dreary

President Eisenhower and Senator Robert A. Taft (left) on the golf course.
After entering the White House, Ike found his former rival to be "a model
of cheerful and effective cooperation." (UPI/Bettmann Archive)

collection of now-forgotten names, they were not, he believed, "natural leaders." Eisenhower recognized that Taft's successor as majority leader, William
F. Knowland, lacked the "sharp mind and the great experience" of the late
senator. The president later amended his private assessment of Knowland. "In
his case," Ike confided to his diary, "there seems to be no final answer to the
question, 'How stupid can you get?'"[22]

The administration's first crisis in its dealings with Joseph McCarthy came in
late February when Charles E. "Chip" Bohlen was nominated to be ambas-

sador to the Soviet Union. A career foreign service officer, Bohlen had served as President Roosevelt's interpreter at the Yalta Conference. Given the timidity the administration, and especially the State Department, later showed in handling the McCarthyites, the nomination of anyone connected with Yalta may appear remarkable at first glance. Moreover, Bohlen had substantive differences with Secretary of State John Foster Dulles. Bohlen had criticized Dulles's proposal to "unleash" Chiang Kai-shek on the Chinese mainland. As State Department counselor, he had authorized a speech by George F. Kennan attacking the Republican commitment to the "liberation" of Eastern Europe. And Bohlen had made known his disapproval of Dulles's demand for "positive loyalty" among State Department employees. On January 23, 1953, when Dulles informed Bohlen that he was being considered for the Russian position, Bohlen himself was surprised. As if seeking to scuttle his own nomination, Bohlen warned Dulles that, if asked, he would defend the Yalta agreements at his confirmation hearings.[23]

Nevertheless, the administration's selection of Bohlen is not inexplicable. A recent biographer of Bohlen has suggested that Eisenhower saw the nomination as a way to challenge McCarthy and to establish presidential dominance in foreign affairs.[24] But Ike rarely borrowed trouble; the real explanation may be less heroic. The Bohlen appointment followed an early administration pattern, demonstrated in the Smith and the Conant nominations, of selecting well-qualified establishment figures regardless of their vulnerability to McCarthyite attacks. Eisenhower apparently considered the diplomat to be "the State Department's foremost specialist on the Soviet Union." The Senate had unanimously approved Bohlen's appointment as State Department counselor only two years earlier. The administration may have seen Bohlen's promotion as a peace offering to congressional Democrats and as a means of reviving sagging State Department morale in the wake of repeated purges and public criticism. Finally, personal considerations ought not to be ignored; Eisenhower and Bohlen had become golfing companions in France while Eisenhower was NATO commander and Bohlen was the American minister.[25]

The administration, Dulles in particular, bungled the nominating process. When Bohlen told Dulles that he would accept the nomination, he reportedly warned the secretary of state to expect Senate opposition. Bohlen urged

Dulles to clear the appointment with key senators before submitting it to the entire body. Dulles had Bohlen reviewed by a panel of three former Republican ambassadors—Joseph Grew, Norman Armour, and Hugh Gibson—but he failed to do the necessary Senate spadework. To complicate matters, the secretary of state assured Eisenhower that, in his "best judgement," the nomination could be sent to the Senate "without waiting for the final FBI clearance." In fact, the FBI did not begin its routine investigation of Bohlen's background until after his nomination went to the Senate on February 27, 1953. Ironically, in almost twenty-five years of government service, Bohlen had never been subjected to a security investigation. Once Senate opposition began to surface, Dulles considered withdrawing the nomination.[26] Eisenhower, judging Bohlen "one of the ablest Foreign Service officers" he had ever met and overconfident of his ability to win over Bohlen's critics, ultimately decided that "there was nothing to do but fight it out."[27]

Closed hearings on the nomination began before the Senate Foreign Relations Committee on March 2. Predictably, Republicans Alexander Wiley of Wisconsin and H. Alexander Smith of New Jersey quizzed Bohlen about his role at Yalta. Sympathetic Democrats sought to minimize his involvement as that of a mere interpreter. Bohlen, however, would not avail himself of that escape route and, true to his words to Dulles, refused to repudiate the Yalta agreements. Still, Bohlen thought the first day of the hearings went well, with only Homer E. Ferguson of Michigan likely to vote against him.[28]

When Wiley leaked Bohlen's defense of Yalta to the press, a storm of protest erupted from conservatives. Apparently fearful that Bohlen would be apt to appease the Soviets, R. W. Scott McLeod, the State Department's security officer, complained about the nomination to Sherman Adams and confided to Styles Bridges that he had refused to grant Bohlen a security clearance. On March 7, Senator Knowland telephoned Dulles to warn him that Bridges, the president *pro tem* of the Senate, would soon deliver a speech opposing the State Department counselor. Amid the controversy over Bohlen's role at Yalta, rumors circulated about alleged "derogatory information" in the diplomat's security file. On March 5, for example, FBI agents interviewing Drew Pearson had asked the columnist if he believed that Bohlen was a homosexual. Pearson said no.[29]

At his weekly meeting with GOP legislative leaders on March 9, Eisenhower managed to persuade a reluctant Taft to support Bohlen. Privately convinced that the opposition to the appointment was "perfectly reasonable," Taft concluded that the ambassadorship was not a "sufficiently important position to make an issue of." The Ohio senator did not want to lead a fight likely to cripple the new administration. Loyalty to the president meant less to other Republicans. The day after the leaders' meeting, the Foreign Relations Committee, at the insistence of Ferguson and Knowland, postponed a scheduled vote on the nomination. With Bohlen facing a second round of committee hearings, Styles Bridges told reporters that "top" officials in the administration wanted Bohlen's name withdrawn. Shortly thereafter, Senator McCarthy announced that he was "going to oppose the nomination on the ground that Bohlen was too important a part of the old Acheson machine in the State Department to properly represent the Administration."[30] On March 13, Sherman Adams conceded to Dulles that because of the "morals" charge against the embattled nominee, the administration was "on very shaky grounds."[31]

Despite the protests, Eisenhower reiterated his support for Bohlen at his March 16 leaders' meeting, two days before the resumption of the Senate hearings. Yet the controversy deeply troubled the administration. When Dulles telephoned Taft, apparently after the leaders' conference, to assure him of the president's commitment to Bohlen, the secretary of state also told the Ohio senator that the administration did not intend to keep Bohlen in Moscow for very long. And Dulles feared that the ambassador-designate might ask to have his name withdrawn, thus leaving the president "in an embarrassing position." Perplexed by the controversy, Eisenhower sought the counsel of Douglas MacArthur, Jr., who dismissed the charges against Bohlen as "incredible."[32] As late as March 16, neither Dulles nor Donald B. Lourie, the under secretary of state for administration, had seen the FBI report on Bohlen. When Dulles informed Eisenhower the next day that J. Edgar Hoover, based on what the FBI director conceded was only a "suspicion," could not give Bohlen a "complete security clearance," the president suggested that they ask Bohlen to resign from the State Department for reasons of "health." Convinced, however, that a resignation "would look bad too," Eisenhower decided to stand by his nominee, but he admonished Dulles that the administration should never make another appointment "until we all have . . . these clearances before us and know that we aren't going to get into this again."[33]

Clearly, Dulles lacked the heart for the battle. When the Foreign Relations Committee held its second hearing on the nomination, Dulles refused to ride to Capitol Hill in the same automobile with Bohlen and told the nominee that he did not want to have his picture made with him. Dulles conceded to the committee that Scott McLeod had brought certain "derogatory information" about Bohlen to his attention. Summarizing Bohlen's FBI report, however, the secretary of state testified that nothing suggested that Bohlen was "not a good security risk," although Dulles made it plain that he would not place Bohlen in a policy-making position. After hearing Dulles, the committee approved the nomination, somewhat surprisingly, by a vote of 15 to 0.[34]

The committee's unanimous decision failed to silence either Bohlen's conservative critics or some simply loquacious senators. Georgia Democrat Walter F. George told reporters that Dulles's testimony had involved "rumors and hearsay" about Bohlen's associations with "dissolute persons," an obvious euphemism for homosexuals. McCarthy charged that it would be a "serious mistake" for the president not to withdraw the nomination. Asked to respond to McCarthy at his weekly press conference on March 19, Eisenhower insisted that Bohlen "seemed . . . to be a very fine appointment." The next day, the right-wing Democrat Pat McCarran asserted on the Senate floor that Scott McLeod had in fact refused to clear Bohlen as an acceptable security risk. For his part, McCarthy acted unimpressed that Eisenhower, Dulles, and even Brownell had each approved Bohlen after finally seeing his FBI file. "I know what is in that file," McCarthy told reporters. "I have known what's in his file for years."[35]

Obviously, McLeod and perhaps others within the executive branch were leaking information about the case to Bohlen's Senate opposition. On March 19 and again on the twenty-first, McLeod, embarrassed by the leaks and unhappy at Bohlen's selection, suggested to Jerry Persons that he himself might resign. Persons apparently told McLeod that the security officer and Dulles would have to resolve the matter themselves. White House Press Secretary James Hagerty wanted Dulles to fire McLeod; Eisenhower let Dulles know the president would support him if he did. But a letter of apology from McLeod and a warning from Sherman Adams, who feared the political consequences of a forced resignation, led Dulles to forgo the opportunity of severing McCarthy's principal channel into the State Department.[36]

When the entire Senate took up debate on the nomination on March 23, McCarthy suggested that Dulles and McLeod be placed under oath and submitted to lie detector tests "to get to the bottom of this very confusing picture." McCarthy's novel suggestion drew a quick and angry rebuff from Taft, but several senators joined McCarthy in demanding that the Senate be allowed to see Bohlen's FBI file. Taft agreed to a compromise under which the Foreign Relations Committee would select two senators to review the file and report back to the full Senate.[37] Fearful of the chilling effect such action might have on informants, the Justice Department had consistently opposed opening security files to Congress. More particularly, Herbert Brownell, not wanting to give the Democrats any ammunition for a charge that the administration was soft on security, objected to allowing a member of the minority party to see Bohlen's record. The attorney general seemed willing to sacrifice a few votes in Bohlen's favor to preserve the confidentiality of the FBI files.[38] Eager to settle the controversy, however, Eisenhower, with the support of Dulles and Taft, instructed Brownell to make Bohlen's file available pursuant to the compromise plan. On March 24, Taft himself and Democrat John J. Sparkman of Alabama went to the State Department and reviewed the diplomat's dossier.[39]

The report of the committee of two, along with Eisenhower's persistence, seemed to wear down most of the opposition. Taft told his colleagues that the only derogatory information in Bohlen's file related "solely to the fact" that Bohlen had "at times been friendly with and . . . entertained at his home persons . . . considered by the investigators or by the Department as bad security risks." Taft assured the Senate "that Mr. Bohlen was a completely good security risk in every respect." During a press conference on March 26, Eisenhower told reporters that he had visited in Bohlen's home, enjoyed "his very charming family," and believed him to be "the best qualified man for that post" that the president could find. The final round of Senate debate the next day demonstrated the agony the affair was causing many Republicans. Reluctantly deciding to follow the president, Homer E. Capehart of Indiana stated,

Eisenhower confers with Secretary of State John Foster Dulles (left) and their new ambassador to the Soviet Union, Charles E. Bohlen (right), shortly after Bohlen's confirmation by the Senate. (Eisenhower Library/National Park Service)

"These are times that try men's souls." Bourke B. Hickenlooper of Iowa, who had voted to confirm Bohlen in committee, announced during the debate that he would now oppose confirmation. "Those who had any substantial part in the nefarious operations at Yalta," he believed, "must go." McCarthy persisted in his opposition to Bohlen but, after Nixon intervened, agreed not to deliver a speech accusing Bohlen of homosexuality. At the end of three days of debate, Bohlen was confirmed by a lopsided 74-to-13 vote.[40]

As Sherman Adams recognized, "the decisiveness of the vote failed to reflect the dissatisfaction that the nomination had stirred up among the Republicans." The vote split Senate Republicans 37 to 11, with prominent party figures like Styles Bridges and Everett Dirksen joining the minority. The defections of Barry M. Goldwater of Arizona and John W. Bricker of Ohio seemed particularly to worry Eisenhower. Bohlen believed that McCarthy's tactics during the debate had offended much of the Senate and represented the beginning of his growing alienation from the majority of that body. More plausible is the likelihood that the struggle reinforced White House concerns about confronting congressional Republicans. The Bohlen affair, like several other incidents, led Eisenhower to consider the formation of a new political party dedicated to "the middle way." But his thoughts quickly returned to the more immediate goal of winning five or six senators away from the Mc-Carthyites so that the splinter group would "be reduced to impotence." The president knew that only Taft's influence had "held the mass of Republicans squarely in line" during the Bohlen vote. And when the roll call was over, Taft sent word to the White House: "No more Bohlens."[41]

Although the Bohlen nomination represented the administration's first major triumph over McCarthy, the senator's investigation of the International Information Agency (IIA) soon found the White House in full retreat. An outgrowth of the Office of War Information, the IIA constituted the propaganda arm of the State Department. Through the Voice of America (VOA), the IIA transmitted short-wave radio programs in some forty languages to eighty-seven countries, many of them behind the Iron Curtain. The agency's propaganda activities also included an international library system of over 190 libraries in the major cities of approximately sixty-five nations. With an annual budget of $100 million, the IIA employed ten thousand people, roughly 40 percent of the State Department's total work force.[42]

Even before Senator McCarthy launched his investigation of the IIA in mid-February 1953, the agency had experienced a checkered history. Members of Congress feared its potential to serve as an organ of the executive branch; State Department traditionalists resented its incursions into conventional forms of diplomacy. Since the tangible results of propaganda activities were difficult to identify, many budget-minded politicians probably suspected that the whole operation was a giant boondoggle. Worse yet for the agency, John Taber, the chairman of the House Appropriations Committee, had voiced a widely held opinion when he denounced the IIA as "decidedly pinko."

Senator Taft, who defended McCarthy's investigation of the agency, believed, according to Drew Pearson, that "it should have been cleaned out or abolished long ago." In reality, the IIA had been repeatedly investigated and reorganized before Eisenhower took office. Criticism of the agency was by no means limited to congressional red-baiters. At the time McCarthy began Senate hearings on the program, Eisenhower had appointed a Committee on Foreign Information Activities, under William H. Jackson, to conduct yet another investigation. James Hagerty complained that IIA officers abroad often knew little about the countries in which they served, did little to cultivate the local press, and were outclassed by their British, French, and Soviet counterparts.[43] The government's overseas information services presented, in short, what might be called a perfect target of opportunity for Senator McCarthy.

On February 16, McCarthy opened hearings on the alleged conspiracy behind the locations of Baker East and Baker West, which were, respectively, the Atlantic and the Pacific sites of two huge VOA transmitters that were designed to penetrate Russian jamming and to broadcast into the Soviet bloc. Expert opinion on the optimum locations of the transmitters had been divided; at least one VOA engineer, Lewis McKesson, had favored sites in Florida and southern California over the points eventually selected, Cape Hatteras, North Carolina, and Seattle, Washington. The weight of scientific authority, including a study by Dr. Jerome B. Wiesner, the director of the Research Laboratory of Electronics at the Massachusetts Institute of Technology, supported the agency's decision. Nevertheless, McCarthy, using McKesson as his star witness, attempted to demonstrate that the North Carolina and Washington sites were the worst possible locations that could have been selected and that such malfeasance could be explained only as an act of sabotage by Communist agents within the IIA. McCarthy's evidence of disloyalty in the organization also included the presence in IIA libraries of books by Communist authors like William Z. Foster and alleged fellow travelers like philosopher John Dewey, educator Robert Hutchins, and historians Henry Steele Commager, Arthur M. Schlesinger, Jr., and Foster Rhea Dulles, a cousin of the secretary of state.[44]

With no apparent direction from the president, the administration commenced on an unseemly course of capitulating to McCarthy. Carl McCardle, the assistant secretary of state for public affairs, immediately issued a sweeping directive prohibiting IIA agencies from making use of the works "of any Communists, fellow travelers, et cetera." Books by suspect authors were ordered removed from IIA libraries. To be sure, C. D. Jackson advised against the "immediate liquidation" of the VOA; Jackson feared that such action would be interpreted "as evidence of panic on the part of the Administration, particularly on the part of the Secretary of State." Jackson, however, recommended that Robert L. Johnson, then the president of Temple University, be appointed as a kind of receiver to preside over the restructuring of the information program. For his part, Eisenhower tried to evade the controversy. When asked at his weekly press conference on February 25 whether McCarthy's investigation was "helping the fight against Communism," the president replied, "I will not answer without a bit more preparation."[45]

On March 3, Johnson took office as the new IIA director and shortly thereafter dismissed six employees as security risks. A new director and a few firings, however, could not, without White House support, stem the disintegration of the embattled agency. A wave of resignations soon swept the organization. Early in April, Herbert T. Edwards, the chairman of the IIA's film division, and Reed Harris, a senior aide to Johnson, were forced from their positions. McCarthy had held Edwards responsible for "widespread waste and Communist propaganda" in his department; Harris had been guilty of leftist activities in the 1930s. A few days after Bohlen was confirmed as ambassador to the Soviet Union, Nixon, Jerry Persons, and William P. Rogers once more entertained McCarthy at Rogers's home. They thought they won there a pledge from the senator to begin cooperating with the administration. If any such agreement existed, it was short-lived and did not include the IIA. On April 14, for example, McCarthy boycotted a meeting that Nixon had arranged for the senator, Johnson, and Johnson's chief aide, Martin Merson. Late in April, Johnson and Merson did manage to win an audience with C. D. Jackson. But even the president's special assistant for psychological warfare, who was no friend of McCarthy's, refused to take the plight of the IIA to Eisenhower. According to Merson, Jackson told them "that he wouldn't dream of approaching the President on the subject." It was Eisenhower's policy, Jackson explained, "not to offend anyone in Congress."[46]

On March 17, a new directive from Assistant Secretary McCardle deleted the "et cetera" from the kinds of writers banned by the IIA, but the revised policy did nothing to still the swelling controversy over the stocking of the overseas libraries.[47] Ironically, a program designed to enhance American prestige abroad or, in the language of the cold war, to win the hearts and minds of men to the cause of freedom, rapidly deteriorated into a propaganda debacle. Nervous IIA librarians actually burned a handful of books; this unthinking embrace of Nazi tactics horrified many Europeans. Perhaps more damaging to the image of the United States was an IIA library tour made by Roy Cohn and G. David Schine, an investigator for McCarthy's subcommittee and a self-appointed anti-Communist ideologue. Visiting twelve cities in six European countries within seventeen days, Cohn and Schine ostentatiously demanded separate rooms, since, they said, they were not from the State Department, a snide allusion to charges of rampant homosexuality within the diplomatic service. At one point, Schine supposedly chased Cohn around a hotel lobby and pounded him over the head with a rolled-up newspaper. Whether true or not, the story aptly illustrates the unflattering press coverage the pair received in Europe. At least one American official, Theodore Kaghan, the acting director of public affairs of the U.S. High Commission in Germany, denounced Cohn and Schine as "junketeering gumshoes." A left-wing playwright in the 1930s, Kaghan subsequently resigned under pressure from Scott McLeod.[48]

McCarthy and Johnson continued to wrangle over library policies into the summer of 1953. While McCarthy claimed that there were thirty thousand books by three hundred pro-Communist authors in the IIA holdings, Johnson asserted the right of IIA libraries to stock works by Communist authors if doing so served "the ends of democracy." In one of his more anti-intellectual rejoinders, McCarthy alleged, "When the State Department purchases a book by a Communist author, it is . . . placing its stamp of approval upon his writings." The bewildering series of directives and policy statements spawned by the controversy probably led to the removal of no more than 1 percent of the IIA's holdings, but by May 1953, the flow of books to the overseas libraries had dropped from fifty thousand a month to three hundred. In June

1953, a citizens' panel appointed by Johnson to investigate the affair reported that the agency was "utterly shaken in morale."[49]

Amid growing pressure to defend the IIA and to denounce McCarthy, Eisenhower held his tongue for weeks. Speaking for many of the president's supporters, Harry A. Bullis, who had urged Eisenhower to take a hard line against communism during the 1952 campaign, complained: "It is a fallacy to assume that McCarthy will kill himself. It is our belief that McCarthy should be stopped soon."[50] Finally, delivering the commencement address at Dartmouth College on June 14, Eisenhower responded publicly to McCarthy's assault on the foreign information program. Before delivering his address, Eisenhower had been drawn into a discussion of the censorship controversy with John J. McCloy, the former high commissioner to Germany, New York Judge Joseph M. Proskauer, and Lester B. Pearson, the Canadian secretary of state for external affairs. The president heard McCloy relate how he had purposefully included works critical of American officials in American libraries in Germany; indeed, McCloy believed the diversity of material found in American libraries was the key to their popularity. Apparently touched by McCloy's comments, Eisenhower departed from his prepared text to admonish the Dartmouth students, "Don't join the book burners." How, he asked, could Americans fight communism without knowing "what it is, and what it teaches"? As for American writers critical of their country's institutions, Eisenhower added, "Even if they think ideas that are contrary to ours, their right to say them, their right to record them, and their right to have them at places where they are accessible to others is unquestioned, or it isn't America."[51]

One need not doubt the sincerity of Eisenhower's comments, but they constituted an uncharacteristically libertarian posture for the president. The very next day, he told Dulles that his Dartmouth remarks had not been directed toward the State Department's information program "but to the general proposition of freedom of thought." At a June 17 news conference, Eisenhower tried to return publicly to what he would have called "the middle way." Asked if his Dartmouth speech represented an attack on McCarthy, Eisenhower predictably responded, "I never talk personalities." Moreover, he denied that he had intended to defend books that attempted to "propagandize

America into communism." Yet he went on to suggest that everyone should read the works of Karl Marx, as well as Stalin's *Problems of Leninism*. Presumably the president would ban only the more obscure Marxist theorists. Eisenhower promised to discuss the issue with Dulles, a promise he repeated when the book controversy came up at another press conference two weeks later. "There is no question," Eisenhower then assured the press, "as to where I stand."[52]

The cabinet belatedly took up the issue on June 26. John Foster Dulles explained there that Congress had created the IIA information centers as "special purpose" libraries to promote an understanding of American life, so that even the Bible or the works of Shakespeare might be inappropriate for an IIA bookshelf. Dulles's remarks to the cabinet, and a memorandum he sent to the president the next day, seemed calculated mainly to distance the secretary of state from the turmoil surrounding the information program. Dulles admitted that early in March he had told Robert Johnson that the IIA should use works by Communist authors "only with great care," that magazine articles detrimental to the United States should not be used, and that periodicals "receptive to international Communist propaganda" should be banned. Johnson translated Dulles's advice into guidelines that produced consequences—the book burnings and the attendant public outcry—that, the secretary of state claimed, "were not called for by any reasonable interpretation of the directives." Dulles attributed the overreaction of IIA librarians to an inordinate fear or offending Congress and "a deliberate effort to discredit the anti-Communist policy by trying to make it appear absurd." Expressing a desire "to bring policy abroad into conformity with policy at home," President Eisenhower, still chafing at public criticism of the IIA, asked Dulles to prepare yet another briefing on the information program for discussion at the next cabinet meeting.[53]

In the interim, Johnson issued a July 8 directive that, among its several provisions, specifically prohibited the burning of books and refused to impose a uniform ban on works by Communist authors or on books considered "controversial" or critical of American institutions and policies. Both C. D. Jackson and Martin Merson hoped that Dulles would solicit Eisenhower's endorsement of Johnson's temperate order. After conferring with the president, however, the secretary of state simply authorized Johnson to announce that Eisenhower approved of the IIA director making the statement but that he had not expressly approved its contents.[54] Nevertheless, Johnson's statement provided the basis for Dulles's presentation to the cabinet on July 10. A vigorous debate ensued. C. D. Jackson defended Johnson, but Charles E. Wilson, the secretary of defense, argued that the federal government ought not to be in the library business at all. Dulles and Harold E. Stassen, the director of the Foreign Operations Administration, took an expansive view of the role of the IIA information centers. Vice President Nixon made the salient observation that Congress would never fund general-purpose libraries. Yet despite the contention within the cabinet, most of those present probably agreed with the secretary of state that the success of the new policy would hinge on the individual eventually selected to manage the information program on a permanent basis.[55]

The administration, to be sure, wanted to replace Robert Johnson, who was ready to return to private life, and to establish a new United States Information Agency (USIA) separate from the State Department. Convinced that a new director could "change the aura of the organization literally overnight," Eisenhower approached Philip Reed, the chairman of General Electric, and D'Arcy Brophey, of the Heritage Foundation. Both men turned down the offer. Reed told C. D. Jackson that "no one in his right mind would take the job." Jackson conceded that Reed was correct "in theory." Promising to "back the right new director to the fullest," Eisenhower, however, eventually recruited the apparently sane Theodore C. Streibert, one of the founders of the Mutual Broadcasting System and a former consultant to the VOA, as Johnson's replacement.[56] In August, an independent USIA was established. Despite severe budget cuts and twenty-five hundred dismissals, Streibert managed to bring a measure of stability to the operation. After McCarthy's assaults began to ebb, Streibert discovered a supportive president, who met monthly with the director to discuss USIA programs and lobbied Congress for adequate funding.[57] By the spring of 1954, Streibert, at the urging of the White House, could deny McCarthy's request that a biography of the senator be placed in the USIA libraries.[58]

All in all, McCarthy's investigation of the government's propaganda activities proved to be little short of catastrophic. Frederick Woltman, of the *New York World-Telegram and Sun*, called the probe "one of the most disgraceful, scatter-brained, inept, misleading and unfair investigations in Congressional annals." After spending $8,434,000 on the Baker transmitters, a beleaguered State Department abandoned the entire project. Before leaping in front of a truck, Raymond Kaplan, a VOA engineer who had worked on the Baker program, left behind an eerie suicide note: "Once the dogs are set upon you, everything you have done from the beginning of time is suspect."[59] The damage done to morale within the information program was incalculable. Pro- and anti-McCarthy factions formed within the agency as many employees, rightly convinced that the administration would not protect them, sought to curry favor with McCarthy by leaking information to the Wisconsin senator. And the persecution of the IIA constituted a critical episode in the erosion of the prestige of the United States abroad, a by-product of the Communist controversy that we shall later consider in detail.[60]

Martin Merson's assertion that the IIA affair was essentially an attempt by Republican conservatives to embarrass Eisenhower in "a plain back-alley fight for political power and control" is difficult to substantiate. Nevertheless, many believed that the GOP Right hoped to use McCarthy to reestablish its control of the party. Given the agency's political vulnerability, the information service provided McCarthy and his cohorts in Congress the ideal opportunity to flex their muscles at the expense of the White House, especially when Senator Taft failed to come to the president's aid. As Emmet Hughes wrote in his diary, how could the administration make a stand against the Wisconsin Republican on this "soggy, fog-bound Information Program"?[61] Dwight Eisenhower apparently concluded that the risks of vigorously defending the troubled agency were prohibitive.

A doctrinaire respect for the separation of powers bolstered President Eisenhower's attempts to cooperate with Republican conservatives in Congress. During his first months in office, the president repeatedly defended Congress's right to investigate American communism. There were, to be sure, limits to the administration's forbearance. When J. B. Matthews, a member of the staff of the McCarthy subcommittee, published an article in the *American Mercury* that alleged massive Communist infiltration of the Protestant clergy, Emmet Hughes and William P. Rogers hatched a scheme in which the president of the National Conference of Christians and Jews would send a letter of protest to the White House, and Eisenhower would reply by repudiating the charges. Sherman Adams approved the plan, and Eisenhower cooperated in its execution with apparent pleasure. Yet the White House played a minimal role in Matthews's dismissal. Had not Nixon and Rogers kept McCarthy occupied in a meeting the afternoon the administration issued its denunciation of Matthews, the Wisconsin senator, under pressure from his own subcommittee members, would have fired him without any prodding from President Eisenhower.[62]

The president demonstrated somewhat more initiative when Senator McCarthy clearly threatened to intrude on executive prerogatives, especially in the field of national security policy. After Don Surine of McCarthy's staff complained that a civilian group Eisenhower had appointed to advise the National Security Council (NSC) lacked proper security clearance, the president vetoed a conciliatory letter Bobby Cutler had dictated and ordered his national security adviser to respond to the inquiry with a curt telephone call.[63] Eisenhower also stood by Allen W. Dulles, the director of the CIA, when Dulles made William A. Bundy his liaison with the NSC. Dean Acheson's son-in-law, Bundy had contributed four hundred dollars to Alger Hiss's legal defense. When Vice President Nixon intervened on Bundy's behalf, McCarthy agreed to forgo his threatened investigation of the CIA.[64] Allen Dulles showed more mettle in dealing with McCarthy than did his brother, the secretary of state; at one point, the CIA director reportedly told Eisenhower he would resign if McCarthy was not silenced. Yet even Allen Dulles could not avert, in the words of one historian of the intelligence organization, "a vast internal purge of the Agency" as the cost of avoiding public hearings before the Wisconsin Republican.[65]

As the imbroglio over the IIA had suggested, Eisenhower would do little to resist invasions of executive discretion when the momentary political advantage lay with Senator McCarthy. On March 27, McCarthy announced that he had reached an agreement with the Greek owners of 242 merchant ships to cease their carrying trade with the People's Republic of China, North Korea, and the Far Eastern ports of the Soviet Union. Predicting a reduction of 10 to 45 percent in the amount of imports entering Communist harbors, McCarthy claimed that the agreement would have "some of the effect of a naval blockade" and would help bring about an American victory in Korea. The Greeks presumably were motivated by more than a desire to avoid being hauled before McCarthy's subcommittee, although that undoubtedly was a consideration. Many of the shipowners had purchased surplus vessels from the U.S. government at the end of World War II, only to default on their loans. Accordingly, some of the Greeks hoped to exchange their trade boycott for easier terms. McCarthy seems to have been flagrantly intruding on the collection efforts of the Justice Department and wholly ignoring the State Department's statutory monopoly on the conduct of American foreign policy. McCarthy told reporters that he had not advised the State Department of the negotiations because of their "extremely delicate" nature. Understandably, Harold Stassen criticized McCarthy for "undermining" the diplomatic position of the administration. Although calling the senator's actions "misguided," Eisenhower, at an April 2 press conference, disagreed with Stassen's characterization of McCarthy's conduct. Because he could not legally commit the United States to anything, McCarthy could not, Eisenhower rationalized, literally undermine American policy. Telling reporters that the White House was "getting better cooperation with the Senate and House every day," the president asserted that, with regard to the rift between Stassen and McCarthy, he was "not the slightest bit unhappy."[66]

The State Department tried unsuccessfully to negotiate a rapprochement with the senator.[67] McCarthy, who had promised further trade agreements, now turned his efforts to securing a British boycott of Communist China. At the urging of Senators W. Stuart Symington of Missouri and John L. McClellan of Arkansas, two Democratic members of his subcommittee who saw an opportunity to embarrass the administration, McCarthy sent Eisenhower a letter demanding a statement of policy regarding Western trade with Communist countries. Privately, Eisenhower felt increased trade might reduce international tensions. As Symington and McClellan had anticipated, however, the letter created a dilemma for the White House. No public official in the early 1950s wanted to be perceived as in any way appeasing a Communist nation, yet it was difficult to demand that America's capitalist allies abandon a lucrative field of commercial enterprise. At a White House staff meeting on May 22, Cutler lamented that McCarthy's activities would eventually leave the United States "without any Allies." He and C. D. Jackson supported a stiff rebuke of McCarthy. According to Staff Secretary Lawrence A. Minnich, Adams and most of the rest of Eisenhower's inner circle believed the issue was "too complicated for use in straightening out the Senator." In other words, public opinion on the trade issue seemed to support McCarthy. After explaining to the senator that he had been the victim of a political ambush, Nixon, again acting as the peacemaker, at least managed to persuade McCarthy to retract his letter.[68]

By the summer of 1953, Eisenhower's vacillation before McCarthy's onslaughts clearly seemed to be hurting the administration among the general public. As columnist Stewart Alsop wrote, "What is going on here, in short, is less a reign of terror than a reign of stupidity."[69] Assessing the president's handling of Congress, political scientist Clinton Rossiter concluded that Eisenhower's "experiment in cooperation . . . failed miserably."[70] Few within the White House questioned Ike's personal distaste for his principal senatorial antagonist. Yet, besides all the other reasons he had for avoiding a pitched battle with McCarthy, the president felt a certain lack of responsibility for what was going on around him. To himself and to his closest friends, usually conservative business and military types outside government, Eisenhower explained McCarthy as mainly a creation of the press. If the newspapers would ignore him, as the president tried to do, the senator's influence would dissipate.[71] If Eisenhower's diagnosis was at least partially sound, his prescription proved ineffective. For his part, Senator McCarthy, according to Roy Cohn, despised Eisenhower as a political "lightweight." The truces Nixon seemed invariably to be trying to negotiate between the senator and the executive branch were doomed to collapse because McCarthy had no interest in an accommodation with the president. As Cohn summarized McCarthy's attitude, "He cared nothing about a place on the White House dinner list."[72]

Temperament and style, of course, separated Eisenhower and McCarthy

"Have A Care, Sir"

To many observers, the genial old soldier seemed wholly outmatched
by Joseph McCarthy; Eisenhower's response to the senator's outrages often
appeared woefully inadequate. The actual situation was more complex.
(Herblock, *Washington Post*, March 4, 1954)

more than did fundamental differences about the role of political dissent in a
free society. Even without prodding from McCarthy, Eisenhower, on more
than one occasion, assumed a virulent anti-Communist stance during his first
few months in office. When Robert Taft objected to the dismissal of Communist teachers without evidence that their beliefs had interfered with their
teaching, Eisenhower argued that party membership itself should be grounds
for termination. Moreover, he claimed "that it would be extremely dangerous
to try to limit the power of Congress to investigate" communism in the
schools.[73]

More controversial was the unyielding position President Eisenhower took on the Rosenberg case. Julius and Ethel Rosenberg had been convicted of conspiracy to commit espionage as part of an atomic spy ring that also included Klaus Fuchs, Harry Gold, and David Greenglass. Only the Rosenbergs refused to cooperate with government prosecutors, and only they received death sentences. The Rosenberg case became a radical cause célèbre, and supporters of the couple inundated the White House with requests for clemency. Advised by Brownell that evidence, which the government could not make public, conclusively established the defendants' guilt and advised by J. Edgar Hoover of Communist influence within the clemency campaign, Eisenhower twice denied the Rosenbergs' pleas for mercy. The president had no reason to doubt their guilt, but the imposition in peacetime of the death penalty for espionage was unprecedented. Moreover, the president's statements in denying the clemency petitions—first the assertion that the Rosenbergs' crimes "could very well result in the deaths of many, many thousands of innocent citizens" and later that the defendants were guilty of "immeasurably increasing the chances of atomic war"—employed precisely the kind of rhetoric that a fearful public did not need to hear in 1953.[74]

The Rosenberg case, in particular the thought of executing a mother with two young children, triggered vocal protests throughout Europe. Eisenhower claimed to be "somewhat astonished" at the notoriety that the case had supposedly obtained among Italians in particular. But he defended the double death penalty against critics at home and abroad. Eisenhower relied on a report prepared for President Truman by the Psychological Strategy Board that stressed the gravity of the Rosenbergs' crimes and the need to take a strong stance against Soviet aggression. President Eisenhower also embraced a widely circulated rumor that Ethel Rosenberg had masterminded the entire conspiracy. Had Eisenhower given the Rosenberg file closer scrutiny, he would have learned that Ethel played only a minor role in the plot and that J. Edgar Hoover, fearful of the public's reaction, had initially opposed her execution. The president might also have discovered that Klaus Fuchs, not the Rosenbergs, constituted the more serious breach of American security. Concerned that the United States not appear "weak-kneed," Eisenhower, however, thought that the death of the Rosenbergs would serve as a deterrent to future Soviet espionage.[75]

Regardless of the president's own anti-Communist crusading and despite the censure he received then and later for not "standing up to McCarthy," the point should be made that much of McCarthy's constituency was not appeased. In June 1953, Tom Coleman, writing to Leonard Hall, complained that too few changes had been made in the State Department since Eisenhower had taken office. "You must remember," Coleman admonished Hall, "that Dulles is not greatly respected here in Wisconsin." When the Republicans lost a special election in Wisconsin's Ninth Congressional District by a wide margin, most people writing to the party's national headquarters blamed the defeat on Eisenhower's adherence to Truman's foreign policy, his failure to reduce taxes, and his failure to support Senator McCarthy. As one Connecticut Republican tried to impress on Hall, "McCarthy . . . is admired and trusted more than you people seem to realize." Whatever the polling data or election results might have suggested, the mail from the Republican grass roots was overwhelmingly sympathetic to McCarthy throughout 1953. And virtually none of it criticized Eisenhower for not "standing up" to the senator. The comments of Mrs. Loyd R. Haight of Ritzville, Washington, typified the views of many exasperated Republicans: "If it weren't for Senator McCarthy and his followers, I'd give up."[76]

The 1953 off-year elections highlighted a problem Eisenhower had first encountered in the presidential race: party conservatives faithful to McCarthy provided a poor barometer of the opinions of the electorate as a whole. A postelection survey conducted in Wisconsin's Ninth District, which the Republicans had lost for the first time in history, concluded that McCarthy "had no major influence on the election results." In fact, McCarthy, whose approval rating was slightly below that of the administration, may have hurt the ticket. More interestingly, respondents expressing disapproval of McCarthy overwhelmingly favored the Democratic candidate, whereas those who approved of McCarthy split almost evenly between the two parties. After the party's stunning loss in Wisconsin, along with defeats in another special congressional election in New Jersey and a string of losses in state and municipal elections, Hall admitted that the Republican party was "in trouble."[77] For anti-Communist conservatives, however, the election returns did not indicate a need for a shift in tactics. "We must keep the [Democrats] on the defensive on communism," Senator Karl Mundt wrote Hall. "After all, what other issue have we?"[78]

A cautious man, Dwight Eisenhower normally preferred not to seek out opportunities to fan the fires of the Communist controversy; shortly after taking office he vetoed a proposal by Richard Nixon to reopen the Hiss case.[79] By November, frustration with McCarthy and a deteriorating political environment combined to lead Eisenhower and Brownell into their own ill-conceived effort to exploit the politics of anticommunism. After discussing the case with the president, the attorney general delivered a speech accusing former President Truman of having appointed a Communist agent, onetime Assistant Secretary of the Treasury Harry Dexter White, as the executive director of the International Monetary Fund. For a number of reasons—a grand jury had refused to indict White, the charges against him were seven years old, and he had been dead since 1948—Brownell's allegations raised a brief storm of protest in both the United States and Europe. Many observers interpreted Brownell's speech as no more than a resumption of the GOP's 1952 campaign tactics of trying to discredit the Democrats by linking them to communism and corruption. Leonard Hall had, in fact, worked with Brownell to provide a "publicity build up" for the attorney general's speech and to ensure a sympathetic reaction from key congressional committees. Brownell had hoped to upstage McCarthy.[80] At what was probably his most heated press conference to that point in his presidency, Eisenhower, on November 11, 1953, confessed his ignorance of the details of the case and denied the charge that Truman would have knowingly appointed a Communist to high office. Eisenhower likely failed to anticipate the tumult that Brownell's speech would make. Years later, the former chief executive tried to defend Brownell's actions on the dubious ground that they served to alert the nation to the dangers of subversion.[81] By November 1953, surely the American people had been alerted often enough.

Eisenhower and Brownell had entered a contest in which they were rank amateurs compared with Joe McCarthy, and he regained the spotlight before the end of November. In a nationally broadcast speech attacking Truman and the Democrats, McCarthy unexpectedly turned his fire on the Eisenhower administration. Although praising the administration for dismissing hundreds

of security risks, McCarthy complained that the State Department had retained John Paton Davies on its payroll as an adviser to the U.S. high commissioner in Germany. McCarthy also charged that the administration had failed
to secure the release of supposedly hundreds of American flyers shot down
over Manchuria by the Chinese during the Korean War. Finally, McCarthy
suggested that U.S. aid to non-Communist countries be made contingent on
their refusal to trade with the People's Republic of China.[82] Describing the
speech as "an open declaration of war" on the administration, C. D. Jackson
expressed to Adams the hope that the address would "open the eyes of some of
the President's advisers" who seemed to view the senator as "really a good
fellow at heart." Others within the White House shared a growing sentiment
in favor of a final showdown with the senator. James C. Hagerty recorded in
his diary that the president himself professed neither anger nor surprise at
McCarthy's outburst, but Eisenhower did declare himself ready to wash his
hands of the GOP's "radical right."[83]

During his first year in office, Dwight Eisenhower, to be sure, had openly
defied the McCarthyites by sending Charles Bohlen to Moscow, but generally
the new president sought to avoid confrontations while establishing his own
anti-Communist credentials. His policy had yet to bear fruit. By December
1953, Joseph McCarthy's popularity had reached its peak. Ike, on the other
hand, stood in no better stead with his party's conservatives than he ever had.
A final solution to "the McCarthy problem" remained months away. Meanwhile, throughout the federal government, the administration would conduct
its own campaign against the international Communist conspiracy.

Securing the Federal Work Force

Whatever chance Dwight Eisenhower had to silence more strident anti-Communists depended on his ability to convince the public that the new administration would make good on Republican campaign promises to drive the reds and "pinks" from the federal government. Accordingly, reform of the employee loyalty program, which the GOP had inherited from Harry S. Truman, became a priority for Eisenhower. Given the importance of personnel policy and the chasm that existed between Eisenhower and the Republican conservatives who dominated the anti-Communist crusade, the security program might logically have become a focal point in the struggle between the White House and the McCarthyites. Perhaps surprisingly, it did not. The president's willingness to defer to Congress and his own obsession with national security neutralized the issue as a point of contention between the administration and congressional anti-Communists. As we shall now see, however, the program remained controversial; Eisenhower tried to maintain his distance from it, in part because he preferred a detached style of executive leadership and in part because detachment made political sense.

Before taking office in January 1953, the president-elect appointed an advisory Special Committee on Government Organization, consisting of his brother Milton, Nelson A. Rockefeller, and Arthur Flemming. The employee loyalty program fell within the jurisdiction of the committee, which recommended that the establishment of a new loyalty system await a study of the issue by a proposed bipartisan panel of judicious elder statesmen like John W. Davis, Owen Roberts, and Learned Hand. Milton Eisenhower, Rockefeller, and Flemming also urged the president to take an aggressive stance on the issue.[1]

It was not to be. Despite the prompting of Henry Cabot Lodge and a few others within the administration, Eisenhower showed little enthusiasm for a special committee. Conservative critics argued that the demand for such a body was a mere ploy by "Left Wing organizations and New Deal columnists" to delay needed efforts to ferret out subversives. Moreover, they argued, a special commission would be a "direct affront" to Congress in light of its refusal to fund the ill-fated Nimitz commission, a blue-ribbon panel Truman had appointed to study the entire internal security controversy. And the suggestion that Eisenhower take the lead on the issue encountered powerful and immediate opposition. Sherman Adams vetoed the Rockefeller committee's recommendations in a January 5, 1953, memorandum to Herbert Brownell.[2]

Yet, during his first weeks in office, President Eisenhower came under pressure from Congress to address the security issue, and he was himself worried about the government's ability to protect its secrets. Lodge, for example, warned Eisenhower early in January that Republican Senator Homer E. Ferguson of Michigan was "still red hot about communists" among Americans working at the United Nations.[3] Representative Edward H. Rees of Kansas and Senator George W. Malone of Nevada had introduced legislation to create a nonpartisan commission to administer the employee loyalty program. At the same time, the administration was concerned about the case of William Remington, a Commerce Department employee cleared by a regional loyalty board but later convicted of lying to a congressional committee about giving classified documents to Elizabeth Bentley, an ex-Communist turned well-traveled informant.[4] A February 18, 1953, meeting of the National Security Council typified the anxious tenor of the times. There the president "confessed that he was frankly frightened" that a secret report by the technical staff of the Congressional Joint Committee on Atomic Energy had been leaked to a Princeton professor. Only three persons could have been responsible for the leak, he believed, and if they had been in the armed services, the culprits would "have been shot."[5]

As president, Eisenhower preferred to act in less dramatic fashion. To be sure, Brownell, along with Vice President Nixon, persuaded Eisenhower to expand the loyalty program from one that attempted to expose the disloyal to one that focused on likely "security risks." Anyone, Nixon observed, could sign a loyalty oath. Even an otherwise patriotic employee, it was feared, might prove untrustworthy. A civil servant who was, in Brownell's words, "a homosexual or an alcoholic or was leading an irregular, abnormal life . . . was automatically a subject for blackmail." Convinced that anyone who was "no good" could be fired under existing laws, Eisenhower apparently did not feel that the new emphasis on "security" constituted a drastic change in the existing system.[6]

At first the president, surely hoping to put the issue behind him, moved quickly, if quietly, to reform the Truman program. At a January meeting with GOP legislative leaders, Eisenhower informed the Republican congressional hierarchy that henceforth the test of suitability for federal employment would include not just loyalty, but the absence of any personal characteristics that might render an employee unreliable. Expressing the belief that government employment represented "a privilege not a right," the president promised the congressional leaders that the administration would proceed "vigorously" to institute a security program covering all employees. By the middle of the month, the administration had already circulated a proposed executive order intended to establish a new security system. When the issue came up at Ike's first cabinet meeting, on January 23, the president set three goals for the program: the protection of the "legitimate rights" of employees, the simplification and uniformity of standards, and an emphasis on security rather than loyalty.[7]

Fairly accurate accounts of the form the new security initiative would take appeared in the press early in February. News accounts led the public to expect final action by Eisenhower within a few days. As reported in the press, the old regional loyalty boards and the central Loyalty Review Board (LRB) were to be abolished. In their place, final authority for decisions on job applicants and incumbents would be vested in the heads of the various departments and agencies. They would be assisted by advisory hearing boards, but unlike the Truman-era loyalty boards, the new bodies would consist of federal employees from outside the affected agency. In the absence of the LRB, the primary responsibility for implementing the program, to the extent any centralization of authority existed, rested with the attorney general, not with the White House. The new program would be comprehensive, and by stressing reliability rather than loyalty, it promised to "crack down on employees whose personal habits made them security risks even though their loyalty" was not questioned.[8] While the administration was enjoying the customary honeymoon with Congress and the Washington press corps, and basking in the generally favorable reaction to the president's first State of the Union Address, the influential columnist Walter Lippmann pronounced the emerging security program "a cool and lucid recognition of the lessons which can be learned from the trials and errors of the Truman administration."[9]

At first glance, the White House seemed to be contemplating a complete break, to the apparent satisfaction of Congress, from the much-criticized Truman program. Senator McCarthy was reported to have "acquiesced for the present" in the administration's plans. Expressing a widespread feeling, Senator Taft declared himself willing to "try it and see if it works out all right." Notwithstanding the proposed overhaul of the existing administrative machinery, similarities would remain between the Democratic and the Republican personnel programs. Going beyond considerations of mere loyalty, the Truman administration in 1950 had discharged ninety-one State Department employees for alleged homosexual activities. In postwar America, Senator Kenneth Wherry of Nebraska could claim that Stalin had a list, taken from Hitler, of homosexuals around the world who could be enlisted for espionage, sabotage, or terrorism. It should not be forgotten that the Truman and Eisenhower administrations shared a concern about homosexuals in government, a worry that rivaled their fears of Communist infiltration. In accusing the new administration of ignoring the procedural rights of government workers, the liberal *New Republic* could conclude, "The pattern and direction of the Eisenhower program remains essentially the same as marked the Truman program."[10]

Just as Eisenhower appeared on the verge of implementing the proposed reforms, the administration seemed to have been temporarily paralyzed by internal dissent and, perhaps, an overabundance of political caution. After the first press reports of the new program appeared, Hiram Bingham, the chairman of the LRB, wrote Eisenhower to urge the retention, not the elimination, of the agency. In a series of meetings at the Department of Justice during mid-

February, the Department of Defense and the Central Intelligence Agency objected to the use of hearing panels composed of government employees from outside of the agency involved. How, they asked, could outsiders appreciate the delicate policy issues and protect the highly classified information likely to be in question in a security investigation of an employee at the Pentagon, the CIA, or the State Department? Seth Richardson, the Republican appointed by President Truman to be the first chairman of the LRB, argued that retention of the board was necessary to prevent the substantive review of personnel decisions from falling to the courts.[11] Indeed, many within the executive branch feared that abolition of the LRB would make it impossible to maintain uniform standards or to protect adequately the rights of employees. Personnel officers from approximately fifty agencies met early in March to express their collective judgment that the proposed order was "very dangerous." One officer noted, "It assumes that each department head will be fair."[12]

Reputedly still "apprehensive" of how McCarthy would receive the new program—and embroiled in controversy over the Bohlen nomination and the VOA investigation—the administration soon displayed evident caution in approaching the security issue. The desire to build a consensus behind a new presidential directive produced unexpected delays as various agencies lobbied for revisions. Robert Cutler, for example, convinced Eisenhower that the NSC should not, contrary to initial expectations, be responsible for continually monitoring the program to detect any failures to protect either national security or the rights of employees. While debate continued within the administration, Brownell took the political lead. In a speech on March 17 to New York's Friendly Sons of Saint Patrick, the attorney general cited the Remington case as evidence of the inadequacy of the old system. A month later, in a speech to the American Society of Newspaper Editors, Brownell promised a new program "in the next few days" and defended the use of outside hearing officers. "An employee cannot be assured a fair hearing," he asserted, "when the hearing board, as in the loyalty program we are tossing out, is responsible to the head of the employing department or agency."[13]

On the same day that he spoke to the newspaper editors, the attorney general sent Eisenhower the final draft of a security order. Brownell's proposal went beyond Public Law 733, the statutory basis for the Truman program, to encompass all federal employees. Government workers and job applicants would be subject, at minimum, to a "national agency check"—an examination of the fingerprint files of the FBI and written inquiries to local law enforcement agencies, former employees, references, and schools. A "full field investigation" would be authorized when information existed suggesting that "the employment of any person" might not "be clearly consistent with the interests of national security" or, in the vernacular of the 1950s, when a file contained "derogatory information." In addition, applicants for positions designated as sensitive by the department or agency chief would also be subject to a full field investigation.[14]

Section 8(a) of the order stated the possible grounds on which one might be denied government employment. Subsections (2) through (7) proscribed a predictable range of offenses: espionage, treason, disclosing classified information, advocating the overthrow of the U.S. government, and membership in a subversive organization or maintaining a "sympathetic association" with any such group. It was the far-reaching Section (8)(a)(1), however, that expressed the breadth of the Eisenhower program and its preoccupation with the putative security risk as opposed to the conscious traitor. Aimed at any type of behavior likely to suggest that an individual was "not reliable or trustworthy," this provision would disqualify from federal service individuals who failed to cooperate with a security investigation or whose shortcomings might include personal immorality, mental illness, the "habitual use of intoxicants to excess, drug addiction, or sexual perversion."[15]

A set of proposed regulations accompanied the order. Intended for adoption by the various departments and agencies, these rules governed procedural issues. Under the new regulations, an administrator who received an adverse report on an individual from the agency's security officer could decide against further investigation or action, transfer the individual to a nonsensitive job, if appropriate, or discharge the employee. In the event someone was transferred or dismissed, he or she could request a hearing. On this point, those who had favored the use of outside hearing officers prevailed. The new hearing boards would consist of relatively high-ranking civil servants drawn from a special roster maintained by the Civil Service Commission. Hearing panels could consider incriminating evidence not made available to the accused, a practice that inflamed civil libertarians. The boards lacked the power to subpoena witnesses and could not guarantee an employee the right to face his or her accusers. The regulations provided, however, that a board, in reaching its decision, should "consider," apparently as a mitigating circumstance, any denial of the right to confrontation.[16]

Brownell unveiled the final draft to the cabinet on April 24, where much of the discussion centered on "coordinating" any action with Republican leaders in Congress, a task that fell to Eisenhower. Three days later, the president and the attorney general met with a congressional delegation that included Senator McCarthy and Representative Harold Velde of the House Committee on Un-American Activities. None of the legislators interposed any significant objections to the program, but they did urge that the hearing panels be composed exclusively of members of the "new team."[17] Explaining the new program, now codified as Executive Order No. 10450, at a press conference the same day, Attorney General Brownell promised that security cases could now be expedited: "The standards and rules are more explicit." The president appeared to have his new system off to a successful beginning. If the internal debates over Executive Order No. 10450 had not substantially altered its terms, the attendant delay at least seemed not to undermine the administration politically. The respected journalist Roscoe Drummond pronounced the plan a "roadblock in the path of subversives." More important, Senator McCarthy conceded: "It is a tremendous improvement over the old method. . . . It shows that the new Administration was sincere in the campaign promises to clean house."[18]

On June 3, 1953, the president and members of the cabinet appeared on network television to report to the American people on the accomplishments of the first five months of the Eisenhower presidency. Addressing the question of domestic subversion, Attorney General Brownell told the nation that the employee security program constituted only part of a larger plan to protect "the security of our homes." Along with the prosecution of Communist party leaders, the registration of foreign agents, and the deportation of alien subversives, the administration also stood on guard against ostensibly loyal employees whose "personal habits" were "such that they might be subject to blackmail" or who might "associate themselves with known subversives." Eisenhower deferred to Brownell during the television broadcast, but a week later in a speech to the Young Republicans at Mount Rushmore, the president proclaimed that the privilege of government employment was "being categorically denied anyone not worthy of the American people's trust."[19]

At the end of the year, the administration reported that 1,456 employees had been discharged as security risks, although Eisenhower could not publicly identify the number dismissed under the various provisions of Executive Order No. 10450, since they were "not charged with just one idea." How many ideas the administration was willing to tolerate is unclear, but by January 1954 the president could note in his State of the Union Address that the number of security-related dismissals had risen to 2,200. At subsequent press conferences, Ike proved unable, or unwilling, to break down the latter figure. Confessing at one point that it had not occurred to him that there would be "this kind of intense interest," he did mention at another press briefing that some of the 2,200 had "probably resigned without knowing of these derogatory remarks on their record."[20]

As Eisenhower's answer suggested, the administration was playing a "numbers game," in part by reporting as a security dismissal any termination of an employee whose file contained derogatory information, even though the employee might have been fired under normal civil service procedures and never informed that he or she was a suspected security risk. Indeed, some agencies routinely disposed of security cases on other grounds. According to one Senate study, between May 28, 1953, and June 30, 1955, the Civil Service Commission reported 3,586 security-related dismissals when, in fact, only 343 employees had been terminated under Executive Order No. 10450. During the same period, the administration claimed that 5,684 individuals whose files contained derogatory information had resigned. But only 662 of them had been told that they were suspected security risks. Such bureaucratic sleight of hand created numbers suggesting a proper level of vigilance on the administration's part, but the loose definition of a security risk had an apparently unexpected consequence. Approximately 40 percent of the discharges categorized as security risks were soon found to have been hired after Eisenhower took office. In particular agencies, the results of such reporting techniques seemed even more embarrassing. Senator Olin D. Johnston of South Carolina claimed that of 449 purported security dismissals at the Veterans Administration as of early 1955, 386 had been hired by the administration. At the same time, there appeared to be a disproportionate number of security cases involving nonsensitive jobs. With less than 700 sensitive positions, the VA reported over 1,800 security-related firings and resignations.[21] Treasury Department attorney Elbert Tuttle, later a distinguished federal judge, privately confessed his embarrassment in responding to congressional inquiries, since "so many of the dismissals were of people who didn't hold sensitive positions." Eisenhower ultimately claimed that 8,008 security risks were terminated during 1953–54, when the program was operating at full tilt. Of these, 3,002 were dismissed and 5,006 resigned.[22]

The "numbers game" originated in blatantly political calculations. At a September 17, 1953, NSC meeting, Richard Nixon proposed that the Civil Service Commission periodically report security-related dismissals to the NSC; the vice president hoped to use the information to discredit the Truman administration and to upstage McCarthy. Likewise, Henry Cabot Lodge, arguing that the administration needed to "end the politically-inspired witchhunts and red-baitings and enhance its prestige for future elections," advocated a "coordinated and steady series of press releases" from different departments about their implementation of the security program.[23] Philip Young, the chairman of the Civil Service Commission, initially acquiesced in efforts to publicize Eisenhower's anti-Communist activities, but as the months wore on, he and others began to question the political usefulness of such tactics. Reluctantly acknowledging to Sherman Adams the necessity of releasing new figures on the program before the 1954 congressional elections, Young lamented that the numbers would "be unintentionally and deliberately misunderstood, misinterpreted, and misconstrued by members of both political parties." Yet the White House's lack of candor surely compounded the confusion. The administration delayed releasing figures on the specific grounds for alleged security-related terminations—only a minority were for the subversive activities, as opposed to "character defects," specified in the president's security order. At the same time, the highly decentralized nature of the program hindered efforts by the press to obtain a comprehensive view of its operations.[24]

President Eisenhower generally gave department heads a free hand in administering the program, but a few individual cases engaged the White House, at least to a limited extent. When agricultural attachés at American embassies abroad were transferred from the State Department to the Department of Agriculture, one of them, Wolf Ladejinsky, was dismissed on security grounds by Secretary of Agriculture Ezra Taft Benson, even though Ladejinsky had passed Scott McLeod's rigid scrutiny at State. In fact, Ladejinsky had earned wide respect for his contributions to the modernization of agriculture in postwar Japan. James Hagerty privately dismissed the charges as "ridiculous." Amid claims of anti-Semitism against Benson and the USDA security officer J. Glenn Cassity, Sherman Adams, who wanted to keep the White House out of the affair, intervened to find Ladejinsky a new position. He was promptly hired by Harold Stassen at the Foreign Operations Administration, the agency responsible for managing American aid to South Vietnam. Neither Benson nor the president's staff fully apprised Eisenhower of the details of the controversy, which was short-lived but embarrassing. Yet Eisenhower resolutely defended Dulles, Benson, and Stassen to the public while instructing Brownell to take steps to achieve greater interdepartmental coordination.[25]

The administration, in fact, tinkered almost constantly with the program through Eisenhower's first term. Under pressure from Robert Cutler, the Civil Service Commission amended its procedures to require investigators to report an individual's membership in any organization that raised "a question of loyalty." This was intended to preclude the employment of individuals who belonged to groups, like the Progressive party, that were allegedly infiltrated by Communists but that had not been listed by the attorney general as subversive. As the estimated cost of the program by October 1953 approached $75 million, Brownell ruled that full-field investigations could be limited to employees with access to top-secret information. A year later, Eisenhower revised his initial security order to include as a basis for dismissal the refusal to testify, on Fifth Amendment grounds, before a congressional committee. The administration also quibbled over a policy for the suspension of employees about whom derogatory information existed. Secretary Dulles believed that he was required by law to suspend employees who were under investigation and that suspension removed them from the federal payroll. Ultimately the Justice Department's view prevailed—suspension was required only after formal charges were filed and suspended employees could receive leave pay, with retroactive full pay if cleared. In 1955, when the administration had almost completed its review of current employees, a whole series of reforms was made in the program. Though not substantially altering the program, the changes did reflect a growing, if modest, appreciation of the rights of employees. No charges could be brought against an employee, for instance, unless they had first been approved by the agency's chief legal officer, and no one below the level of assistant secretary could be empowered to suspend a worker.[26]

From Eisenhower's perspective, the mundane problems of delay and bureaucratic inertia loomed larger than the celebrated cases of controversial figures like John Paton Davies and John Carter Vincent. Finding that the program needed "intensified management attention," a study by the Civil Service Commission in October 1953 concluded that the implementation of Eisenhower's security order had "been relatively limited up to the present time." Despite the commission's report and Henry Cabot Lodge's pleas to expedite the program, the president expressed his satisfaction with the pace of progress, although he confided to Brownell that Lodge's entreaties, motivated in part by fears that the Democrats might exploit the issue in the 1956 election, disturbed him "just a little bit." In reality, as late as the spring of 1955, reviews of individuals cleared in full-field investigations by the Truman administration, cases supposedly accorded a high priority, were not yet complete.[27]

The problems Philip Young highlighted in a presentation to the cabinet in January 1954—the lack of a generally accepted definition of a security risk, the absence of a defensible policy regarding the release of information, and the need to expedite the review process—plagued the administration throughout Eisenhower's first term. Indeed, by the time the program hit stride in

1954, it had begun to lose momentum. After the censure of McCarthy in December of that year, the Communist threat somehow grew less urgent; at an NSC meeting shortly after the censure vote, Brownell expressed his belief that "the storm was over." Yet the search for security persisted after McCarthy's downfall. As late as 1956, President Eisenhower was still urging department heads to accelerate the adjudication of security cases.[28] Indeed, near the end of Ike's first term, the political scientist Robert N. Johnson, a student of the administration's security program, concluded, "The gradual subsidence of spectacular congressional investigations in the loyalty-security field is due mainly to the fact that, since Eisenhower's inauguration, the executive branch has taken precisely the position on these questions that the extremists in Congress had previously advocated, thereby stealing their thunder."[29]

One case overshadowed all the rest. If the procedure by which the government revoked the security clearance of J. Robert Oppenheimer did not constitute a typical personnel decision, it in no sense represented an aberration. Viewed in the context of America's postwar paranoia about communism, the Oppenheimer case assumes an unmistakable air of inevitability. Hundreds of less prominent people suffered more, but the branding of Oppenheimer as untrustworthy serves as a painful illustration of the abuses to which the Eisenhower security system was subject.

A renowned physicist, J. Robert Oppenheimer had served as the wartime director of the Los Alamos atomic laboratory. Considered central to the success of the Manhattan Project, "Oppie" was widely regarded as "the father of the atomic bomb," but he had long been the target of suspicion. His brother and his sister-in-law were Communists, and his wife, Kitty, was an ex–party member. Before and for a brief time after his marriage, Oppenheimer had engaged in an affair with yet another Communist, Jean Tatlock. In addition to his questionable associations, the physicist had hesitated, while working at Los Alamos, before relaying to security officers some remarks by a friend, the radical writer and literary critic Haakon Chevalier, about the possibility of transmitting scientific and technical information to the Soviet Union. Ulti-

Famed physicist J. Robert Oppenheimer before a 1949 HCUA
hearing. His case would later become one of the most controversial of the
Eisenhower years. (Library of Congress)

mately, controversy developed over whether Oppenheimer had accurately reported Chevalier's suggestion. Yet despite constant FBI surveillance—he was followed incessantly, his telephone bugged, his mail opened—no evidence existed that Oppenheimer had ever leaked anything to anybody. At the end of World War II, the now-famous scientist became chairman of the Atomic Energy Commission's General Advisory Committee (GAC) and later director of the Institute for Advanced Study at Princeton University. After an informal investigation in 1947, the Atomic Energy Commission unanimously acceded in the judgment of its deputy general counsel, Joseph Volpe, that even though Oppenheimer's background was "awful," the physicist could not, on balance, be considered a security risk.[30]

During his service on the GAC, Oppenheimer took some controversial positions and made some powerful enemies. In 1949, along with a number of other distinguished scientists, he expressed opposition to the development of a hydrogen bomb. The arguments against "the Super" were not wholly moral or humanitarian. Critics of the H-bomb questioned its military usefulness; technological advances had made the atomic bomb almost as deadly as the H-bomb. Smaller than the proposed new weapon, the atomic bomb seemed to some a more versatile device, possessing a potential for tactical, battlefield use. Besides alienating scientists like Edward Teller, who favored the development of a new thermonuclear weapon, Oppenheimer's views infuriated the U.S. Air Force, which saw Oppenheimer's apparent preference for tactical weapons as a challenge to its commitment to strategic bombing and hence to its claims to primacy among the military services. Oppenheimer made an even more formidable foe in Lewis L. Strauss, a Wall Street tycoon, retired navy admiral, and member of the AEC. At a commission hearing in 1949, Oppenheimer, who, to say the least, lacked a certain sensitivity to conventional social mores, needlessly ridiculed Strauss's opposition to the export of radioactive isotopes to the Norwegian government. It was an affront Strauss did not soon forget, and many of Oppenheimer's defenders later attributed his troubles with the AEC to Strauss's desire for retribution.[31]

By the spring of 1953, Robert Oppenheimer's rift with the air force had become public, leading the members of Senator McCarthy's investigations subcommittee to consider launching a new investigation of the scientist. Mc-

Carthy himself visited J. Edgar Hoover to discuss the possibility of a Senate probe; the FBI director advised him "that this was not a case which should be prematurely gone into solely for the purpose of headlines." Meanwhile, the Wisconsin senator received assurances from the administration, possibly through Richard Nixon and William Rogers, that the case "would not be neglected." The brewing controversy might have been avoided—Oppenheimer was currently working for the AEC simply as a consultant under a contract scheduled to expire in June 1953. The outgoing AEC chairman, Gordon Dean, however, extended Oppenheimer's contract for another year shortly before leaving office. Ironically, Eisenhower replaced Dean by promoting Commissioner Strauss to the AEC chairmanship.[32]

If McCarthy had been momentarily placated, William L. Borden had not. On November 7, amid the public debate over Brownell's charge that Truman had harbored the alleged Communist Harry Dexter White in his administration, Borden sent Hoover a letter detailing all the old accusations against Oppenheimer. Borden, the former executive director of the staff of the Congressional Joint Committee on Atomic Energy, dutifully noted Oppenheimer's opposition to the H-bomb and, more damagingly, attempts the physicist had supposedly made to persuade other scientists not to work on the project. Based on his review of Oppenheimer's record, Borden concluded that "more probably than not," the former director of the Los Alamos laboratory was, and for years had been, "functioning as an espionage agent" of the Soviet Union.[33]

By some accounts, J. Edgar Hoover, accompanied by Attorney General Brownell, immediately notified President Eisenhower of Borden's letter, but in any event, it seems to have made little initial impact as it circulated through the bureaucracy.[34] Most of Borden's allegations had been rejected by the AEC in 1947, and parts of his letter were patently illogical, such as the implication that Oppenheimer, in contributing to American development of the atomic bomb, had been "acting under Soviet instructions."[35] Nevertheless, Borden found a receptive audience in Secretary of Defense Charles E. Wilson, a Washington novice. With a copy of a new FBI report in hand, an agitated Wilson called Eisenhower on December 2 to warn him that Oppenheimer might be "a security risk of the worst kind." The defense secretary added that he had learned from Strauss that McCarthy knew about the Oppenheimer problem and might "pull it on us." Years later, Eisenhower claimed that he had summarily dismissed the political ramifications of Wilson's remarks, and perhaps he did. Aware that "Oppenheimer had long been under observation" because of his connections "with the communist movement some years back," the president decided to order Brownell to consider the propriety of a criminal indictment. Yet Ike confided to his diary, "I very much doubt that they will have this kind of evidence." Eisenhower also concluded that, pending an investigation of the charges against Oppenheimer, the government would be "forced to sever all connections with him."[36]

On December 3, 1953, the president convened a high-level meeting in the Oval Office attended by Wilson, Strauss, Brownell, Cutler, Arthur Flemming, and congressional liaison Jerry Persons. In their discussions, "no weight," Eisenhower later wrote, was given to Oppenheimer's opposition to the H-bomb. The president received the impression from his advisers that Borden's letter indeed raised few issues that had not already been examined and dismissed. Convinced that no evidence suggested that Oppenheimer was disloyal, Eisenhower nevertheless concluded, "This does not mean that he might not be a security risk." Accordingly, Eisenhower ordered that "a blank wall" be placed between the physicist and any classified information, effectively suspending him from government employment. Yet Ike recognized that such action, if Oppenheimer indeed proved to be a spy, "would not be a case of merely locking the stable door after the horse is gone; it would be more like trying to find a door for a burned-down stable."[37]

Notwithstanding Eisenhower's assertion that he and his closest aides had given "no weight" to Oppenheimer's objections to the H-bomb, the formal charges against Oppenheimer stated that he had continued to oppose the project even after it was approved "as a matter of national policy," that he had attempted to persuade "other outstanding scientists" not to work on the new weapon, and that his efforts had "definitely slowed down its development." Refusing to leave public service under a cloud of suspicion, the embattled physicist demanded a formal hearing, as was his apparent right under Executive Order No. 10450 and AEC regulations. As AEC chairman, Strauss selected the members of the hearing panel—Gordon Gray, a Democrat and the president of the University of North Carolina; Thomas Morgan, also a Democrat and the former chairman of the Sperry Corporation; and one Republican, Ward V. Evans, an eccentric and archconservative chemistry professor at Northwestern University. Eminently respectable, Gray, once the secretary of the U.S. Army, would serve as the board's chairman.[38]

As the hearing approached, Strauss unsuccessfully sought a ruling from Brownell that any appeal from the decision of the hearing board could be resolved by the AEC chairman, not the entire commission. The services of the FBI, which apparently included the bugging of the office of Oppenheimer's lawyers, were made available to the AEC staff. The agency retained Roger Robb, a prosecuting attorney with a reputation as an aggressive trial lawyer, to represent the staff at Oppenheimer's hearing. For their part, Oppenheimer's attorneys, besides being denied the right to confidential communications with their client, were also denied access to classified material relating to Oppenheimer's past—a collection of some three thousand pages of documents that Robb could use and that the panel could consider. The 1946 Administrative Procedure Act generally obligated agencies to abide by the "blank pad rule" requiring administrative bodies to base decisions solely on the record before them. But the act specifically exempted the AEC, and in any event such procedural niceties seem to have been exceptional in security cases.[39]

On April 6, 1954, a few days before the hearings were scheduled to begin, Senator McCarthy delivered a speech asserting that Communists in the government had managed to delay the American production of an H-bomb by eighteen months. The senator was, James C. Hagerty feared, "skating pretty close to [the] Oppenheimer case"; the White House press secretary hoped that the matter could be resolved "before McCarthy breaks it and it then becomes our scandal." At a press conference the day after McCarthy's speech, Eisenhower denied any knowledge of a delay in the H-bomb project. In reality, anxiety was mounting within the administration about the possibility that Oppenheimer actually had hindered development of "the Super." Within the next two days, before the *New York Times* broke the story of the AEC proceedings, the White House hosted a series of nervous meetings. President Eisenhower himself discussed the case with Brownell, Strauss, and Sherman Adams. Brownell advised Eisenhower that the government lacked the evi-

dence to prosecute Oppenheimer for espionage but might file a perjury indictment. The president seemed especially concerned about maintaining "orderly" procedures and forestalling an attack by McCarthy on the entire
scientific community. "That goddammed McCarthy," Ike told Hagerty, "is
just likely to try such a thing." Yet, with the senator closing in on Oppenheimer, the odds that the AEC might ultimately clear the physicist were
diminishing.[40]

The hearings commenced on April 12 with a witness list that read like a
Who's Who of the nation's emerging military-scientific establishment. James
B. Conant, David Lilienthal, John J. McCloy, and Vannevar Bush, who had
been a science adviser to the Roosevelt administration, testified in defense of
Oppenheimer, as did other well-known public figures. Essentially, the hearing
contrasted two different approaches to the security issue. To Oppenheimer's
critics, a good security risk, like Caesar's wife, had to be above suspicion.
Oppenheimer's lawyers, on the other hand, hoped that the AEC panel would
weigh Oppie's past indiscretions against his undeniable record of service to
his country. As is common in quasi-judicial proceedings, much of the evidence against the scientist consisted of hearsay, but Edward Teller, Oppenheimer's principal antagonist in the H-bomb controversy, and General
Leslie R. Groves, the former director of the Manhattan Project, did testify that
they would not vote to continue the physicist's security clearance. And under
Roger Robb's skillful cross-examination, aided by the attorney's singular
access to the security files on Oppenheimer, questions soon emerged about his
veracity, especially on his reporting of Chevalier's overtures in the early
1940s.[41]

At the beginning of the hearing, Chairman Gray perceived that Morgan and
Evans were likely to vote against Oppenheimer; Evans said it had been his
experience that subversives usually proved to be Jewish. Gray felt "mildly
uncomfortable" with Robb's piecemeal use of classified documents in cross-
examining Oppenheimer, but he concluded that the physicist had not been
prejudiced by it. After adjourning the hearings on May 6, the panel recon-
vened on May 17 to reach a decision. To the surprise of Gray and Morgan,
Evans had now decided to vote in Oppenheimer's favor. They suspected that
the professor's colleagues in the Chicago area had pressured Evans to change

his vote. For their part, Morgan and Gray might have disregarded the charges of which Oppenheimer had been found innocent in 1947, thus limiting their deliberations to his subsequent opposition to the H-bomb and his probity at the hearing. Acknowledging that Oppenheimer had been subjected to "a sort of double jeopardy," Gray said later, "would have been the easy way out." As it was, Gray and Morgan could not be accused of looking for an easy way to reach a decision. In their majority opinion, they found that Oppenheimer was undoubtedly loyal, that he had not attempted to sabotage the H-bomb project, and that he seemed "to have had a high degree of discretion, reflecting an unusual ability to keep to himself vital secrets." Nevertheless, Gray and Morgan managed to produce enough evidence—including Oppenheimer's unsavory relations, his lack of enthusiasm for thermonuclear weapons, and his evasive behavior at the hearing—on which to rest a decision that his clearance should be permanently revoked. After restating the board's findings in a somewhat more coherent fashion, AEC General Manager Kenneth Nichols forwarded them to the commission with the recommendation that the majority opinion be affirmed. On June 29, 1954, over the dissent of Henry De Wolf Smyth, the only scientist among the five commissioners, the AEC upheld Gray and Morgan.[42]

Throughout the affair, Dwight Eisenhower manifested little personal animosity toward Robert Oppenheimer. At a press conference in April and at another one in June 1954, Eisenhower expressed his admiration for Oppenheimer's scientific achievements. Insensitive to the demands of intellectual specialization, the president, apparently wanting to find the physicist a nonsensitive position, asked Strauss whether they might try to interest Oppenheimer in desalting seawater. To be sure, Oppenheimer's continuing, if irregular, association with the controversial Haakon Chevalier troubled Eisenhower. When Ike saw that Oppenheimer and his attorneys were seeking to sway public opinion—as was the AEC—the president commented to James Hagerty, "This fellow Oppenheimer is sure acting like a communist." Paramount in Eisenhower's mind, however, was loyalty to his subordinates, along with maintaining at least the appearance that subversion could be effectively fought through calm and orderly administrative procedures. On learning that the AEC had upheld Gray and Morgan, Eisenhower telephoned Lewis Strauss

to commend him on his performance and to express "the hope that the handling of the Oppenheimer case would be such a contrast to McCarthy's tactics
that the American people would immediately see the difference."[43]

It cannot be said that everyone did. Editorial reaction to the decision was
mixed; many scientists were appalled.[44] In reality, the Oppenheimer case
embodied many of the worst features of the administration's security program. Criticism of government policy and unconventional personal characteristics were somehow transformed into a defective patriotism. Security
cases fell subject to congressional politics and, perhaps as important, to intra-
agency jealousies. The procedural safeguards present in criminal cases, or for
that matter in ordinary civil litigation, were often lacking. The Eisenhower
administration inherited most of these failings from the Truman era, but it
added at least one of its own—the absence of any procedure for the review of
an agency's decision. Apparently having second thoughts about the AEC's
ruling, Eisenhower later that summer considered, and then abandoned, the
notion of appointing a special committee to review the Oppenheimer affair
and "related cases." Within the White House, Bernard Shanley, aware that
Oppenheimer had been held to be loyal and discreet, concluded that the
decision "did not make a great deal of sense." Convinced by Strauss that the
crux of the controversy was Oppenheimer's attempt to prevent other scientists
from working on the H-bomb, Eisenhower himself must surely have been
perplexed by Oppenheimer's acquittal on that charge. He was sensitive to the
wounds the affair had engendered and later attributed, in part, the rejection of
Lewis Strauss's nomination as secretary of commerce to the bitterness of
Oppenheimer's defenders.[45]

Oppenheimer's contract expired only a few weeks after the Gray board
entered its decision; the government might prudently have simply refused to
renew his position and to have forgone the security investigation. As it was,
the administration exposed itself to the ugly charge that the proceedings
against Oppenheimer were motivated principally by a desire to destroy the
influence within the scientific community of an eccentric and recalcitrant
physicist. Senator Clinton P. Anderson of New Mexico, who served on the
Joint Committee on Atomic Energy and who led the opposition to Strauss's
appointment as commerce secretary, later accused the AEC chairman of bow-

ing to the "McCarthy hysteria." George F. Kennan, who knew Oppenheimer as a colleague at the Institute for Advanced Study, described the judgment against him as an act of "personal vindictiveness and shameless, heartless, political expediency." AEC attorney Harold P. Green, who helped draft the original charges against Oppenheimer and then resigned from the agency in dismay over the course the proceedings were taking, subsequently denounced the commission for basing its decision more on "a mythology of security" than on established legal principles. If Dwight Eisenhower, whose "blank wall" order unwittingly consigned Robert Oppenheimer to the AEC's censure, had hoped to use the affair to distinguish his administration from the McCarthyites, the president, in the eyes of many observers, fell far short of his goal.[46]

One of the objectives Eisenhower set for the security program at the beginning of his tenure in office was the protection of the legitimate rights of government employees. Amid the army-McCarthy confrontation, Eisenhower repeated this theme in a March 1954 directive instructing his cabinet members to "observe every requirement of law and ethics" regarding their employees. He reminded high-ranking officials of their duty to protect subordinates "against attacks of a character under which they might be helpless." The president insisted that "no hope of any kind of political advantage, no threat from any source," should cause department heads to deviate from these principles.[47]

Much in the record suggests that Eisenhower sincerely attempted to administer a security program marked by decency and civility. Forgoing personal vendettas, he treated Robert Oppenheimer charitably in his memoirs. Ike apparently wanted Ezra Taft Benson simply to admit his mishandling of the Ladejinsky case but hesitated to wound the pride of his secretary of agriculture.[48] In a seemingly unlikely meeting with the nation's best-known Socialist, Eisenhower listened patiently to Norman Thomas's complaints about discrimination against Socialists in government employment. Indeed, the president dutifully conveyed Thomas's charges to the cabinet and expressed his agreement with Thomas that Socialists should not be subject to discrimination, "except in policy making positions." He added, somewhat incongruously, "Because of the broad range of the term there are some Socialists who are actually more conservative than some American middle-of-the-road people."[49]

Eisenhower once considered an amnesty plan for ex-radicals and former fellow travelers, and he repeatedly advocated the transfer, when possible, of minimum security risks to nonsensitive positions. Apparently only Justice Department opposition prevented the president from ordering that those questionable associations, short of actual Communist party membership, that were terminated before 1948 be disregarded in security cases involving employees in nonsensitive positions. At cabinet meetings, Ike expressed concern about the premature or extended suspensions of workers, and he urged transfers when the charges were "not extremely serious" or "when the individual had a record of long service and when no clear finding of 'risk' was possible." Presumably under some pressure from the White House, the attorney general eventually ruled that transfers were legally permissible if "ameliorating circumstances" were present and if the derogatory information involved did not suggest active disloyalty.[50]

Eisenhower, like many of his advisers, quickly tired of the "numbers" game. Although in the fall of 1953 the president was advocating that the security review of employees be "conducted as openly as possible," by 1954 he had concluded that the "compilation of statistics . . . would inevitably lead to recriminations" and that it seemed "most desirable to avoid public reports until an exceptional need arose." At an NSC meeting in March, Eisenhower flared, "Why the hell should we take credit for any of these firings?" Attempting to do so had only created political embarrassments for the administration; the president added, "There was no rational excuse for taking credit for what was plainly our duty."[51]

Finally, in light of frequent complaints among Republicans about both the lack of patronage during the Eisenhower years and the difficulty of recruiting the party faithful for government jobs, it appears unlikely that Eisenhower saw the security program as a device for purging the federal payroll of Democrats and New Dealers. To be sure, Ike could on occasion wield his patronage powers like a veteran ward boss. Indeed, Eisenhower urged cabinet officers to be certain of the partisan loyalties of their security officers. Otherwise, as one aide described it, "There will be a studied effort to hang onto those believing in the New Deal philosophy and to eliminate those who show any respect for the ideas of self-dependence and self-reliance."[52]

Nevertheless, Eisenhower moved slowly to replace incumbents in policy-making positions. The Republican National Committee, the president believed, had to "recognize that patronage" was "not going to save the country." As late as 1958, James Reston, by then no great friend of the president's, reported that the administration had yet to exploit fully the resources of the GOP.[53] The expansion of the civil service system had placed a higher percentage of employees beyond the reach of arbitrary dismissal than had been the case in the 1930s and 1940s. Leonard Hall complained to Eisenhower that lack of patronage was stifling the party at the local level. The Senate Republican Policy Committee, protesting that Philip Young was hostile to any patronage request by a Republican politician, went so far as to press for his resignation. When Young eventually left office, Eisenhower replaced him as chairman of the Civil Service Commission with a relatively apolitical career government employee, Roger W. Jones. At the same time, Robert K. Gray, a White House aide who assisted Sherman Adams with personnel matters, observed that the party regulars who parlayed political connections into positions as agency heads would often, after a few weeks in office, come to resist White House pressure to "clean house" as an unsavory and unwarranted intrusion of partisanship into the administrative process.[54]

Even so, the security program drew sharp criticism from influential voices in the press, from a variety of liberal groups, and on occasion from conservatives generally supportive of the administration. Journalist Anthony Lewis, who won a Pulitzer Prize for his exposés of the security program, complained that the division of authority over personnel matters within the administration made it difficult to obtain accurate information. Noted attorney Eleanor Bontecou, the author of a study of the Truman administration's loyalty program, found Executive Order No. 10450 "one more broken promise to government employees in so far as it invalidates previous clearances." Walter P. Reuther threatened to withdraw the cooperation of the Congress of Industrial Organizations in selecting labor attachés for service abroad unless the administration stopped using security considerations to eliminate politically unacceptable candidates.[55] During his Senate subcommittee investigation of the program, South Carolina Democrat Olin D. Johnston blasted the administration for confusing loyalty, security, and suitability and thereby doing "great harm to the career civil service." Senator Hubert H. Humphrey of Minnesota headed a separate investigation that brought forth criticism from prominent civil libertarians such as Ernest Angell, chairman of the board of the American Civil Liberties Union, and Joseph L. Rauh, vice president of the Americans for Democratic Action.[56]

Partisan politics motivated much of the vituperation directed at the program, but even former Senator Harry P. Cain, a conservative Republican then serving on the Subversive Activities Control Board, expressed dismay at Wolf Ladejinsky's treatment and emerged as a vocal critic of the security program. Merlo J. Pusey, in a favorable early assessment of the Eisenhower presidency, concluded that administration procedure for the coordination of security decisions among agencies constituted a "make shift arrangement." Cataloguing the problems of the program, Pusey lamented, "The Government has not yet taken full advantage of the country's best traditions in reconciling the demands of security to those of freedom and justice." Likewise, Arthur Krock of the *New York Times*, who was initially sympathetic to Eisenhower, responded to criticism of Strauss's handling of the Oppenheimer case and Dulles's dismissal of the career diplomat John Paton Davies by arguing that Executive Order No. 10450 had left Strauss and Dulles little discretion. Krock repeated the familiar plea for a nonpartisan study to "end repetitions of the deplorable case of John Paton Davies." Krock's criticism so disturbed Eisenhower that he raised it at a cabinet meeting. It was, Secretary of Commerce Sinclair Weeks complained, a case of the "administration doing the right thing but coming off second best publicity-wise."[57]

There were simply too many lengthy suspensions of harmless people like Abraham Chasanow, a navy hydrologist whose case necessitated a formal apology from the Navy Department, and too few counterintelligence coups. Although the program was primarily designed to remove security risks from government service, not to catch outright spies, the capture of a Soviet agent would probably have spared the administration considerable ridicule. Worse yet, a handful of Russian operatives actually managed to elude the program and to receive security clearances. As it was, the most serious threat to security that the program unveiled was perhaps that posed by an NSC employee, Joseph S. Peterson, Jr. After an inconclusive Civil Service Commission investigation, the FBI took up the trail, only to have it take a comic twist. Peterson had indeed leaked classified documents, but to the Dutch, not the Russians, and those documents pertained to the efforts of the U.S. government to decipher a secret code used by Dutch intelligence. Such results were obtained only at great price. One nonpartisan private study of the program found that it had cost $37 million in fiscal 1954–55 alone, had undermined American prestige abroad, and had discouraged scientific advances in government by driving talented researchers out of the civil service.[58]

Holes nevertheless existed in the security program, suggesting a certain hypocrisy in Washington's handling of the whole affair. Few loyalty or reliability requirements were imposed on congressional employees; some alleged security risks simply migrated from the executive branch to Capitol Hill once they came under a cloud. Given his reputation for gambling, womanizing, and excessive drinking, Joe McCarthy presumably could not have been cleared for government employment under Executive Order No. 10450. Nor could Roy Cohn have passed such a test. A homosexual who died many years later of acquired immune deficiency syndrome, the flamboyant lawyer was precisely the kind of government official who supposedly horrified anti-Communists. Moreover, rumors had abounded in Washington for years of a homosexual relationship between the nation's chief law enforcement officer, J. Edgar Hoover, and Clyde Tolson, his deputy and confidant. In Hoover's case, official Washington apparently concluded that his personal life was a private matter. Such tolerance was not widely granted.[59]

The cliché upon which Eisenhower rested the security program—that government employment was a privilege, not a right—proved a shaky foundation. It led him to defend the denial of an employee's right to confront an adverse witness at a security hearing with the argument that security proceedings were not concerned with "anything about the legal rights [of the employee] or the application of the Bill of Rights." During one of the frequent cabinet debates over the definition of a security risk, the president interjected the simplistic notion that the issue was merely whether a person was "worthy of a job with the federal government or not—a type of decision . . . made daily in every walk of life."[60] In reality, of course, the federal government faced a unique responsibility in balancing the demands of national security with those of civil liberty. As early as its 1952 decision in *Wieman* v. *Updegraff*, the U.S. Supreme Court began moving away from the "privilege, not right" maxim to the doctrine that the absence of a constitutional right to federal employment could not justify the violation of those rights ordinarily enjoyed by American citizens. Ike remained oblivious to the trend.[61]

President Eisenhower seemed to possess few philosophical compunctions with which to resist congressional pressures for a more repressive system, and his unwillingness to engage Congress on the issue further undermined his goal of protecting the rights of employees. When Congress pushed an issue, the administration's tendency was to concede. Under pressure from Senator Pat McCarran and others to attack Communist subversion at the United Nations, Eisenhower established an International Organizations Employee Loyalty Board to screen Americans working for the UN, an act that continued a peculiar precedent set by the Truman administration of allowing the United States to veto the hiring decisions of an international organization. When Representative Edward Rees, chairman of the House Civil Service Committee, demanded that employees who took the Fifth Amendment before congressional committees be discharged, the White House stalled for several months and then obligingly amended Executive Order No. 10450. Soon after Senator Karl Mundt introduced legislation to expedite the processing of security cases, Eisenhower signed Executive Order No. 10550, giving an agency ninety days after the completion of a full-field investigation to report to the Civil Service Commission. The program itself had been in part a reaction to congressional worries; a continuing subservience to Congress merely continued a tradition.[62]

Eisenhower's reluctance to challenge Congress represented only one side of his "management style." The other was his refusal to involve himself in the operation of the program. From the time Sherman Adams objected to the Rockefeller Committee's proposal that the president assume an active role on the security issue, there existed a consistent pattern, if not deliberate strategy, of presidential noninvolvement. In October 1953, the president vetoed the suggestion that the White House decide when exceptions should be made in the general policy against releasing specific information in security cases. By January 1955, the program had become a public relations problem for the administration; Philip Young suggested that either the Justice Department or the White House begin to coordinate press releases. He preferred the former, he added, "because of the feeling" that it was "desirable to keep the operations of the program as var [*sic*] removed from the President as possible."[63]

Such a strategy had obvious political advantages. Any kind of personnel security program must have seemed destined to generate complaints, especially from civil libertarians. By maintaining his distance from the program, Eisenhower spared himself a measure of controversy. But at the same time, with few genuine reservations, he allowed his administration to embrace a security system that few anti-Communists could fault.

5

★ ★ ★

John Foster Dulles and the
Diplomacy of Anticommunism

Shortly before taking office, President-elect Dwight Eisenhower told his incoming cabinet that the new administration would have to be sensitive to the "relationship between security problems and foreign relations." As Eisenhower saw the issues, they were "really one and the same."[1] Undoubtedly, domestic anticommunism fed heavily on American concerns about Soviet expansionism and, in turn, provided a powerful constituency for a militantly anti-Communist foreign policy. Nowhere did the nexus between the Communist controversy and American diplomacy seem more intimate than at the State Department. Yet the Eisenhower administration's search for security at Foggy Bottom stemmed only in part from paranoia generated by the McCarthyites; much of it was self-induced. As earlier chapters have suggested, the administration shared with the McCarthyites an obsession with security and a minimal concern for civil liberties. On occasion, the administration's anti-Communist crusading even went beyond the demands of some conservatives. Admittedly, differences did exist between the president and the GOP Right, a group that had almost, but not quite, monopolized anti-Communist extremism. But other issues—like the Bricker Amendment, which would have restricted the president's power to conduct foreign policy—seem to have been more important in defining the rival Republican factions than the question of internal security. At least with regard to the administration's policing of the State Department, anti-Communist conservatives, with few exceptions, could find little to criticize.

By 1953, right-wing critics had been pounding away at the State Department's allegedly pro-Communist policies for years. When Eisenhower entered the White House, the department's prestige, and the morale of its employees, stood at a low level. The veteran diplomat Robert D. Murphy, returning to the United States after serving in Japan, later recalled, for example, being asked by a friend in Milwaukee how he could bring himself to work "in that nest of commies and homosexuals."[2] No substantial evidence of subversion within the department had surfaced since the Hiss case, and within the Foreign Service especially, a select career organization with rigid entry requirements, the possibility of Soviet infiltration remained negligible.[3] Nevertheless, the new secretary of state, John Foster Dulles, gave no indication that the government might be able to relax its vigilance against Communist influence within its foreign policy-making apparatus. Citing a recent remark by President Eisenhower that "this nation stands in greater peril than at any time in our history," Dulles greeted his new colleagues at the State Department with a demand for what he called "positive loyalty." Within a few weeks, twenty-three more State Department employees, most of whom were apparently suspected homosexuals, had been dismissed as security risks.[4]

President Eisenhower may have initially preferred John J. McCloy as secretary of state, but within a relatively short time, John Foster Dulles became closer to the president than anyone else in the administration, with the possible exception of Sherman Adams. Eisenhower quickly conceded that Dulles, for years the leading Republican spokesman on international relations, well deserved "his reputation as a 'wise' man." For his part, the former New York lawyer assiduously cultivated his relationship with the president. Given a direct line to the White House, Dulles talked daily with Eisenhower and rarely made an important move without presidential approval. Strong-willed and unflappable, Dulles served the president as an intellectual resource, as an able emissary, and, at times, as a lightning rod for political attacks.[5] Yet despite the intimacy that the two men enjoyed, Eisenhower maintained years later that he could not recall discussing with Dulles how to handle Senator McCarthy's attacks on State Department personnel. Whether strictly accurate or not, Eisenhower's recollections illustrate the distance that both he and the secretary of state tried to maintain between themselves and the security issue.[6]

According to Thomas E. Dewey, Secretary Dulles, like most lawyers, simply "didn't have the instinct of an executive."[7] Few secretaries of state have devoted themselves to the management of the department. Dulles, a devout Presbyterian, often seemed obsessed with what one State Department official described as his "God-ordained mission" to reverse the tide of international communism. Critics have perhaps exaggerated the stridency of the secretary's anticommunism, but Dulles's concern for substantive issues left him little time to trifle with administrative details. It also offered him a rationale for his refusal to confront the McCarthyites. During the course of the 1952 presidential campaign, Dulles's sister, Eleanor Lansing Dulles, herself a distinguished diplomat, had gone to New York to tell the future secretary of state that if Eisenhower did not repudiate Senator McCarthy, she would vote for Adlai Stevenson. Dulles replied tersely that, as a foreign policy specialist, he could not become involved in domestic political issues.[8]

Once he became secretary of state, John Foster Dulles gave at best perfunctory attention to the few security cases that actually reached his desk. George F. Kennan believed that Dulles's insensitivity toward his subordinates flowed not so much from personal animosity as from "a simple lack of interest in them, or concern for them, as human beings."[9] If given a preference, Dulles probably would have entrusted the screening of State Department personnel to the discretion of trusted deputies instead of to the national security bureaucracy that emerged during the early years of the cold war. Nevertheless, Dulles dutifully defended the security program from outside attacks. Responding to the common complaint that unjustified dismissals had discouraged Foreign Service officers from filing controversial reports with the department, the secretary claimed that he had seen "no evidence of any cringing." He repeatedly denied charges that he gave security cases scant attention. As late as 1958, when the personnel program had come under criticism from almost every direction, Dulles expressed the conviction that the department's security procedures were "about as fair as human judgement" could make them.[10]

At the same time, Dulles displayed, in the words of Emmet Hughes, "a painful preoccupation with Congressional relations." According to Robert Murphy, the secretary "tried to get along with Congress at almost any cost." To liberals like David E. Lilienthal, Senator McCarthy seemed to have Dulles, along with the president, "all in a panic, frozen, scared." On occasion, the secretary's caution may even have exceeded the necessary bounds of political expediency. In 1953, after the Russians had asked to have George Kennan removed from his ambassadorship in Moscow, Dulles refused to offer him another post, allegedly on the grounds that the Senate would not confirm the veteran diplomat. Yet when Kennan related Dulles's fears to Senator Homer Ferguson of the Foreign Relations Committee, the conservative Republican reportedly told Kennan, "Why hell, you wouldn't have any trouble getting confirmed."[11] Nevertheless, despite the secretary's efforts to placate congressional anti-Communists, many remained skeptical of his internationalist approach to foreign policy.

Secretary Dulles had worked with Alger Hiss at the Carnegie Endowment and was terrified that McCarthy would use that association to render him politically impotent. Early in his tenure, the secretary confided to an aide that he wanted "to find some basis for cooperation with McCarthy." The administration, Dulles warned, could not assume an "arbitrary position" of defending "past mistakes" and thereby further alienate Republican conservatives.[12] After the Wisconsin senator began to investigate the International Information Agency, Dulles wrote John McCloy, who had urged him to defend the organization, that relations between Congress and the administration were beyond the responsibility of a cabinet officer; the secretary believed that they had to be "part of an overall strategy."[13]

Perhaps the single most plausible explanation for Dulles's timid response to the McCarthyites was neither his distaste for administration nor his fear of offending Congress. It was the secretary's own disdain for the nation's foreign policy–making establishment, especially after a generation of Democratic stewardship. The Republicans entered the State Department in 1953, according to Charles Bohlen, like "a wagon train going into hostile Indian territory." In addition to the familiar GOP complaints about Democratic foreign policy, Dulles had personal grievances; in 1946, State Department officials had recommended Hiss to him for a position at the Carnegie Endowment.[14] Shortly after becoming secretary of state, Dulles acknowledged the difficult times facing the department's employees. He explained, "It will necessarily take considerable time before the new administration can correct the accumulated errors of the last 20 years."[15] Dulles's lack of confidence in his predecessors clearly shaped his response to Senator McCarthy. When, for example, the conservative columnist George Sokolsky telephoned Dulles to advise him that the senator would soon launch an investigation of the Voice of America, the secretary's main concern was that he not be blamed "for things he had nothing to do with."[16]

John Foster Dulles hoped that, with the aid of "a few strong dynamic men with a business background," he could adapt "the foreign service of the United States to the philosophies of the present administration" in a relatively short time.[17] On the recommendation of Representative Walter Judd, perhaps the leading House spokesman for the China lobby, Dulles placed Walter S. Robertson, a Richmond banker, in the sensitive position of assistant secretary of state for Far Eastern affairs. An unyielding supporter of Chiang Kai-shek, Robertson blindly accepted virtually all of the anti-Communist charges against Owen Lattimore, Harry Dexter White, and the other familiar McCarthyite targets. To Robertson, it made no difference whether the accused were Communists or not, since "they were working in the closest collaboration with them, to carry out their objectives."[18] In an effort to relieve Dulles of unwanted managerial responsibilities, Congress created the new position of under secretary of state for administration. Dulles selected Donald B. Lourie for the post. Lourie, an executive with Quaker Oats, initially declined the job because of his "lack of experience and knowledge of . . . foreign relations." Dulles nevertheless persisted until the reluctant businessman accepted the position. Senator McCarthy, for one, praised the appointment. Lourie, the senator believed, could clean out the "bad apples" at State because, unlike Dulles, he had no previous ties to the department.[19]

For his part, Lourie soon came to regret one of his first official acts—hiring Scott McLeod, a former reporter for the *Manchester Union-Leader*, ex-FBI agent, and confidant of New Hampshire's archconservative Senator Styles Bridges, as the State Department's security officer. By most accounts, McLeod quickly proved to be a small-minded provincial wholly out of place in the world of international diplomacy. His skills seem largely to have been limited to promoting himself within the Republican establishment. According to Emmet Hughes, Lourie discovered McLeod, virtually by accident, through a neighbor who was also a former FBI agent. The story sounds apocryphal, especially since the influential Bridges was working to find his protégé a position in the administration.[20] Yet Hughes's account is essentially accurate. When McLeod's attempt to sabotage Charles Bohlen's nomination as ambassador to the Soviet Union became known within the White House, Sherman Adams asked Dulles how the security officer had been selected; Dulles replied that Lourie had hired him and explained that the under secretary "did not have much political experience or background."[21]

As chief security officer, McLeod considered every job at the State Department to be a sensitive position and ordered full-field investigations for all employees. Almost always able to force an individual out of the department without a hearing, McLeod complained publicly, "The common error is to feel that there is some analogy between the security-*integrity* system and the judicial system."[22] McLeod kept on his desk a photograph of Senator McCarthy, inscribed "To a Great American," and made no secret of his right-wing sympathies, becoming, in fact, a fairly popular public speaker. Addressing an American Legion convention in Topeka, Kansas, in August 1953, McLeod assured his audience that, "for the first time in twenty years," Harold Velde, William Jenner, and Joseph McCarthy had "the complete and unequivocal support of the State Department."[23] Before leaving for his new post in Moscow, Charles Bohlen, then the president of the Foreign Service Association, complained personally to President Eisenhower about the security officer's antics. The president reportedly agreed that the selection of McLeod had probably been a mistake but lamented that to dismiss him now would raise "a great big stink."[24]

To be sure, the president fully understood that McLeod's appointment, and the broader problem of McCarthyism, had created "a great big stink" for the United States throughout the world. After returning from a tour of several European capitals, businessman Philip D. Reed warned Eisenhower in June 1953 that McCarthy had attracted a surprising amount of attention in Europe. Many Europeans, Reed wrote Ike, wondered whether the American "concept of democratic government and the rights of individuals" was "really different from that of the Communists and fascists." While the Communist controversy acutely disturbed America's Western allies, foreign dismay with Senator Mc-

Carthy also surfaced in the Far East. After a tour of the Orient, Senator Alexander Smith of New Jersey and Francis O. Wilcox, the chief of staff of the Senate Foreign Relations Committee, reported to the president widespread concern in Asia about the Wisconsin senator and general bewilderment as to why his influence had not been curbed. Eisenhower relayed such information to Dulles, but otherwise the president assumed no particular personal responsibility for the deterioration of America's image abroad. As Eisenhower told Smith and Wilcox, he simply "hoped that somebody would do something relatively soon."[25]

At a July 9, 1953, meeting of the NSC, however, Eisenhower did express his concern about constant reports of a European obsession with McCarthyism. The president seemed especially concerned that the Republican party shed its foreign image as "isolationist and irresponsible." He suggested that C. D. Jackson explore a possible campaign to restore American prestige and, perhaps, the use of "covert radio to attack and ridicule McCarthy." Secretary Dulles agreed that "many European leaders seemed to believe" that the country was "moving into an American fascism, under McCarthy as a leader."[26] Disturbed about overseas attitudes toward the United States, Dulles solicited the views of several of America's overseas missions. Yet for the secretary of state, the fundamental problem was not Senator McCarthy, and it was certainly not the administration's own aggressive anticommunism. Instead, Dulles advised Eisenhower that foreign hostility toward the United States stemmed mainly from twenty years of Democratic attacks on the GOP as isolationist. Once Europeans came to understand Republican foreign policy, the secretary predicted, they would begin to support the administration. Other members of the NSC seemed less confident, and late in July the council authorized the Psychological Strategy Board (PSB) to make a comprehensive study of the apparently dramatic decline of American prestige abroad.[27]

Within the State Department, the reports from America's foreign missions did not sustain Dulles's assessment of the problem. Fearful that U.S. policies would provoke war with the Soviet Union, or at least prolong the cold war, many Europeans, according to diplomatic sources, believed that the United States took "a naïve and unrealistic approach to the problem of communism." The uproar in the United States over domestic subversion further offended

European sensitivities. Several mission chiefs concluded, "'McCarthyism' has done more to weaken American prestige abroad than any [sic] development." President Eisenhower remained popular, but Europeans constantly asked why he did not publicly denounce Senator McCarthy. Suggesting that the United States appeared generally intolerant of nonconformity, the State Department study warned that the nation's current "attack of anti-Communist hysteria" threatened to undermine the European non-Communist Left's support for American foreign policy.[28]

The PSB's initial survey of the issue tended to corroborate the State Department memorandum. Indeed, the evidence suggested that, as early as 1952, Europeans had "clearly favored Stevenson." As the influential Paris *Le Monde* editorialized, "McCarthyism is only an atrophied expression of the sentiment which carried President Eisenhower to the White House." Alarmed by McCarthy's ability to force a reorganization of the international information program, many people abroad expressed doubts about the ability of American democracy to survive another depression, if coupled with a foreign policy disaster. To Europeans, the seemingly chronic anxieties in the United States about its "negligible Communist party" indicated that the country was either "unsure of itself" or had "no genuine attachment to some of the fundamental values of a democratic society."[29]

At an NSC meeting in October 1953, the council considered a final, more temperate staff report that nevertheless noted a marked decline in American prestige abroad and European misgivings about President Eisenhower's leadership. The president had earlier seemed prepared to accept the notion that Senator McCarthy had become a serious public relations problem for the United States, but he exploded at any suggestion that he had contributed to the country's embarrassment or that his own image had been tarnished by the Communist controversy. Eisenhower blamed those charges on "New Dealers" still staffing American missions overseas, a view apparently shared by others within the administration. After defending the NSC staff, even C. D. Jackson conceded that the Foreign Service contained "a lot of disgruntled eggheads whose last thought" was to "promote the positive side of this Administration's policies." The president heeded Secretary Dulles's warnings about "the great damage" the NSC report might do to the Republican regime if it became public; Ike readily embraced his recommendation that no action be taken on it. Indeed, Eisenhower ordered Robert Cutler not to circulate the document and to recall all of the existing copies. Concerns about the political loyalty of the Foreign Service replaced worries about the impact of the anti-Communist crusade on American prestige. "It would be very helpful," Eisenhower said in concluding the NSC discussion, "to find out who are the traitors in these various missions."[30] Evidence of foreign revulsion to McCarthyism, some of it from Republican appointees, would continue to trickle into the State Department, but the administration took few direct steps to combat it.[31]

Large-scale dismissals and forced resignations of State Department personnel on security grounds began in 1945 and continued into the first two years of the Eisenhower administration. Perhaps some three hundred suspected security risks left the department in 1953 and 1954 alone. One small group of Foreign Service officers, the "China Hands," ranked as the most celebrated casualties of the State Department purge. Never numbering more than three dozen or so at any given time, their specialized training—especially their Chinese language skills and, undoubtedly, their exotic locale—established the China Hands as a unique breed. Journalist Eric Sevareid, who had covered their exploits during the Second World War, described them as "the ablest group of young diplomats" he had "ever seen in a single American mission abroad." Critics, however, held these specialists responsible for the "loss" of China; most of the China Hands, viewing Chiang Kai-shek's cause as hopeless, had advised against continued support of his government in the late 1940s. Other indiscretions could, admittedly, be charged against them. John Stewart Service, for example, had leaked classified documents to a left-wing magazine. Yet a grand jury refused to indict him for any criminal activity, and the Supreme Court later ordered the State Department to reinstate the career diplomat. Beyond question, the China Hands fell victim not to their own shortcomings but to the political reaction to the apparent failure of America's Asian policy.[32]

The persecution of the China Hands, and the political momentum for it, peaked during Dean Acheson's tenure as secretary of state. According to one poll taken shortly after Dwight Eisenhower entered the White House, only 7 percent of those surveyed blamed the Foreign Service's China experts for the fall of Chiang's government. Most of the Asian specialists who survived through the end of the Truman administration had been transferred to positions unrelated to the Far East. John Foster Dulles seemed willing to tolerate many of the survivors. At the same time, the Republican secretary of state revealed but a nominal interest in rehabilitating ruined careers and tarnished reputations. Only the direct intervention of the new American ambassador to Italy, Claire Booth Luce, secured a promotion for Fulton Freeman, a China expert who, in 1951, had been transferred to the U.S. Embassy in Rome. Even with an influential benefactor, Freeman never received another assignment in Asia.[33] Secretary Dulles, moreover, completed the removal from the State Department of two of the best-known China Hands—John Carter Vincent and John Paton Davies.

Under the Truman loyalty program, Vincent, a First World War veteran with thirty years of government service, had been cleared three times by the State Department's loyalty board. Vincent then served as American minister to Morocco and as diplomatic agent at Tangier. Numerous accusations were leveled against the diplomat—indeed, ex-Communist Louis Budenz claimed that Vincent had once belonged to the Communist party, USA (CPUSA). But the gravamen of the charges against him, from the China lobby, the Senate internal security subcommittee, and Senator McCarthy, concerned his hostility toward the Kuomintang. On December 12, 1952, the Loyalty Review Board recommended that Vincent be dismissed. Without making any findings on the specific accusations against the Foreign Service officer, the appeals board expressed "a reasonable doubt" as to his loyalty. And it noted "Mr. Vincent's studied praise of Chinese Communists and equally studied criticism of the Chiang Kai-shek Government" during a time when it was the policy of the United States to support Chiang's regime.[34]

Dean Acheson considered the charges against Vincent to be "unfounded" and feared that the diplomat was being punished for honestly reporting to the department the failings of the KMT government and, among other unpleasant realities, "the combat potential of the Chinese Communists." Acheson could

"China Hand" John Carter Vincent was one of many victims of the anti-
Communist crusade in the Department of State. (Library of Congress)

legally have ignored the decision of the Loyalty Review Board, but that would have left Vincent with no protection from the incoming Republican administration. With the approval of President Truman, therefore, Acheson appointed a special review board to examine Vincent's case yet again. Chaired by the revered jurist B. Learned Hand, the five-member panel included at least one prominent Republican, John J. McCloy.[35]

On Christmas Eve 1952, the outgoing secretary of state met with his successor to discuss the panel's investigation. Acheson believed he won a commitment from Dulles to give serious consideration to the special board's recommendation; the incumbent secretary instructed Judge Hand to proceed with his review. By January 20, 1953, Hand's group had apparently decided informally to clear Vincent. On the same day, the judge wrote Dulles to ask whether his committee should continue its deliberations and submit a formal report. Despite his reported pledge to Acheson, Dulles surely recognized that the panel might well reject the Loyalty Review Board's ruling, thereby making it more difficult for him to dispose of Vincent, who would remain a definite political liability in the secretary's dealings with congressional conservatives even if he was eventually vindicated. The new secretary told Hand, "It will not be necessary for you and your associates to act as a special review group." Citing President Truman's loyalty order, Dulles said that under "established procedures," the responsibility for a final decision in a security case, once the Loyalty Review Board entered its judgment, rested squarely with the secretary.[36]

The evidence suggests that Dulles did not, despite his later assertions, carefully discharge the responsibilities that he had assumed. The record in Vincent's case had grown to considerable proportions—including six volumes of testimony and dozens of FBI reports—yet the secretary, according to Vincent's biographer, saw none of this material until February 20. Dulles may, in fact, never have seen Vincent's personnel file. Yet on February 23, Secretary Dulles met with Vincent and told him that he would be dismissed for poor judgment unless the diplomat agreed to resign his present post and retire from the Foreign Service. Anxious to retain his pension, Vincent agreed to Dulles's terms. On March 4, 1953, Dulles issued a statement accepting Vincent's resignation. The diplomat, he conceded, could not be labeled a security risk or branded disloyal; yet, Dulles claimed, Vincent had demonstrated "a failure to meet the standard . . . demanded of a Foreign Service officer of his experience and responsibility at this critical time."[37]

As Dean Acheson noted in his memoirs, John Foster Dulles did not define the standard by which he had judged John Carter Vincent, and none of Dulles's six predecessors had considered Vincent's judgment to be "defective or substandard."[38] Still, more than mere political expediency motivated Eisenhower's secretary of state. To begin with, Vincent's forced resignation subjected Dulles to criticism from many liberals and further lowered his standing among Foreign Service professionals. Of greater relevance, his decision to allow Vincent to resign, and hence to keep his pension, enraged Pat McCarran, Joseph McCarthy, and many of the more militant anti-Communists. Although Dulles respected Vincent's knowledge of the Far East, he simply did not trust his judgment. At their last meeting, on February 28, the secretary solicited Vincent's views on current Chinese affairs, but he defended Chiang to the diplomat as a democrat and a Christian who had "suffered for [his] faith."[39] Ultimately, Vincent's departure from the Foreign Service constituted part of a politically inspired purge not so much because the administration knuckled under to the McCarthyites but because, sharing so much of their anti-Communist ideology, Dulles found Vincent's opinions unpalatable.

Nor could Dulles sympathize with the views of John Paton Davies, another longtime critic of Chiang Kai-shek. Before Dulles became secretary of state, Davies had served in the American Embassy in Moscow, on the State Department's Policy Planning Staff, and, to his great misfortune, as political adviser to General Joseph W. Stillwell's mission to China. After repeated investigations of the diplomat by the Department of State, the Loyalty Review Board, on December 12, 1952—the same day that it ruled against John Carter Vincent—issued an opinion finding "no reasonable doubt" as to Davies's loyalty.[40] Nevertheless, Davies remained under suspicion. In April 1953, the State Department announced that he was being removed from his post on the staff of the U.S. High Commission in Germany to become the counselor at the U.S. Embassy in Lima, Peru, a clearly less visible position. The transfer failed to silence Davies's critics. Senator William Jenner, for one, wanted him prosecuted for allegedly perjuring himself in testimony before the Senate internal security subcommittee. The major impetus for reopening the Davies case, however, came from Joseph McCarthy, who, in a November 24, 1953, speech, cited the continued employment of the beleaguered diplomat as evidence that the administration was soft on communism. Late in December, Scott McLeod decided to reconsider the charges against Davies, subjecting him to investigation for an almost incredible ninth time.[41]

McLeod met with Davies in mid-January 1954. Hoping to minimize publicity about the case, McLeod persuaded the Foreign Service officer to take a leave of absence during the investigation, thereby avoiding a suspension. Although he expressed personal reservations about such a course, the security officer admitted to Davies, "Our interest would be better served if you were not seen around the building." McLeod also warned him not to allow himself to be used by those who wanted to discredit the security system. For his part, Davies felt little relief when McLeod tried to assure him that the security officer would handle his case "the right way" as God permitted him "to see the right." Indeed, Davies believed that General Eisenhower's failure to defend George Marshall at Milwaukee during the 1952 campaign had signaled his own eventual doom in the event of a Republican victory.[42]

In March, Secretary Dulles appointed a five-member board, with no particular expertise in Sino-American relations, to hear Davies's case. After several days of hearings in June and July, the board, on August 30, 1954, issued an opinion finding the ex–China Hand guilty of "a definite lack of judgment, discretion, and reliability." The board concluded that Davies had been evasive as a witness and had carried his protests against America's China policy outside established channels. Yet the panel obviously considered the substance of his official reports to be at least equally incriminating. As the opinion summarized his China service, "It is the Board's view that Mr. Davies was motivated first, by his intense dislike of Chiang Kai-shek and the corruption he had associated for years with that regime."[43]

Two months later, Secretary Dulles released a statement accepting the board's findings. Publicly, however, Dulles minimized the significance of Davies's reports from China and emphasized his unconvincing demeanor as a witness and his unauthorized protests against American policy.[44] Nevertheless, Davies's dismissal provoked outcries from a variety of sources—among them Eric Sevareid, Arthur Krock of the *New York Times*, diplomatic historian Louis J. Halle, and the board of directors of the Foreign Service Association. Roscoe Drummond reported "the nearly unanimous view of Washington correspondents covering the State Department" that Davies was "the victim of a government security program which ran off the rails."[45]

The story circulated that John Foster Dulles, believing himself more or less bound by the hearing board's recommendation, had fired John Paton Davies only with great reluctance. The secretary himself tried to cultivate the notion that the tribunal's decision had rested "primarily on the basis of Davies's demeanor as a witness," a finding Dulles had little discretion to overturn, since he had not observed Davies's oral testimony. Supposedly, the secretary of state even complained at a cabinet meeting about the need for greater flexibility in the administration of the security program.[46] Undoubtedly, Dulles recognized the human tragedy of the Davies case—the diplomat's public humiliation and pecuniary embarrassment. But his reaction combined compassion with cynicism, and the latter predominated. Rather than complain about the case to the cabinet, the secretary told that body that "there could be no basis for disagreement with the unanimous findings" of the hearing panel. Instead of lamenting the program's rigidity, Dulles noted "the broad area left to administrative judgment."[47] The administration apparently hoped to convey the impression that the hearing board's report was being withheld from the public in order to spare Davies further indignity. In reality, of course, the opinion tended only to substantiate the charge that the diplomat, in the words of one State Department official, was "another in the series of scapegoats for our China policy." Indeed, at an NSC meeting in December, Secretary Dulles conceded that "he could not have proved anything [against Davies] other than information reflecting a degree of unreliability."[48]

To be sure, President Eisenhower and Secretary Dulles agreed that the government could not be expected to carry the burden of proof in a security case. The "abnormal times," Dulles believed, justified a reversal of the presumption of innocence. More sensitive to political attacks than his senior cabinet officer, Eisenhower, during the cabinet's discussion of Davies's case in November, suggested that the administration begin releasing more detailed public explanations of the reasons for security-related dismissals. The president "wanted by all means to avoid any appearance of the program operating as a 'Star Chamber' court." To Dulles, however, the existence of the right to counsel and a limited opportunity to cross-examine opposing witnesses vitiated any allegations of "Star Chamber" proceedings.[49]

The State Department, through the attorney general's office, had discussed the disposition of the charges against John Paton Davies with Senator Jenner, but the White House exerted no apparent influence in the affair. Eisenhower chafed at the dismay moderate observers like Arthur Krock expressed at Davies's treatment. The president considered asking some "expert" like lawyer John W. Davis, a former Democratic nominee for president, to address the nation on the operation of the security system. Yet Dwight Eisenhower never seemed to sense that the controversy over the fate of a handful of career diplomats might necessitate the exercise of presidential leadership. His public response to Davies's dismissal consisted of a brief statement at his weekly press conference; there, in reply to a reporter's question, he expressed the belief that Dulles's decision had been supported by the record.[50]

In time, the banishment from the Far East of a whole generation of China experts was widely seen as contributing greatly to a simplistic American policy toward the People's Republic and an unhealthy preoccupation with U.S. relations with the Soviet Union. More tragically, official ignorance of Asian politics, history, and culture ostensibly helped to compel the United States into the quagmire of Vietnam. More recent observers have assessed the China purge and have questioned its significance to the subsequent course of American diplomacy. The punishments meted out to men like John Carter Vincent and John Paton Davies evidenced the nation's inveterate commitment to international anticommunism; the containment doctrine predated their dismissals. Later American policy, especially in Southeast Asia, seems to have been more a product of what Barbara Tuchman, the popular historian, called "woodenheadedness"—an inability by decision makers to digest the best advice available to them—than of a failure of the intelligence-gathering process. Few scholars, however, are likely to dissent from Warren I. Cohen's description of the purge as "one of the most shameful and destructive episodes in the history of the United States."[51] Convinced of the rightness of his own views and confident of his own ability, Dulles never worried about any loss of expertise within the State Department. Meanwhile, Eisenhower presided over the security program with Olympian detachment, his mythic "hidden hand" all but invisible.

Next to the State Department itself, the favorite institutional target of anti-Communist crusaders seems to have been the United Nations. In 1949, Pat McCarran of the Senate internal security subcommittee inaugurated a long-running investigation of American citizens employed by the UN Secretariat. Two years later, Roy Cohn, then an assistant U.S. attorney, launched a federal grand jury on a similar investigation. McCarran and Cohn uncovered no demonstrable threats to American security at the UN, but their efforts were not without dramatic consequences. Frustration with American anti-Communists contributed to the suicide of Abraham Feller, legal counsel to UN Secretary General Trygve Lie. Not an object of suspicion himself, Feller had grown depressed under the constant strain of defending UN employees from unfounded allegations. Cohn's grand jury returned no indictments, but it did claim to have discovered "an overwhelming large [*sic*] group of disloyal citizens" on the staff of the international organization. The nation's leading red-baiting magazine, *U.S. News and World Report*, helped to popularize such charges, including the ridiculous allegation that perhaps half of the UN's executive leadership consisted of Communists and Communist agents. Claims of subversion spilled out onto those government employees who represented the United States before the UN. When the Eisenhower administration appointed Robert Murphy to replace John D. Hickerson as assistant secretary of state for UN affairs, Murphy found his new staff to be "half-smothered under a cloud of innuendo."[52]

Senator McCarran, Roy Cohn, and their allies had, in short, manufactured a crisis, one the White House and the State Department could not easily ignore. The UN charter, to be sure, vested sole responsibility for personnel matters in the hands of the secretary general, unfettered by interference from member nations. In 1949, however, the United States negotiated a secret agreement with the secretary general under which it could at least advise him of the Communist party membership of any UN employee or job applicant. The need to maintain the confidentiality of the program limited its applicability, and in any event, Dean Acheson was not convinced "that the security of the United States was involved in the type of citizen employed by the United Nations." Acheson also feared triggering Soviet reprisals against White Russians and Eastern European émigrés working for the UN. But after a panel of international jurists advised Trygve Lie in December 1952 that he possessed the legal authority to discharge any employee "likely to be engaged in any subversive activity against the host country," pressure mounted for the adoption of a more comprehensive security system. Only days before leaving office, President Truman issued Executive Order No. 10422, which extended the federal loyalty program to American citizens employed by the UN Secretariat and effectively placed the secretary general of the UN, with regard to matters of personnel security, in the position of a department head with the U.S. government.[53]

As Francis Wilcox later recalled, "Anybody who knew anything about the UN knew that this was not a nest of spies." Indeed, the real threat at the UN came not from American citizens but from Russian nationals, attached to the Soviet delegation or employed by the Secretariat, who used the organization as a base from which to conduct espionage operations unrelated to UN business.[54] Once Henry Cabot Lodge became ambassador to the UN, he repeatedly asserted that the organization was "not a nest of spies" because there was "nothing to spy on in the United Nations." As he pointed out, the United States never provided classified information to the agency. That fact, coupled with Lodge's defense of the security system as justified by "a sense of the general fitness of things," suggested that the UN personnel program, like so much of the search for security, represented in no meaningful sense a counterintelligence operation. It was essentially a transparent device to maintain political orthodoxy by punishing political dissenters.[55]

No one in the Eisenhower administration, with the possible exception of Richard Nixon, possessed more sensitive political antennae than Henry Cabot Lodge. The former Republican senator fully understood the congressional paranoia about the UN; he had warned the administration even before taking

U.N. Ambassador Henry Cabot Lodge (far right) at a White House
press conference in July 1953. The former Massachusetts senator was the
administration's tactical expert on the politics of anticommunism.
(Eisenhower Library/National Park Service)

office that Homer Ferguson of Michigan, as noted earlier, was "still red hot
about Communists in the United Nations."[56] Lodge also undoubtedly recognized the political laurels that might come his way if he could win the credit
for cleansing the world organization of subversive Americans. However one
might justify the UN security program, Lodge believed that only its vigorous
enforcement could restore the confidence of the American public in the
United Nations. Having joined Dwight Eisenhower's inner circle before his
nominal superior, John Foster Dulles, the UN ambassador maintained a considerable degree of autonomy. But on the question of personnel security,
Lodge's performance at the UN meshed perfectly with the administration's
anti-Communist philosophy.[57]

Ambassador Lodge, in short, moved quickly and noisily against the Red menace in his bailiwick. Virtually within hours of assuming his new post, he asked J. Edgar Hoover to undertake full-field investigations of all the employees at the U.S. mission. On January 28, 1953, Lodge presented his credentials to Trygve Lie and also delivered to the secretary general personnel forms to be completed by American nationals on the UN staff. By his third day on the job, the U.S. representative had the almost two thousand Americans employed by Lie lined up in the halls of the UN headquarters for fingerprinting, a supposedly reassuring spectacle. Taking pains to keep congressional leaders informed, Lodge won praise for his anti-Communist initiatives from McCarthy, Jenner, Velde, and others.[58] Within a few months, even Scott McLeod wrote Lodge to express "the high regard" in which the ambassador had "always been held by the security personnel of the Department of State."[59]

Although the UN personnel system focused on loyalty, not on personal traits that might make an otherwise patriotic American unemployable, it shared certain characteristics with the federal employee security program. There was never sufficient money to hire enough security officers and FBI agents to process investigations as rapidly as the administration wanted. Lodge originally hoped to complete the review of existing UN employees and officials by fall 1953, but security investigations continued into 1954.[60] The transition from the Truman personnel program to Eisenhower's caused further delay. Lodge considered Executive Order No. 10422 "completely adequate from every viewpoint." Yet the administration's abolition of the old Truman-era loyalty boards compelled President Eisenhower, in June 1953, to enter Executive Order No. 10459 establishing a new International Organizations Employees Loyalty Board to advise the secretary general on personnel matters. To Lodge's great dismay, the Civil Service Commission temporarily suspended its review of security files pending the release of Eisenhower's order.[61]

Notwithstanding its halting steps to secure the UN work force, the administration received a much-needed respite from its anti-Communist critics when the New York grand jury that was investigating the UN issued its second report in June 1954. The panel returned no indictments and reported that the new administration had dramatically reduced the alleged security problem at the world organization. By late in Eisenhower's first term, the new UN loyalty board had terminated 16 employees; another 162 Americans left the UN under suspicion before the board could act on their cases.[62]

Whether the benefits of the program justified its cost remains debatable. According to one study, the qualifications that investigators looked for in an acceptable candidate—college-educated, "very religious," and noncontroversial—bore little relationship to loyalty. The lengthy screening process placed Americans seeking jobs with the UN at a distinct disadvantage. Member nations were allocated a certain number of positions with the Secretariat; the United States never filled its quota. Reflecting the UN's perspective, Dag Hammarskjöld, Trygve Lie's successor, complained that American security demands made it more difficult for him to maintain an adequate staff.[63]

Predictably, the U.S. anti-Communist crusade led to conflicts with the secretary general and other member nations. Hammarskjöld felt markedly less sympathy toward the American obsession with security than had Trygve Lie. The Swedish diplomat protested the separate U.S. sorties onto UN property by Roy Cohn and the FBI; Hammarskjöld believed it had been a mistake to allow earlier investigations to occur in the UN headquarters, a point Lodge conceded. The new secretary general expressed reservations when the United States announced its decision to conduct hearings overseas on the loyalty of Americans employed abroad by the UN. He feared such proceedings might undermine the authority of officials assigned to delicate missions in explosive areas like the Middle East.[64] In particular, the administration's decision to conduct hearings in Geneva strained relations with the Swiss, who saw the investigations as a dangerous precedent and as an affront to their sovereignty.[65]

The most serious rift between the United States and the United Nations came when the Americans orchestrated the dismissal by the secretary general of a small band of employees who had taken the Fifth Amendment when called to testify before the Senate internal security subcommittee. Successfully defending the secretary general's action to the General Assembly, Henry Cabot Lodge argued that American citizens had a duty to cooperate with a legislative inquiry and that the right against self-incrimination was actually more narrow in the United States than it might be in a constitutional monarchy. Lodge's argument notwithstanding, late in the summer of 1953, a UN administrative tribunal held the firings to be unlawful. Dag Hammarskjöld refused to reinstate the eleven employees involved, but he seemed willing to pay them damages.[66] Congress and the administration were outraged. Vice President Nixon described the tribunal's decision as "catastrophic." Henry Cabot Lodge called it "really incredible." The administration wanted to maintain a free hand in dealing with the security question at the UN, but the tribunal's decision renewed demands for legislation, already passed by the Senate, that would make it a crime for an American citizen to take a position on the UN staff without first being cleared by the attorney general.[67] Although concerned about the political reaction to the tribunal's decision, Hammarskjöld warned the United States against a direct attack on the judgment in the General Assembly. As he told Robert Murphy, the tribunal's authority was "generally accepted by a large percentage of the member countries."[68]

Contrary to Hammarskjöld's advice, Secretary Dulles and Ambassador Lodge worked doggedly to prevent the General Assembly from appropriating funds for damage awards to the discharged employees. The result was to isolate the United States from some of its closest allies. With unconvincing hyperbole, Dulles told Foreign Minister Georges Bidault of France that the United States could not agree "to paying funds over to American Communists who presumably" planned to give the funds "to the Communist party in America and thus attempt to overthrow the U.S. Government."[69] In essence, the tribunal had ruled that the secretary general could not dismiss staff members for availing themselves of a legal right, at least when no existing UN policy had been violated. Dulles argued that a 1946 precedent from the then moribund League of Nations would justify the General Assembly in ignoring the decision of the administrative tribunal. But America's crusade against Communist tyranny had often strained under established legal principles; in their fight to overturn the adverse judgment, Dulles and Lodge preferred to sidestep questions of international jurisprudence and to emphasize political realities—the financial clout of the United States within the UN and the intense unpopularity of the decision in Congress.[70] Few experts, indeed, favored the punishment of UN employees by the secretary general's retroactive policy-making or considered the League of Nation's action to be relevant. Two months into its diplomatic campaign against payment of the awards, the United States had won no significant support. Late in November 1953, Dulles advised Lodge that the British and the French, for example, felt they could not vote "against awards . . . sustained by their best legal advice without losing the respect of their own Civil Service."[71]

Great Britain and France, however, hoped to avoid a final showdown with the United States in the General Assembly. Seeing an opportunity to postpone a confrontation for several months, Foreign Minister Anthony Eden of Great Britain endorsed a proposal by Selwyn Lloyd, the United Kingdom's representative, to refer the controversy to the World Court. Consistent with its position that the issues involved were "political rather than legal," the State Department dismissed the British proposal as "inadvisable and unacceptable"; Henry Cabot Lodge called it "an extremely unfriendly thing to do."[72] Diplomatically isolated, however, Lodge proved helpless to prevent the adoption, in January 1954, of a General Assembly resolution asking the World Court to determine on what grounds, if any, the assembly could set aside a decision by the administrative tribunal.[73]

The State Department estimated that the United States had a "fair chance" to prevail on the narrow jurisdictional question, as opposed to the broader issue of the employees' rights to damages. But in July 1954, the World Court ruled, by a vote of 9 to 3, that the General Assembly could not refuse, on any basis, to implement a decision by the tribunal. As to the earlier decision by the League of Nations, the court found "a complete lack of identity between the two situations."[74] The opinion hardly mollified Congress or the administration, but even William Jenner now conceded that the United States might not be able to block the eventual payment of the awards.[75] Ultimately, the administration agreed to accept the World Court's judgment while persuading the General Assembly to assert its right, in future cases, to review decisions of the tribunal. And in a face-saving gesture for the benefit of the United States, the assembly elected to fund the awards with revenue from various commercial enterprises owned by the UN, thereby avoiding a specific appropriation from money that could be linked to the American contribution to the world body.[76]

The dispute over the tribunal's decision nicely illustrated at least two salient features of the Communist controversy. First, the search for security never comfortably accommodated itself to conventional legal procedures; the crusade against a foe so treacherous as Soviet totalitarianism, anti-Communists believed, had to transcend such mundane restraints. Second, among the industrialized democracies, anticommunism represented a distinctly American phenomenon, especially perhaps in its low regard for the professional diplomat and the career civil servant.

With regard to the endangered American diplomat, the anti-Communist nightmare began during the Truman presidency, of course, but State Department morale reached its nadir in Dwight Eisenhower's first two years in office. From 1953 to 1954, applications for positions with the Foreign Service fell by half.[77] Entry into the diplomatic corps virtually ceased. Assessing the impact of the security program in April 1955, political scientist Hans J. Morgenthau concluded, "The State Department as presently constituted, is hardly competent to serve any government, totalitarian or otherwise."[78] But spirits had begun to revive. In October 1954, the president, seeking to dispel the popular image of an effeminate diplomatic corps, had dedicated a plaque to Foreign Service officers killed in the line of duty. An experienced diplomat, Loy Henderson, eventually replaced the political dilettante Donald Lourie as under secretary of state for administration. Dulles curbed the powers of Scott McLeod; the president later made the State Department security officer ambassador to Ireland.[79]

As secretary of state, John Foster Dulles felt no noticeable responsibility to challenge Senator McCarthy or his anti-Communist allies. Dulles, understandably, worried far more about his own political survival. As he reportedly told Charles Bohlen, "I couldn't stand another Alger Hiss."[80] Almost to the day he died, the secretary remained preoccupied with his country's struggle against Soviet and Chinese communism.[81] For whatever Dulles lacked in sensitivity or flexibility, one point must be conceded in assessing his performance as secretary of state: he did not go as far in purging the State Department of so-called fellow travelers as some conservatives wanted. Walter Judd, for example, generally defended Dulles, but the Minnesota congressman did complain that in rooting out security risks, the secretary "leaned over back-

ward not to be as sharp and tough as he ought to have been."[82] Outside the
Republican Right, Judd represented a minority view.

As for Dwight Eisenhower, his claims to presidential greatness rest in large
part on his conduct of American foreign policy.[83] As he himself recognized,
however, no clear line separated foreign and domestic threats, real or imagined, to the national security of the United States. The Communist controversy soiled American prestige abroad, incalculably undermining American influence. Anticommunism disrupted the very processes by which American
foreign policy was shaped and executed. Yet the convergence of diplomacy
and domestic anticommunism engaged President Eisenhower no more, and
perhaps less, than the purely domestic varieties of McCarthyism and McCar-
ranism. Again and again, a powerful anticommunism shaped his administration's policy. As a steward guarding American diplomacy against the ravages
of anti-Communist extremism, Eisenhower cannot be given high marks.

★ ★ ★

McCarthy

The Decline and Fall

Throughout its first year in office, the Eisenhower administration had repeatedly sparred with Joseph R. McCarthy, but as 1953 came to a close, it had avoided an open break with the Wisconsin senator. Hoping to preserve its uneasy alliance with Republican conservatives, the White House had vacillated before McCarthy's onslaughts against alleged Communist influence within the executive branch of the federal government, in particular his assaults on the International Information Agency and the Voice of America. It was this policy of appeasement that guided Secretary of the Army Robert T. Stevens when McCarthy later turned his fire on the U.S. Army, which, he claimed, had been infiltrated by Communists and Communist sympathizers. Even then, the administration tried to come to terms with McCarthy; President Eisenhower acted decisively to check his formidable opponent only when the army-McCarthy controversy threatened to spread its political fallout into the White House itself. Faced with a worsening political crisis, the president responded with a sweeping assertion of executive privilege, denying McCarthy—and the rest of the nation—access to a broad range of information about the workings of the national government. In a sense, the timidity of the White House probably helped to ruin McCarthy by encouraging him to pursue an increasingly reckless and self-destructive course, but the senator's fall came at the expense of something approaching a national trauma. As a political battle between Eisenhower and the Republican Right, the affair ended in stalemate. Although McCarthy, behind whom party conservatives hoped to expand their influence, was ultimately discredited, Eisenhower proved unable to establish his unquestioned control of the GOP's future. The events leading to McCarthy's downfall can now be detailed.

In August 1953, McCarthy announced his intention to investigate the U.S. Army Signal Corps Engineering Laboratories at Fort Monmouth, New Jersey. McCarthy offered as evidence of subversion at the post little more than what came to be known as the "purloined letter," a letter, supposedly written by J. Edgar Hoover, that purported to identify thirty-five Fort Monmouth employees as security risks. Despite the paucity of evidence, however, the installation offered congressional witch-hunters an inviting target. The atomic spy Julius Rosenberg had once worked for the Signal Corps and had known many of the scientists at Fort Monmouth. Most of the concern about Communist infiltration at the facility was unfounded, but the army had been abysmally slow in processing security cases there; one employee about whom derogatory information was received in 1948 continued to work on classified projects until he was suspended in September 1953. As late as that October, nineteen employees with access to confidential information remained under investigation. Secretary Stevens, perhaps mindful of the weakness of his position, and certainly aware of the conciliatory stance the administration had taken thus far in its dealings with McCarthy, pledged to cooperate with the Senate probe. Indeed, Stevens took McCarthy and his staff on a guided tour of the Signal Corps facility. By the end of October, General Kirke Lawton, the commander at Fort Monmouth, had suspended thirty-three employees.[1]

The army refused to accede, however, to McCarthy's demands for the security files of the employees in question. Nor would the army make available for interrogation the army loyalty board members who had previously cleared certain Fort Monmouth employees. In the spring of 1953, Assistant Attorney General J. Lee Rankin had advised H. Struve Hensel, then a consultant to the secretary of defense, "that the presidency was a continuing office" and that, accordingly, the army should consider itself bound by the Truman administration's policy against the release of loyalty files and the interrogation of loyalty board members. To be sure, Harry S. Truman, in an April 3, 1952, letter, had instructed Secretary of State Dean Acheson not to provide Congress with personnel files, the names of employees under investigation, or the names of loyalty board members. Beyond that, the legal basis for the army's position appeared murky, at best. From a political standpoint, Stevens's reliance on the precedent set by an embattled and unpopular Democrat seemed almost untenable. To bolster the army's position, army lawyer John G. Adams pressed the Justice Department for an executive order codifying the Truman policy. On December 12, Hensel and Adams met with Herbert Brownell and William Rogers. Brownell agreed that board members should not be subject to interrogation and promised to support the army in any confrontation with Congress. Yet despite repeated entreaties from Adams, no formal action affirming the army's right to withhold information from McCarthy's subcommittee on investigations was, for the moment, forthcoming.[2]

The Fort Monmouth investigation would soon share the headlines with the budding military career of G. David Schine. The McCarthy aide had received notice in the summer of 1953 that he was soon to be inducted into the armed services. Almost immediately, Roy Cohn, with the apparent acquiescence of McCarthy, set about trying to secure a commission for Schine and a comfortable assignment in the New York City area. The youthful heir of a hotel magnate, Schine gave his associates ready access to fine restaurants and Broadway plays, but otherwise his value to the McCarthy subcommittee remains in question to this day, as do the motives behind Cohn's efforts on behalf of his friend. In any event, Schine, as a raw recruit in basic training, had a small cadre of senior army officers working to get him a commission. He eluded work details. He received weekend, holiday, and evening passes. On at least one occasion, he left his unit at Fort Dix, New Jersey, to return to his suite at New York's Waldorf Towers. And he went unpunished. Admittedly, the American defense establishment did not wholly surrender to Cohn and the young private. He did not receive a commission or special duties; late in December, John Adams told Stevens, "We have scrupulously kept our hands off the Schine situation." Yet at the same time, the army counselor, in the spirit of compromise that pervaded the administration, was proposing to Stevens "the alternative" the army could "offer the McCarthy group" with regard to Schine's military career.[3]

Administration officials who were closer to the White House than Stevens and Adams still hoped to reach a rapprochement with McCarthy. Toward the end of 1953, Richard Nixon and William Rogers invited the senator to Key Biscayne, Florida, in yet another attempt to bring him under control. Urging McCarthy not to push the army investigation too far, Nixon warned him of the danger of becoming a "one-shot" senator. Nixon and Rogers wanted to channel McCarthy's investigative energies toward certain tax settlements that had been negotiated by the Truman administration. For the moment, the senator seemed to agree to take up the tax issue, but when press reports suggested that he would temper his crusade against communism, the senator called the story "a lie."[4]

Indeed, Francis P. Carr, a lawyer on the staff of the McCarthy subcommittee, telephoned John Adams on January 19 to inform him that if the army did not produce its loyalty board members by January 22, they would be subpoenaed. Adams thought "the McCarthy group" had decided to increase its pressure on the army because it feared that Schine might shortly be sent overseas. With Stevens on a tour of the Far East, Adams contacted William Rogers and insisted, "I must have assistance from outside the Pentagon." The deputy attorney general agreed to arrange a meeting with Brownell.[5]

When Adams arrived at the Justice Department on January 21, he was greeted not only by Brownell and Rogers but also by Sherman Adams, Henry Cabot Lodge, and presidential aide Gerald Morgan. The army lawyer told them of the pressures, among which he included the Fort Monmouth investigation, that McCarthy and Cohn had been applying to the army in an effort to secure favorable treatment for Schine. Sherman Adams suggested that John Adams begin compiling a record of the army's problems with Schine; Lodge and the White House chief of staff apparently agreed that such a document might profitably be leaked to the press and a few key senators. As to the specific issue at hand, Brownell indicated that an executive order safeguarding the confidentiality of the loyalty program would be presented to Eisenhower within "a couple of weeks." Nevertheless, the attorney general conceded that it might be impossible to keep loyalty board members away from the McCarthy subcommittee if they were subpoenaed to testify about official fraud or misconduct, as opposed to their own decisions in particular cases. Still, no one relished an open confrontation with McCarthy. Hoping that the GOP maverick could be persuaded by his fellow senators to withdraw his ultimatum, the group decided to dispatch John Adams and Gerald Morgan to Capitol Hill to seek support from McCarthy's Republican colleagues on the investigations subcommittee—Everett M. Dirksen, Karl E. Mundt, and Charles E. Potter. The strategy apparently worked; McCarthy announced on the following day that he would defer further action on the Fort Monmouth case until Secretary Stevens returned from the Orient.[6]

Senator McCarthy had, in reality, only shifted his focus. He was now on the trail of an army dentist stationed at Camp Kilmer, New Jersey. Irving Peress, in filling out the paperwork before his induction into service in October 1952, had taken the Fifth Amendment when asked if he belonged to any organization that advocated the overthrow of the U.S. government. Apparently, the officials responsible for investigating the loyalty of recruits moved more slowly than did those in charge of inductions and promotions. Pursuant to Public Law 779, better known as the Doctors Draft Act, Peress received a commission as a captain and shortly thereafter a promotion to major. On January 30, 1954, McCarthy hauled Peress before a one-man subcommittee hearing in New York City, where the dentist again refused to answer questions about his political affiliations. The Wisconsin Republican demanded that Peress be court-martialed, but the army, looking for a quick way to dispose of a possible security risk and a definite political problem, gave the major an honorable discharge.[7]

Few controversies could have engaged Dwight Eisenhower's attention, and emotions, as did McCarthy's forays against the service in which the president had spent most of his adult life. At a February 10 meeting at the White House, Eisenhower advised Stevens to admit the army's mishandling of the Peress case and to make a full disclosure of the relevant facts. Stevens should, Ike believed, explain the steps being taken to prevent the recurrence of similar episodes. And he should make plain his confidence in the army and his refusal to tolerate any "browbeating" of his subordinates. After meeting with the president, Stevens announced that he was instructing the inspector general of the army to initiate an "exhaustive investigation."[8]

To McCarthy, this was "Communist jargon," a delaying tactic to protect Pentagon officials guilty of "coddling Communists." On February 18, the Wisconsin senator heard testimony from the commanding officer at Camp

Kilmer, Brigadier General Ralph W. Zwicker, a combat veteran of World War II and a much-decorated hero of the Battle of the Bulge. Reluctant to disclose the details of the Peress case in light of the administration's policy of maintaining the confidentiality of personnel matters, Zwicker triggered a vitriolic outburst that exceeded even McCarthy's normal capacity for verbal abuse. Zwicker, the chairman stated, lacked "the brains of a five-year-old child" and, McCarthy went on, might not be "fit to wear the uniform" of the U.S. army.[9]

After McCarthy finished with Zwicker, perhaps only Richard Nixon, among high-ranking administration officials, still retained hopes for a compromise with the senator. For his part, Secretary Stevens instructed General Zwicker to ignore further demands from McCarthy for additional testimony. With Eisenhower away on a golfing vacation, Nixon and the administration's congressional liaison, Jerry Persons, arranged a meeting in Nixon's Capitol Hill office with John Adams, Rogers, Dirksen, Senate Majority Leader William F. Knowland, and I. Jack Martin of the White House staff. Eisenhower had hoped that, after the death of Robert A. Taft in 1953, Dirksen would become the Senate "champion" for the president's "middle-of-the-road" philosophy. The Illinois lawmaker now agreed to demand Cohn's dismissal and an end to McCarthy's arbitrary use of the subpoena power, his one-man subcommittee hearings, and his abuse of army witnesses. On each point, Dirksen failed to deliver; indeed, Adams believed that the purpose of the meeting was to persuade the army to capitulate to McCarthy and that Dirksen advised the subcommittee chairman to try to have the army lawyer fired. But Dirksen did make good on his promise to host a meeting between Stevens and McCarthy.[10]

When Secretary Stevens, a former New Jersey textile manufacturer, went to Dirksen's office on February 24 for a luncheon meeting with McCarthy, he entered as a political innocent. He left as another casualty of the Communist controversy. At what would become known as the "chicken lunch"—for the menu and the army secretary's bungling—Stevens received from McCarthy, in the presence of Nixon and the Republican members of the subcommittee, the assurance that army personnel who appeared before the McCarthy panel in the future would receive fair and courteous treatment. In exchange, Stevens agreed to provide the names of those officials involved in Peress's promotion and discharge and to make them available to the subcommittee. Yet when Karl Mundt reduced the details of the meeting to a "memo of understanding" for distribution to the press, only the army's concessions to McCarthy were included.[11]

With the release of the Mundt memorandum, the "McCarthy-Stevens row," in the words of James Hagerty, "broke wide open." Immediately perceived by the press as having surrendered to McCarthy, an almost hysterical Stevens called both Nixon and Hagerty on the evening of February 24 to discuss his resignation; they advised him against any rash action. Eisenhower's response to reports of the chicken lunch, he wrote later, "was not pleasant." Not only had Stevens demonstrated considerable political ineptitude, but Eisenhower's fellow Republicans, including the vice president, had embarrassed the administration and created a widespread, albeit erroneous, impression that someone in the White House, if not the president personally, had instructed Stevens to settle his problems with McCarthy at any cost. As Eisenhower told his old friend Lucius D. Clay, the imbroglio was hurting the Republican party with the Democratic voters it needed in order to stay in power.[12]

Yet the president hesitated to bring the full force of his prestige to bear against the administration's congressional antagonists. To be sure, Eisenhower told James Hagerty that McCarthy apparently wanted to be president; Ike added, "He's the last guy in the world who'll ever get there, if I have anything to say." Nevertheless, Nixon persuaded Eisenhower not to issue a statement saying that congressional witch-hunters were as bad as the Communists they pursued. As Nixon, Sherman Adams, and several key aides prepared a more moderate statement setting forth Stevens's version of the chicken lunch, Eisenhower sought relief from the tensions of the week by practicing chip shots on the South Lawn of the White House. Significantly, despite the urgings of Hagerty and White House counsel Bernard Shanley that Eisenhower make a personal appearance, Stevens was forced to issue his statement with only Hagerty and Roger Keyes, the acting secretary of defense, at his side.[13]

Worried that McCarthy was making "people believe" he was "driving the administration out of Washington," Eisenhower, at his weekly meeting with the Republican congressional leadership on March 1, complained that the

army's "blunder did not excuse some of the things that had since happened."
Procedural reform—in particular a rule requiring a favorable vote by a committee majority before a subpoena could be issued—was becoming, the administration thought, its best hope for relief from the McCarthyites.[14] Tele-
phoning William Knowland later in March to press his appeal for a revision of
the Senate rules, Eisenhower told the majority leader, "If we pursue the
course we have taken so far, the Republican party will be wrecked." Convinced that he could expect no help from archconservatives like William E.
Jenner of Indiana and John W. Bricker of Ohio, the president continued to
cultivate Everett Dirksen's support. Yet Dirksen proved to be an unreliable
ally. Meanwhile, the rest of the Republican Senate leadership, James Hagerty
confided to his diary, was "wobbling all around on this."[15]

As he had done throughout his presidency, Eisenhower continued to resist
pressure from his more liberal supporters to engage McCarthy in a verbal
donnybrook, but the early spring of 1954 saw the budding of a new com-
bativeness at the White House. At a press conference on March 3, Eisenhower
assumed his most vigorous public posture to date, commending General
Zwicker, calling on the GOP leadership to support "codes of fair procedure"
for congressional committees, and regretting the turmoil caused by a "disregard of the standards of fair play." Still, the president's essentially temperate
remarks, in the face of McCarthy's outrages, failed to satisfy much of the
press.[16]

Political necessity required that Eisenhower further distance himself from
the Wisconsin senator. Delivering a well-received address to a Democratic
fund-raising dinner in Miami on March 7, Adlai Stevenson charged, "A group
of political plungers has persuaded the President that McCarthyism is the best
Republican formula for success." The Republican party, the former Illinois
governor continued, was "divided against itself, half McCarthy and half
Eisenhower." The Eisenhower half quickly intervened to ensure that Vice
President Nixon, not Senator McCarthy, would deliver the GOP's formal
response to Stevenson. After Eisenhower made the appropriate arrangements
with legislative leaders, Sherman Adams apparently telephoned the chairman
of the Federal Communications Commission to guarantee that McCarthy
would not receive network television time. Finally, on March 11, the army

released John Adams's memorandum detailing the efforts made by McCarthy and Cohn to secure preferential treatment for David Schine. With the release of the Adams chronology, the junior senator from Wisconsin, Eisenhower later wrote, went "on the defensive for the first time." Along with such initiatives inevitably came increasing intraparty tensions. Fearful of losing the advantage of the Communist issue, many Republican members of Congress urged the White House not to attack McCarthy. William Knowland threatened to resign as Senate majority leader when Adams's memorandum was made public, ostensibly because he had not been forewarned but in reality, Eisenhower thought, because the Republican leader was still hoping for a "compromise" with his Wisconsin colleague.[17]

The counterattack on their Wisconsin ally threatened hopes of Republican conservatives to gain control of their party. Henry Cabot Lodge and C. D. Jackson believed that McCarthy ultimately intended to destroy Eisenhower; Lodge thought it no coincidence that an attack had been launched on the organization with which Ike was so intimately linked.[18] Eisenhower heeded such advice. Although he recognized that "Old Guardism and McCarthyism" were "not necessarily" synonymous, he also believed that a handful of Republican reactionaries were supporting McCarthy because they were "so anxious to seize on every possible embarrassment for the Administration." The GOP's Old Guard, the president thought, "hates and despises every thing for which I stand." Eisenhower had never enjoyed great strength among the Republican Right; his growing estrangement from the McCarthyites further undermined his position within the party. The president received "less than deafening" applause when he addressed his fellow Republicans at a 1954 Lincoln Day dinner in Washington. For their part, many Republican conservatives undoubtedly shared Roy Cohn's later assessment that the controversy over subversion represented a "gut issue" capable of returning "a powerful right-wing bloc" to Congress.[19]

In rallying to McCarthy's banner, Republican conservatives committed a tactical blunder. To be sure, the senator's popularity reached an all-time high in January 1954, with respondents in a Gallup survey rating him favorably by a margin of 50 to 29 percent. But even at his peak, the senator showed signs of political weakness. By pluralities, Americans disapproved of his "methods," believed he was hurting U.S. relations with allies, and purported to be less, rather than more, likely to vote for a Republican congressional candidate endorsed by McCarthy. Among one key group, the college-educated, the controversial legislator received an overall negative rating. Even before the start of the now famous army-McCarthy hearings, the senator's popularity had begun to erode. By March 1954, McCarthy's positive standing in the Gallup Poll had dropped from 46 to 36 percent.[20] Reports reaching the White House indicated a dramatic decline in his political clout. George Etzell, a member of the Republican state committee in Minnesota, publicly stated that he did not want McCarthy to come to Minnesota to campaign against incumbent Democratic Senator Hubert H. Humphrey. After returning from an extensive tour of the nation, one journalist told Sherman Adams, "Where Joe missed the boat was in getting too rough with a gentleman whose personal popularity was much greater than his own." The remaining McCarthyites were probably more zealous than the growing ranks of the disaffected, but for most Americans, a struggle between the senator and the president would be no contest at all.[21]

On March 12, 1954, Senator McCarthy responded to the release of the Adams chronology with copies of eleven memoranda of dubious authenticity—the originals never surfaced—that conveniently purported to rebut the army's charges point by point. Denying that he had sought preferential treatment for David Schine, McCarthy charged at a midday news conference that Robert Stevens and John Adams had tried to use his former aide as a "hostage" to "blackmail" him into stopping his investigation of the army. According to one of McCarthy's memoranda, unsigned but dated November 6, 1953, Secretary Stevens had even offered to provide the subcommittee with "plenty of dirt" on the air force and the navy, if only McCarthy would leave the army alone.[22]

The Senate could hardly allow the army's charges and McCarthy's countercharges to pass without a formal inquiry, a responsibility that fell, by default, to the permanent subcommittee on investigations. During a stormy executive session on March 16, the subcommittee decided that Karl Mundt, its second-ranking Republican, would assume the chairmanship pending a resolution of the army-McCarthy dispute. Mundt wanted to remove the controversy to the Armed Services Committee, but that body refused to accept it. Cohn was suspended, and the subcommittee agreed to seek new counsel. At the same time, the panel reached two critical procedural decisions. First, John L. McClellan of Arkansas, the senior Democrat on the subcommittee, won adoption of a resolution providing that the army-McCarthy investigation would proceed to the exclusion of all other business, thus minimizing McCarthy's ability to employ diversionary tactics. Second, the hearings would be open to the public and subject to live television coverage. Wanting to settle the matter quickly and quietly, Everett Dirksen proposed that the subcommittee conduct a closed hearing, to be followed by the resignation of a scapegoat from each side—Cohn for the McCarthyites and John Adams for the army. McCarthy, Charles E. Potter, and the Democrats joined together to defeat the Dirksen proposal. It was as if all concerned, except the Wisconsin senator, knew that he could not withstand the scrutiny of the klieg lights.[23]

When Eisenhower faced the press on March 17, he defended Stevens's "integrity and honesty" but conceded that the secretary might have made some mistakes. Privately, Ike believed that press coverage of the McCarthyites had "exaggerated, out of all proportion . . . , their importance to the nation as a whole."[24] Nevertheless, the president displayed, as the investigations subcommittee prepared for the army-McCarthy hearings, a hitherto uncharacteristic interest in the affairs of the Senate. The day after his press conference, Eisenhower telephoned Karl Mundt to discuss the selection of a temporary replacement for Roy Cohn. Both men wanted a special counsel of unimpeachable stature; Eisenhower suggested the venerable John W. Davis, a former Democratic presidential nominee and a distinguished constitutional lawyer. Telling Mundt that nothing was "hurting our position more," the president admonished the South Dakota senator that the subcommittee was a "Republican committee" and that Mundt, Dirksen, and Potter could not afford to mishandle their responsibilities. On March 20, Eisenhower commended Senator Knowland for his pronouncement that McCarthy should not be allowed to vote as a subcommittee member during the course of the hearings or to question witnesses. "Everybody in the United States," Eisenhower told the majority leader, "will approve what you said." Over the heated objections of congressional liaison Jerry Persons, Eisenhower expressed the view at a March 24, 1954, press conference that McCarthy should not be allowed to sit as a judge in his own case. The White House had passed the point of considering a compromise with the McCarthyites. On March 25, several key White House aides, including Persons and James Hagerty, were invited to a Capitol Hill luncheon with a handful of McCarthy loyalists. There Herman Welker of Idaho and Bourke B. Hickenlooper of Iowa proposed a settlement of the case on essentially the same terms Dirksen had recommended on March 16—the dismissal of Cohn and Adams. Their entreaties had no apparent effect on the White House staffers, and when Hagerty returned to his office, he released a statement describing the luncheon as merely a "social" gathering.[25]

Within the confines of the subcommittee, however, certain compromises were possible. McCarthy agreed to resign, technically, from the panel, but he was allowed to name his own replacement, Idaho's Henry Dworshak, a quiet foot soldier in the McCarthy infantry. Moreover, McCarthy received the right to cross-examine witnesses. The loyalties of the subcommittee were confused and divided. Besides Dworshak, McCarthy could usually depend on the support of Mundt; the White House could not. When Eisenhower and his advisers debated the position the administration should take on McCarthy's right to sit on the subcommittee, Ike decided against expressing his opposition in a letter to Mundt. As Eisenhower told his staff: "You can't trust that fellow. He plays everything against the middle." So too did Everett Dirksen. Despite White House efforts to woo him, Dirksen wanted to protect McCarthy from the ordeal of a lengthy public investigation. Dirksen had, after all, been elected to the Senate over the political corpse of Scott W. Lucas, one of the first Democrats to speak out forcefully against McCarthyism. In the middle of the controversy fell a moderate Republican, Charles E. Potter of Michigan. Potter had lost both legs to a German artillery shell in the Colmar pocket. He would not be sympathetic to Schine's demands for a special assignment. Led by John McClellan, the subcommittee's Democrats lined up in solid opposition to the pro-McCarthy Republican majority. A crusty conservative with an impregnable political base, McClellan was not intimidated by McCarthy, or anyone else. A former prosecutor committed to orderly procedures, the ranking Democrat liked to boast, "I can be as hard as anybody in rooting out Communists

but I'll never violate the Bill of Rights." Next in seniority came W. Stuart
Symington of Missouri. Formerly the secretary of the air force and a Pentagon
loyalist, Symington emerged in the hearings as McCarthy's most fervent
antagonist. The junior Democrat, Washington's Henry M. Jackson, was more
reserved, but he would pursue McCarthy through the hearings with the earnest
demeanor of a young district attorney.[26]

Karl Mundt explored some strange leads in trying to find a temporary
replacement for Roy Cohn as subcommittee counsel. It proved difficult to
obtain a lawyer of the caliber Eisenhower desired. The position paid little,
entailed considerable political risk, and required that a candidate have no
public record on what was one of the two or three most controversial issues of
the day. Mundt unsuccessfully approached Deputy Attorney General William
Rogers, American Bar Association President William Jameson, and New
York Judge Robert Morris, an old McCarthy ally. The temporary chairman
suggested to Eisenhower that the subcommittee might attempt to borrow a
federal district judge, but Chief Justice Earl Warren objected. Mundt finally
selected Samuel P. Sears, a Massachusetts Republican, but Sears resigned
almost immediately when it was learned that he had solicited funds for Mc-
Carthy in 1952. Ultimately Mundt, through the intercession of Everett Dirksen, located Ray H. Jenkins, a colorful and successful criminal lawyer from
Knoxville, Tennessee. A Taft Republican, Jenkins admired McCarthy, but he
had, thus far, kept his opinions to himself.[27]

Robert Stevens, Milton Eisenhower advised his brother, would need "the
best lawyer in the United States." Milton recommended Thurmond Arnold,
the old New Dealer. On the suggestion of Brownell and Governor Thomas E.
Dewey of New York, however, the army retained Joseph N. Welch, a liberal
Republican hostile to McCarthy. A graduate of Harvard Law School and a
self-made Brahmin, Welch headed the trial section of the old-line Boston law
firm Hale and Dorr. Courtly and sixty-three years old, Welch, not Jenkins,
would appear before the television camera as the proverbial folksy, small-
town lawyer.[28]

While the other players prepared for the hearings, McCarthy continued on
his political descent. To be sure, the senator did embark on a speaking tour
that demonstrated his ability to rally enthusiastic crowds of true believers—

Irish Catholics in Chicago, Young Republicans in Milwaukee, oil millionaires in Houston. Yet a Gallup survey taken after the release of the Adams chronology showed that Americans now disapproved of the nation's most outspoken anti-Communist by a margin of 46 to 38 percent. Old supporters started to abandon him. J. Edgar Hoover told Eisenhower that McCarthy had become an impediment in the war against subversion. Worse yet, McCarthy was deteriorating physically and, one must presume, mentally. Working virtually around the clock, he was drinking almost as steadily, seeming to draw strength not from food and rest but from tension and alcohol.[29]

The hearings began on April 22, 1954, in an overflowing Senate caucus room before a network television audience. One of the first political spectaculars of the video age, the hearings overshadowed the Viet Minh's capture of the French garrison at Dien Bien Phu and the Supreme Court's decision in *Brown* v. *Board of Education* to become, in the words of columnist Walter Lippmann, "a national obsession." The issues appeared simple. Did McCarthy and his staff seek to win special favors for David Schine? Did the army attempt to use Schine, or other improper means, to thwart a congressional investigation? Yet for two months, the subcommittee would explore almost every possible detour while ignoring the fundamental questions raised by McCarthy's career: did Communist subversives really threaten American national security, and if so, how ought the United States to deal with them?[30]

Secretary Stevens, who was on the stand for days, seemed ill-prepared and evasive. It became clear that the army, in its treatment of Schine, had gone to extraordinary lengths in attempting to appease McCarthy and, especially, Roy Cohn. Senator McCarthy fared miserably. First, the nation had an opportunity to see a red-baiter in action, not just the headlines he liked to create. Instead of bold-faced type declaring "Army Shields Reds, Senator Charges," Americans now saw a fading demagogue badgering witnesses, interrupting lawyers, upbraiding his fellow senators, and incessantly disrupting the proceedings with irrelevant "points of order." Second, Joseph Welch skillfully managed to mire McCarthy in what today would be called "the sleaze factor." There was the "purloined letter" supposedly written by J. Edgar Hoover about security risks at Fort Monmouth; if it was not a forgery, McCarthy had received it in violation of federal laws protecting government secrets. There were the elev-

McCarthy confers with Karl Mundt (left), as Roy Cohn (center) looks on, during the opening days of the army-McCarthy hearings. (AP/Wide World Photos)

en memos that McCarthy's secretary could not remember typing or filing. And there was a doctored photograph showing Stevens and Private Schine in an amicable pose. As journalist Drew Pearson assessed the hearings, "[The army] comes off badly—though McCarthy comes off a little worse."[31]

Critics continued to urge Eisenhower to attack McCarthy publicly, but by April no need existed for the president to do so.[32] McCarthy was destroying himself. On April 5, in a nationally broadcast address, Ike sought to assuage the fears that McCarthy and others—including the president himself at times—had aroused. American Communists, Eisenhower said, constituted only a tiny percentage of the nation's population. Unsubstantiated allegations made behind the shield of congressional immunity, he noted, could result in "grave offenses" against individual rights. Stopping short, however, of recommending concrete action to put an end to McCarthyism, the president instead reassured the nation that "public opinion" would ultimately "straighten this

The army-McCarthy hearings, May 1954. Senator McCarthy swears to
tell the truth, before a skeptical audience. (AP/Wide World Photos)

matter out." Eisenhower secretly followed the course of the hearings through
Charles Potter. The Michigan Republican briefed Eisenhower on the first day
of the hearings and again in early May. The president, according to Potter,
initially thought that Stevens would perform well as a witness and that the
hearings would be brief. Convinced that the White House had failed to support Stevens adequately, Potter feared that Eisenhower might not fully understand the situation on Capitol Hill. But Ike knew enough to "feel ashamed for
the United States Senate," a sentiment he did not conceal at a May 5 press
conference. The president hoped the benefits of the hearings, he told reporters, would at least be "comparable" to what the country had "suffered in loss
of international prestige, and . . . self-respect."[33]

Few Republican leaders could see any benefits in the army-McCarthy confrontation. Leonard W. Hall, the party's national chairman, wrote an acquain-

tance, "I don't think anyone believes that the current hearings are helping Senator McCarthy, the cause of anti-communism, the Republican Party or the country."[34] Beginning early in May, Everett Dirksen commenced his own campaign to bring the hearings to a close. As unveiled to the subcommittee on May 11, the Dirksen proposal provided that further public sessions would be limited to the testimony of McCarthy and Stevens, that any other testimony would be heard in executive session, and that Senator McCarthy would be allowed to resume his other investigations. Both John Adams and White House speechwriter William Bragg Ewald, Jr., later wrote that Fred A. Seaton, the deputy secretary of defense for legislative affairs and a politician with close ties to the White House, had pressured Stevens to agree to the Dirksen plan. Despite his disgust with the whole affair, however, Eisenhower would not order the army to compromise. Instead, the president sent word to Stevens, through Charles Wilson: "Do what you think is right." Believing that the hearings would clear his name and vindicate the army, Stevens refused to budge. Dirksen complained to the White House, but to no avail. On May 11, the Democrats and Chairman Mundt—who had promised not to terminate the proceedings without the agreement of all the principals—defeated the Dirksen compromise 4 to 3.[35]

President Eisenhower might not have given Stevens such discretion if he had foreseen the next path the hearings would take, although there had been warning signs. On May 3 and again the next day, Roy Cohn, representing himself, repeatedly pressed Stevens for the legal basis of the army's refusal to make loyalty board members available to congressional investigators. On May 7, the army responded with a legal memorandum that was short on case law but stated that at a January 21, 1954, conference attended by "members of the White House executive Staff," William Rogers, John Adams, and the attorney general, "Mr. Brownell took the position that the success of the loyalty program required that security board members . . . be protected from the dangers inherent in the congressional review of their actions." The January 21 meeting surfaced again as Ray Jenkins questioned John Adams on May 12, the day after the subcommittee rejected the Dirksen compromise. Apparently, Adams believed the immunity of the loyalty boards derived from the traditional common-law rule that judges could not be summoned to give testimony

Eisenhower greets Secretary of the Army Robert Stevens (left) at Washington's National Airport in mid-May 1954 and expresses his continued confidence in the army and the secretary. (AP/Wide World Photos)

about their decisions. "The boards are quasi-judicial in nature," he explained to the subcommittee. "They have somewhat the function of an appellate court." And Adams volunteered some details on the January 21 meeting: that Sherman Adams and Henry Cabot Lodge had been present, that they had discussed David Schine, and that it had been suggested that the army lawyer prepare a written summary of the Schine affair. Jenkins did not bore in on the particulars of the meeting, but Adams had implicated the White House. On the mention of Lodge's name especially, *Time* magazine reported, "the senators' political radarscopes blipped wildly." Obviously, the meeting possessed no relationship to Lodge's duties at the United Nations. Moreover, as the manager of Eisenhower's tough 1952 preconvention campaign, Lodge had attracted the political enmity of both Democrats and anti-Eisenhower Republicans.[36]

Adams, as we have seen, had been trying since the fall of 1953 to force the Justice Department to clarify the administration's policy on the power of Congress to demand witnesses and documents from the executive branch. With regard to the ability of Congress to subpoena loyalty board members, Adams told the subcommittee that "two schools of thought" existed within the administration. Indeed, it was beginning to appear that one school existed for material embarrassing to the White House and another existed for everything else. Concerned about the release of the transcripts of telephone calls monitored by the Department of Defense, Herbert Brownell had advised Sherman Adams on May 2 that if the subcommittee sought to obtain "telephone conversations with the White House or the Department of Justice, the Administration should not allow them to be turned over." Along with Brownell's advice, the White House received a lengthy memorandum from William Rogers detailing numerous incidents in which presidents had withheld information from Congress.[37] Fearful that he might be called to testify, Ambassador Lodge indicated to the president on May 7 that he would not honor a subpoena. Eisenhower replied three days later that the UN ambassador's position was "exactly correct." Yet as late as May 11, Eisenhower instructed Charles Wilson to provide Congress with all the facts relevant to the Peress case, except those touching on national security. The president did not, he told the defense secretary, want the army to appear guilty of a "cover-up."[38]

Nevertheless, once John Adams offered the subcommittee an opportunity to pursue the army-McCarthy controversy into the Oval Office, the administration moved immediately to limit further disclosures. Sherman Adams ordered Seaton to collect for transmittal to the White House all records pertaining to "the inquiry before the subcommittee." On the same day, Eisenhower directed Wilson not to permit the disclosure before the Mundt panel of the substance of any conversations between employees of the executive branch that involved their official duties. Such confidentiality was essential, the president said, to the preservation of the separation of powers and the free exchange of advice.[39]

Jenkins kept John Adams on the stand for all of May 13 without questioning him about his meeting with Sherman Adams and Lodge. The next day, a Friday, gave Stuart Symington a chance to cross-examine the army lawyer, and Symington went directly to the reason for Lodge's presence at the January 21 meeting. As Adams was conceding that no UN business had been under discussion, Welch, citing oral instructions from the Department of Defense, told Adams to say no more about the conference. The Democrats immediately objected, with Henry Jackson making the credible point that Adams, by disclosing the meeting and revealing some of its details, might legally be held to have waived any privilege. But on Welch's instructions, Adams dodged further questions about the meeting until the subcommittee recessed for the weekend.[40]

When the hearings resumed on May 17, John Adams returned with a letter, freshly prepared by the White House staff, in which President Eisenhower instructed Charles Wilson that Defense Department witnesses were not to testify about conversations with other executive branch employees or to produce related documents. The army also submitted a memorandum incorporating Rogers's arguments in his earlier report to the White House. Eisenhower's directive stunned the subcommittee. Speaking for the Democrats, Senator McClellan charged, "The issuance of this Executive Order is a serious mistake." If it was to be issued, McClellan argued, it should have been done at the beginning of the hearings. Even the Republicans were taken aback; Charles Potter feared that Stevens and Adams were being "used as whipping boys" for the decisions of more senior administration officials. Confused and anxious to negotiate a modification of Eisenhower's order, the subcommittee voted to recess until the following week.[41]

He had tried to "stay out of this damn business on the Hill," Eisenhower told the Republican leaders at their weekly meeting on May 17. Knowland and the House GOP leader Charles A. Halleck expressed reservations about the scope of the order, but Ike asserted that Sherman Adams and other executive aides, like military staff officers, possessed "no political existence" beyond the president. Ike admitted that he "couldn't tell the Senate its business," but he asserted, "A person like Governor Adams has no responsibility to the legislature." Eisenhower clung stubbornly to principle and, to be sure, expediency. He defended his order at a press conference two days later and, despite the personal intercession of Everett Dirksen, refused to modify his decision.[42]

Eisenhower seemed personally offended at the possibility that two of his closest aides might be called to testify, as if the prospect threatened to invade his own privacy. As he told James Hagerty, "Any man who testified as to the advice he gave me won't be working for me that night." This was the other side of Eisenhower's rigid view of the separation of powers. Loath to involve himself ostentatiously in congressional affairs, he deeply resented legislative scrutiny of the upper reaches of the administration. Ironically, for so mild-mannered a chief executive, Eisenhower's instructions to Wilson represented an unprecedented assertion of presidential prerogative. No longer was the administration merely seeking to prevent the exposure of sensitive personnel files, the disruption of an administrative tribunal, or the abuse of a hapless general.[43] Now the administration, through Attorney General Brownell, claimed that the president enjoyed an "uncontrolled discretion" over the release of information from the executive branch, although the attorney general quickly had to correct his statement that the courts had "uniformly" recognized such a right. In reality, the administration's argument rested on past incidents in which presidents had resisted Congress but avoided litigation. No definitive judicial decisions supported Eisenhower's claims. What soon became known as "executive privilege," wrote one constitutional scholar, was a "myth," an unwarranted assertion of executive supremacy "altogether without historical foundation."[44]

Notwithstanding later criticisms, the order stood; it was widely perceived that the president, after months of public temporizing, had finally dealt a deadly blow to the nation's leading political rabble-rouser.[45] McCarthy's startled reaction to the May 17 directive—"Mr. Chairman, I must admit that I am somewhat at a loss to know what to do at the moment"—contributed to that impression. Yet the senator's bewilderment was evidence more of his declining powers than it was of the efficacy of Eisenhower's action. At his peak, McCarthy had needed little to send Washington into turmoil—an ex-Communist willing to talk, a leaked document, a bald-faced lie. Now he seemed less resourceful, less intimidating. The hearings themselves, apart from their incalculable psychological damage, may have hurt McCarthy less

COMMUNIST PARTY ORGANIZATION U.S.A-FEB. 9, 1950

As the army-McCarthy hearings drone on into June 1954, McCarthy
describes the Communist party infrastructure in the United States to a bored Joseph
Welch (center). (UPI/Bettmann Archive)

than they did the Republican party. The senator's favorable rating slid to about
a third of the population before the hearings began, and remained there. The
pollster George Gallup estimated that McCarthy would retain the undying
allegiance of about 30 percent of all Americans. But as David M. Oshinsky
has perceptively noted, McCarthy's influence had long depended on "the
appearance of mass support," and by the late spring of 1954, that appearance
was dissolving.[46]

In mid-May, *Look* magazine published a summary of the research of Louis
H. Bean; the social scientist argued that McCarthy had actually hurt the
Republican candidates for whom he had campaigned in 1952. Then, in June,
voters in Maine's Republican primary hammered another nail in McCarthy's
coffin. Incumbent Senator Margaret Chase Smith, a longtime foe of her
Wisconsin colleague, won renomination over McCarthy's candidate, Robert
L. Jones, by a five-to-one margin. Local issues may have predominated in the

minds of Maine voters, but many national observers saw Smith's decisive victory as yet another rebuff to McCarthy.[47]

For his part, Eisenhower mixed restrained public denunciations of McCarthyism with a growing personal contempt. The president had earlier ridiculed the notion that McCarthy represented a menace to "our system of government." But McCarthy's call for government employees to ignore Ike's secrecy order of May 17 infuriated the president, who privately compared the senator to Adolf Hitler and labeled his plea "the most disloyal act . . . ever . . . by anyone in the government of the United States." In a well-received speech at Columbia University, Eisenhower warned against censorship, "hysteria, and intimidation" in the war against subversion. Near the end of the hearings in mid-June, Charles Potter, disgusted with his GOP colleagues' efforts to defend McCarthy, told Eisenhower that he might vote with the Democrats to deliver a report critical of the Wisconsin Republican. Frustrated himself, the president told James Hagerty, "That's all right with me."[48]

Despite the attention, the army-McCarthy hearings, at least from a procedural standpoint, proved to be less important in McCarthy's ultimate downfall than did an earlier investigation by the Subcommittee on Privileges and Elections of the Senate Committee on Rules and Investigations. In February 1951, the subcommittee, then controlled by the Democrats, began questioning Senator McCarthy in a wide-ranging investigation that encompassed alleged financial misconduct and violation of state and federal election laws. Beset by partisan divisions and McCarthy's obstructionism, the panel's inquiry proved inconclusive. Then on June 11, 1954, Senator Ralph E. Flanders, a Vermont Republican, introduced a resolution calling on the Senate to strip McCarthy of his chairmanships unless he remedied his "contempt" of the Subcommittee on Privileges and Elections. The impact of McCarthyism on America's position in the world had begun to concern Flanders while he was visiting Australia and New Zealand. Many observers there, Flanders later recalled, saw McCarthy as "something like a new Hitler," a demagogue capable of leading the

United States down "the Nazi path." On returning home, Flanders attacked his colleague in a Senate speech on March 9 and eventually, as the army-McCarthy hearings droned on, set in motion the forces that would lead to the censure of the Wisconsin senator.[49]

Most Republicans resented Flanders's efforts to force their party to deal directly with the McCarthy issue. William Knowland denounced Flanders's resolution as "unfair and unprecedented." Knowland and Homer E. Ferguson of Michigan, another conservative Republican, pleaded with Flanders to withdraw it. Flanders soon found himself ostracized by the Senate GOP, forced to eat alone with his wife in the Senate dining room. Vice President Nixon predicted that the resolution would not pass "in its present form" and perhaps not in any form. Secretary of the Treasury George M. Humphrey, widely regarded as one of the most influential figures in the administration, quietly went to Capitol Hill to urge Flanders to drop his attack on McCarthy.[50]

The president, meanwhile, sent the Vermont senator a brief, and confidential, message of support. Privately, Eisenhower questioned the propriety of a censure motion lacking specific charges, as did Flanders's.[51] Eisenhower refused publicly to endorse the anti-McCarthy initiative and, by all accounts, maintained his distance from the affair.[52] Political scientist Fred Greenstein has depicted the president as the mastermind of a massive and surreptitious campaign to depose McCarthy, but much of his evidence consists of Ike's rather timid verbal assaults on blatantly paranoid anticommunism. Those statements impressed none of McCarthy's contemporary critics, even if they stung his supporters. In all fairness, the administration did contribute to McCarthy's destruction. Representatives of the White House, if not the president himself, plotted army strategy with Welch and his assistants. Yet few of Eisenhower's intimates, in the words of reporter Robert Donovan, believed "that the president followed any carefully planned, deliberate strategy toward McCarthy."[53]

The divisions within the administration, along with the likelihood that presidential meddling in so delicate a Senate proceeding might trigger a pro-McCarthy backlash, counseled against White House intervention. To be sure, a few people on the "fringes of the administration," as William Knowland later recalled, assisted Senator Flanders.[54] The Vermont senator received crucial legal and political support from the National Committee for an Effective Congress, which claimed the longtime Eisenhower supporter Paul Hoffman as its leading fund-raiser. Concerned that McCarthy was driving liberal and independent voters away from the GOP, Hoffman thought that the White House might be able to persuade Ferguson, Potter, and Eugene D. Millikin of Colorado to join in the Flanders motion. But the president, his contempt for McCarthy by now well known, left the Senate to its own devices.[55]

On its own, the Senate moved deliberately. Faced with the virtually unanimous opposition of the Republican leadership, Senator Flanders modified his resolution to call simply for the censure of McCarthy. At the same time, demands were growing within the Senate for the inclusion in the resolution of a bill of particulars and for hearings on the Flanders resolution, both of which were seen as delaying tactics put forward by McCarthyites. Flanders and his supporters acceded to the demand for a set of specific allegations. Then, on August 2, 1954, the Senate voted 75 to 12 to refer the censure resolution to a select committee. As handpicked by Knowland and Texas Democrat Lyndon B. Johnson, the minority leader, the committee consisted of three Democrats and three Republicans, all respectable members of the Senate establishment. Utah's Arthur V. Watkins would head the panel. A Taft Republican and former member of the internal security subcommittee, Watkins boasted of having as much experience investigating Communists as did McCarthy. Unlike Karl Mundt, Watkins would manage his committee with a stern hand; the select committee hearings, which would not be televised, proceeded without the fanfare that accompanied the army-McCarthy confrontation.[56]

The Watkins Committee hearings were played out against the background of the coming congressional elections—the first real political test of the administration's handling of the Communist controversy. As early as November 1953, Eisenhower had publicly disputed Leonard Hall's assertion that Communists in government would be the principal issue in 1954. Undoubtedly, the president feared turning the election into a referendum on McCarthyism, with the GOP taking the pro-McCarthy position. Hall's campaign strategy, Henry Cabot Lodge warned the president, was "a virtual admission" that the administration had accomplished "nothing constructive" of its own.[57] When Eisenhower and Nixon met with a group of Republican congressmen in

May to assess the party's prospects for the fall, it was clear that McCarthy's popularity had declined precipitously. Yet the senator retained significant pockets of support at the grass-roots level; throughout 1954, mail to the RNC was overwhelmingly pro-McCarthy. As former Congressman O. K. Armstrong advised Hall after returning from a tour of the Midwest and West, McCarthy still possessed "a big following . . . one not to be antagonized needlessly." And even Lodge believed that anticommunism, minus McCarthy, represented "a marvelously popular issue."[58]

Eisenhower responded to such advice with a little election year red-baiting of his own. As he had done before, the president sought to ignore, and to preempt, McCarthy. On June 10, Eisenhower told a national gathering of local party workers that the administration had been "intensifying legal action against the members and leaders of the Communist conspiracy." On August 30, the president, appearing before an American Legion convention in Washington, D.C., pledged to "wage a relentless battle against subversion and infiltration." Eisenhower said less about the issue during a fall campaign swing through the West, but he did assure a Republican rally in Denver that the government was "dealing decisively with 'the Communist menace.'" Ike also agreed to campaign in Illinois for the Republican Senate candidate, an archconservative McCarthyite who was challenging incumbent Democrat Paul H. Douglas. The president, however, insisted that the Republican nominee, Joseph T. Meek, not bring McCarthy into Illinois.[59]

For the most part, however, President Eisenhower left the administration's anti-Communist crusading to Richard Nixon. On September 15, the vice president embarked on a tour designed to take him into thirty-one states over the next forty-eight days. All across the country, Nixon warned that a Democratic Congress would impede the war against communism and bragged that "thousands of Communists, fellow travelers, and security risks" had been "thrown out" of the government by the administration. In December 1953, the RNC had received indications from a survey of Ohio party members that Eisenhower's initial desire to minimize communism as an issue would not, at least in the Midwest, help to turn out a "big Republican vote." Both Eisenhower and the vice president later sensed a pervasive apathy among Republicans. Nixon attributed it to the divisions and embarrassment created within the party by the controversy surrounding Joseph McCarthy. The remedy, it seemed, was for the administration to take the initiative in the search for subversives.[60]

Eisenhower believed that the survival of the Republican party depended on the rejection of its "dyed-in-the-wool reactionary fringe" but not, apparently, in the abandonment of the anti-Communist stance with which the conservatives were associated. He feared that a Republican defeat in November would encourage the "extreme right wing" to try to seize control of the organization.[61] The actual results proved less menacing. Although the Republicans lost control of Congress, by a narrow margin, the results were especially disappointing for the Old Guard. Meek lost in Illinois, and the conservative stalwart Homer Ferguson met defeat in Michigan. At the same time, an avowed anti-McCarthy Republican, Representative Clifford Case, made an impressive showing by bucking the Democratic tide and winning a Senate seat in New Jersey. James Hagerty concluded that the party's association with McCarthy had hurt the GOP in New York and other large industrial states. But in most of the country, Communists in government seems not to have been a significant issue.[62]

On September 27, 1954, the Watkins Committee had issued a report recommending that McCarthy be censured for his refusal to cooperate with the investigation of the Subcommittee on Privileges and Elections and for his harassment of General Zwicker. Notwithstanding the ordeal of the army-McCarthy hearings, the Watkins Committee report, and the election returns, a host of sincere McCarthyites rallied for a last-ditch defense of their hero. So too did some conservatives who simply saw the Wisconsin senator as a useful weapon in their battle with the Eisenhower wing of the GOP. Senators reported a massive influx of pro-McCarthy mail. Arthur Watkins received thirty thousand letters, two to one against censure.[63] The conservative journalist David Lawrence questioned the jurisdiction of the Watkins Committee in recommending sanctions against McCarthy. Some thirteen thousand McCarthy sympathizers attended a rally at Madison Square Garden in New York City on November 13. The journalist William S. White described the anticensure forces as "the largest reemergence and coming together of essentially right-wing groups since before the United States entered the Second World War."

Most of these groups shared the foreign policy priorities of the Republican Old Guard—noninvolvement in Europe but support for an active role in Asia. "All or nearly all," White reported, "oppose President Eisenhower almost as vehemently as they opposed Presidents Roosevelt and Truman."[64]

Eisenhower's refusal to attack McCarthy publicly, his support for a stringent employee loyalty program, and his own lapses into red-baiting could never placate the hard-core McCarthyites because the appeal of the Wisconsin senator transcended the narrow issue of Communists in government. To many conservatives at the Republican grass roots, New Deal liberalism had been indistinct from socialism, which, one pro-McCarthy correspondent wrote Kansas Senator Frank Carlson, was "the next step to communism." Since so many of them saw so little difference between a New Dealer and a Communist, McCarthy's supporters easily equated McCarthyism with a general conservative assault on the changes that had taken place in American politics and foreign policy in the last twenty years. Liberals had been dismayed by Eisenhower's public diffidence toward McCarthy, but Republican conservatives chafed at the president's failure to support McCarthy wholeheartedly and his affiliation with the eastern wing of the party. If Ike was not the conscious agent of an anti-McCarthy conspiracy, some McCarthyites thought, "the Republican New Dealers, pinks, intellectuals and liberals were taking him for a ride."[65]

It was not surprising, then, that Eisenhower, according to James Hagerty, "hit the roof" when he learned that William Knowland would oppose censure as a threat to the investigative power of the Senate. In reality, Knowland feared alienating conservative support for his principal political objective, a strong U.S. commitment to the defense of Formosa.[66] To be sure, Eisenhower publicly minimized the possibility that the censure issue might split the GOP. He showed no interest when, before the November elections, New Jersey Senator H. Alexander Smith suggested a meeting between Attorney General Brownell and Senator McCarthy in another attempt to reconcile the senator and the administration. "Actually of all the awkward times for a meeting to talk over differences," Eisenhower told Smith, "this would be about as awkward as any."[67] Evidence exists that after the election, with McCarthy's influence clearly curbed, the administration may have considered some kind of compromise, which most senators would have welcomed. According to McCarthy's lawyer, Edward Bennett Williams, who reportedly discussed the issue with Bernard Shanley, the White House seemed eager to settle the controversy as quickly as possible. The Wisconsin senator, however, characteristically refused to apologize for his past behavior or to agree to anything less than a complete vindication by the Senate. On December 2, the Senate voted 67 to 22 to condemn McCarthy for contempt of the Subcommittee on Privileges and Elections and for contempt of the Watkins Committee.[68]

Before the end of the week, Eisenhower broke his silence on the censure controversy by summoning Arthur Watkins to the White House. After a brief meeting—in which the president agreed once more to the release of the identities of those involved in promoting Peress—the White House issued a statement praising Watkins's handling of the select committee. Neither did the McCarthyites forget Watkins. In 1958, when he ran for reelection, pro-McCarthy Republicans fielded an independent candidate, former Utah Governor J. Bracken Lee, who enjoyed the support of wealthy conservatives in Texas and California. Watkins and Lee split the Republican vote, and the Democrat, Frank E. Moss, won the election.[69]

As the vendetta against Watkins demonstrated, although McCarthy's censure had neutralized the senator as a political force, it had not silenced the Republican Right. Eisenhower made a modest contribution to the destruction of Joseph McCarthy, and thereby to the continuing vitality of the Republican party. But the president failed to win the Old Guard away from its favorite witch-hunter or to remake the GOP in the moderate image he had fashioned for himself. All of the twenty-two votes opposing censure came from Republicans, splitting the party's Senate membership in half. Except for Leverett Saltonstall of Massachusetts, all of the Republican leadership—Knowland, Dirksen, Millikin, and Styles Bridges—voted for McCarthy.[70]

The historian Gary Reichard has ranked Senate Republicans in the Eighty-third Congress based on their general support of the Eisenhower administration. Among those he identified as voting with the president at least 80 percent of the time—half the Republican membership—the censure resolution passed 14 to 8. Among GOP senators who supported the administration on less than 80 percent of key roll-call votes, the censure resolution lost by a two-to-one margin.[71] The censure vote, in short, represented a power struggle between party factions divided over other issues. Internal security policies rarely split the Republicans—a vote to censure McCarthy was in no sense a vote against repressive anti-Communist legislation. Surveying the political landscape after the censure battle, Eisenhower expressed doubt that half of all Republicans were on the extreme Right, but he believed that "a fairly good hunk of Republican strength" might have to be jettisoned if the party was to win over Democrats, independents, and new voters.[72] That goal Ike would never achieve.

★ ★ ★

The Communists

and the Constitution

McCarthyism, to recapitulate, ought not to be confused with anticommunism. McCarthyism merely represented one particular political manifestation of America's crusade against domestic subversion, although as such, it symbolized anticommunism in its most spectacular form. McCarthyism was an anti-Communist truncheon for Republicans to use against Democrats and for GOP conservatives to wield against moderates and liberals within their own party. With regard to the former, McCarthyism exploited, to some extent, divisions between the parties over internal security policy.[1] Within the Republican party, the administration rarely allowed itself to be outflanked on domestic communism; the issue provided the GOP Right with little ammunition to use against the White House. Yet anti-Eisenhower Republicans generally indulged Joseph McCarthy's attacks on the administration. McCarthy's fall from grace deprived the Republican Right of the Wisconsin senator's unique skills—mainly his remarkable ability for creating controversy and for intimidating official Washington. In fact, the ex-Marine became a distinct liability to the cause he had championed.[2] But anticommunism survived as a central theme of American public life. To be sure, the movement changed after Senator McCarthy departed from the stage. Drawing on a long-standing consensus against political radicalism, anticommunism waned as a matter of public controversy, but it persisted as a more or less settled policy for national security bureaucrats to implement quietly.[3]

Much of this will perhaps be illustrated by an examination of the legislative, judicial, and extralegal steps taken by the Eisenhower administration in its efforts to curb the American Communist party. Such a perspective not only illuminates the distinction between McCarthyism and anticommunism but also helps to explain Eisenhower's treatment of his leading Republican adversary. The administration's anti-Communist initiatives were not undertaken primarily as a response to pressure from the McCarthyites, or solely as an attempt to undercut Senator McCarthy. Many of the steps the administration took to curb domestic subversion came after the senator's influence began to erode dramatically.[4] A sincere, if misguided, obsession with the nation's security, more than anything else, motivated Eisenhower and his inner circle. They partook fully of the cold war anxieties pervading the nation's politics. This obsession constituted perhaps the single most fundamental reason for Eisenhower's failure to satisfy his liberal critics by confronting McCarthy publicly and decisively. However much disgust the president felt toward the worst of the red-baiters, it was considerably less than many liberals felt, because on the issues of internal security and civil liberties the administration stood closer to the McCarthyites than it did to the liberals.

Although the administration had formulated what would be its basic legislative strategy for dealing with internal subversion as early as March 1953, it nevertheless moved deliberately in submitting its proposals to Congress.[5] During hearings before a subcommittee of the House Judiciary Committee in May, representatives of the Department of Justice did make plain their support for the increased use of wiretaps in national security cases and their opposition to any legislation that would require court approval before the installation of a listening device. As William Rogers sought to explain to the subcommittee, investigations of espionage rings were usually national in scope; the requirement of judicial authorization for electronic surveillance would place an undue burden on the government and increase the risk of leaking sensitive information.[6] Yet in the area of internal security, the administration did not press its legislative agenda during its first year in office. At a September meeting of the NSC, National Security Adviser Robert Cutler warned of "6500 known dangerous subversives" in key industrial facilities around the country. At the same time, Vice President Richard Nixon argued that new antisubversive measures should be "one main object of the administration." Rogers, nevertheless, told the council that "a complete legislative program" would not be ready to submit to Congress until early 1954.[7]

In October, Attorney General Brownell wrote Bryce Harlow to suggest that President Eisenhower include in his next State of the Union Address a witness immunity bill and a wiretap bill. Witnesses appearing before congressional investigating committees freely invoked the privilege against self-incrimination—"Fifth Amendment Communists," McCarthy called them—often withholding testimony to protect friends and former associates. Judges, frequently hostile to legislative witch-hunters, interpreted the Fifth Amendment broadly, sometimes allowing witnesses to refuse even to state their addresses or places of employment. As to the electronic eavesdropping, the Supreme Court had ruled in the 1928 *Olmstead* case that the use of evidence obtained by a wiretap did not violate the constitutional provisions against unreasonable searches or self-incrimination, only to hold in the 1937 *Nardone* case that the admission of such evidence did violate Section 605 of the Communication Act of 1934. That provision prohibited the interception and disclosure of a telephone message. Brownell now proposed that the attorney general be allowed to compel a witness to testify on a grant of immunity from prosecution. Brownell also proposed that evidence obtained by wiretaps authorized by the attorney general in intelligence investigations be admissible in criminal cases. Under consideration for months, these bills represented the heart of the administration's legislative package.[8]

When Brownell presented his recommendations to the NSC in November, John Foster Dulles and Harold Stassen expressed "very considerable reservations" about the broad discretion the wiretap bill would give the attorney general. Both the secretary of state and the director of the Foreign Operations Administration preferred the New York procedure, in which a court order was necessary before a tap could be placed on a telephone. Eisenhower expressed the view that if the taps were limited solely to espionage matters, "he was inclined to pooh-pooh the objections of the civil liberties people." Yet when

Dulles pointed out that an electronic device could hardly be selective in the kind of evidence it collected, even the president conceded that judicial authorization should be "requisite to the admission of wire-tap evidence in court." And Eisenhower expressed skepticism that a dedicated Communist could, under any circumstances, be compelled to testify against the interests of the party. Nevertheless, the NSC agreed that the administration should seek the adoption of a witness immunity bill as well as a wiretap bill, the latter subject to further consideration of the need to obtain court approval.[9]

A month later, however, when Brownell presented his legislative proposals to the cabinet, he repeated the Justice Department's opposition to any law subjecting electronic surveillance to judicial regulation. The department, in fact, was willing to forgo the use of wiretap evidence, if necessary, in order to retain the ability to tap whenever it wished. And despite the debate over the issue within the NSC, no one at the cabinet meeting challenged Brownell. Likewise, the cabinet routinely approved the witness immunity bill, although concern surfaced about the political attractiveness of the measure. As Richard Nixon observed, it would raise "a great hue and cry from the liberals."[10]

In reality, Brownell's anti-Communist initiatives not only offended liberals but also went beyond what many Republican conservatives believed to be necessary. Perhaps Brownell's desire to centralize more and more authority in the attorney general, at the expense of the courts and Congress, worried legislators more than did the obvious threat to civil liberties. In any event, the attorney general faced some probing questions when the White House convened a legislative summit meeting late in December 1953. Even the president recognized the potential for abuse in the witness immunity bill. Homer Ferguson, apparently reflecting the views of most of the legislators at the gathering, argued for a federal law modeled after a Michigan statute that empowered a trial judge, not a prosecutor, to compel testimony through a grant of immunity. But the wiretap bill attracted the most attention. A majority of the states, after all, prohibited wiretapping by law; only a handful followed the New York practice of permitting even court-approved taps. Eugene Millikin led the attack. Electronic eavesdropping, he argued, constituted "an invasion of privacy and a violation of American tradition." Some safeguards, the Colorado senator urged, should be established to protect the public. William Knowland seemed to win from Brownell the concession that, at the minimum, the president's approval, not simply that of the attorney general, should be required for the installation of a tap. Even Joseph McCarthy, at the suggestion of Bernard Shanley, suggested that the Department of Justice curtail the general use of wiretaps in criminal investigations. McCarthy proposed that wiretaps be limited to kidnapping and national security cases and that only in the latter should they be installed without court approval. The Shanley-McCarthy compromise won the day.[11]

In his State of the Union Address of January 1954, Eisenhower skirted the more controversial security measures. He did call on Congress to adopt an expatriation bill that would revoke the citizenship of anyone convicted of conspiring to advocate the violent overthrow of the government. Shanley and Gerald Morgan had lobbied persistently for the inclusion of such a provision in the president's speech, and the idea received an initially favorable reaction. In his memoirs, Eisenhower wrote that although he had known that "some so-called liberals would object seriously," he had also called in his address for the adoption of a witness immunity bill. Eisenhower believed, he wrote, "that our nation had a fundamental obligation to protect itself against palpable disloyalty." In reality, the president's address dismissed the remainder of the antisubversive package with the observation that the attorney general would soon present to Congress recommendations for "needed legal weapons with which to combat subversion" and, the president concluded opaquely, "to deal with the question of claimed immunity."[12]

Clearly, Eisenhower would defer to Brownell on questions of security policy. In the second session of the Eighty-third Congress, the attorney general committed the administration to one of the most sweeping, if not repressive, packages of antisubversive legislation in American history. During a broadcast address in April 1954, Brownell told the nation that progress had been made in the battle against communism but that there were legal "loopholes" that needed "to be plugged to complete the task of destroying this threat to our nation's security." Besides the witness immunity and wiretapping bills, Brownell also wanted to expedite the deportation of naturalized and alien subversives. The attorney general proposed limiting judicial relief from a deportation order to a single application for a writ of habeas corpus, to be sought within sixty to ninety days of the decision of the Board of Immigration Appeals. When the attorney general appeared before a House judiciary sub-committee to testify for the measure, conservative Representative Francis E. Walter told him that Senator Ferguson had convinced the panel that Brownell's proposal was unconstitutional. The administration, through the head of the Justice Department, further recommended that peacetime es-pionage be made a capital offense, that perjury statutes be amended so that inconsistent statements by a witness—without additional evidence—could support a conviction, and that the government be allowed to require the dismissal of alleged subversives from nonsensitive positions in defense plants, to name only some of the two dozen measures that the administration ultimately advanced.[13]

To many cold warriors, however, an obvious void existed in the administra-tion's program. For years they had argued that the most effective method of fighting subversion would simply be to make membership in the Communist party a crime, and on February 7, 1954, Representative Martin Dies, the dean of congressional anti-Communists, introduced such a bill, HR 7894. As one might expect, the idea of outlawing the Communist party had been entertained by the administration; the NSC had taken up the idea in November 1953, and the cabinet had discussed it the following month. John Foster Dulles, Harold Stassen, and Under Secretary of State Bedell Smith seemed responsive to the heavy-handed approach, but the administration quickly adopted more subtle tactics.[14]

Attorney General Brownell opposed Dies's bill, as well as a temporizing measure to create a special commission to study the desirability of outlawing the Communist party. As he advised the president, Brownell feared that legislation establishing "a conclusive and irrebuttable presumption" that equa-ted party membership with a conspiracy to overthrow the government might violate due process of law. So too might legislation that failed to distinguish between the party member who was knowingly plotting revolution and the unwitting dupe who merely thought he had joined a left-wing political organi-zation. More important, how could the government, consistent with the Fifth Amendment, require Communists to register with the Subversive Activities Control Board (SACB) under the McCarran Act if party membership constituted a crime? The McCarran Act, the Smith Act, and existing immigration legislation provided an adequate legal bulwark for internal security, Brownell told a subcommittee of the House Judiciary Committee, but, he added, if party membership was prohibited, the McCarran Act's "entire operation . . . would be jeopardized, unless . . . a grant of immunity . . . so broad as to vitiate the legislation now proposed" was added.[15]

In short, the administration opposed outlawing the Communist party as a threat to the McCarran Act and the SACB, which was hardly a libertarian concern. The 1950 law had itself been the partial outgrowth of a celebrated bill cosponsored by Senator Karl Mundt and Representative Richard Nixon in 1948. Brownell believed, as he told the cabinet in April 1954, that the government would have a "strong power" to use against subversion if the Supreme Court upheld the SACB's decision ordering Communists to register with the board. It would be far easier to register and monitor the country's twenty-five thousand Communists, the attorney general suggested, than it would be to drive them underground and then try to prosecute them as criminals.[16]

The greatest threat to the McCarran Act, however, came not from Martin Dies or the supporters of a special commission to study the issue but from a group of disgruntled Senate Democrats. Exasperated at repeated charges that they were soft on communism, many liberal Democrats resented the administration's delay in pushing its own antisubversive program until the onset of the 1954 midterm political campaign. Accordingly, early in August, Hubert H. Humphrey of Minnesota introduced a bill declaring the CPUSA to be a conspiracy to overthrow the government and punishing party membership by up to five years in jail and a ten-thousand-dollar fine. Humphrey offered his bill as a substitute for a measure proposed by Senator John M. Butler of Maryland, with administration support; Butler's bill would have empowered the SACB to pronounce a labor union "communist-infiltrated" and thereby deprive it of its standing before the National Labor Relations Board. Such remained the climate in Washington that, even with Joseph McCarthy fighting for his political survival, no senator wanted to be seen opposing a bill that appeared to strike at the heart of the Communist conspiracy. Humphrey agreed to combine his bill with Butler's. On August 12, the Senate, over the opposition of the White House, the attorney general, and FBI Director J.

Edgar Hoover, passed the hastily drafted package, without the benefit of hearings or serious debate, by a vote of 85 to 0.[17]

At his August 16 meeting with legislative leaders, President Eisenhower labeled the Senate measure "the worst can of worms" he had ever seen. But few observers believed that the president would veto such a popular bill if it cleared the House, and in any event, Congress might well override his veto. Working with Homer Ferguson in the Senate and GOP leaders in the House, the administration had already devised an alternative to the Senate bill. The essence of the Butler bill would be retained and the Communist party would be stripped of all its legal rights, but no penalties would be imposed for party membership. The administration's plan would, therefore, offer each member of Congress an opportunity to record a vote to "outlaw" the Communist party without endangering the operation of the McCarran Act. As White House counsel Bernard Shanley observed, the term *outlaw* meant "nothing in the law." After forty minutes of debate on the sixteenth, the House passed the administration's bill with only New York Democrat Abraham J. Multer and North Dakota Republican Usher L. Burdick dissenting. Eisenhower made public his preference for the House initiative at a press conference on August 17, when he expressed the warning that Congress should not enact legislation that would impair the enforcement of the Smith Act, which was not precisely Brownell's main concern. At a House-Senate conference, the conservative Democratic Senator Pat McCarran led a successful effort for the adoption of the administration's proposal. The Senate unanimously passed the resulting conference committee bill, and the House approved it 265 to 2 before the end of August.[18]

Although the Communist Control Act of 1954 had been primarily an exercise in damage control for the administration and although it contained the kind of evidentiary finding—that the CPUSA constituted "an instrumentality of a conspiracy to overthrow the government"—that Brownell had warned the president might be unconstitutional, Eisenhower sought to make the most of the bill's passage. With congressional elections approaching, the White House took the unusual step of making a short film in which the president hailed the adoption of the act. Eisenhower also seized the opportunity to review the administration's accomplishments in the search for security: its expatriation bill; legislation modernizing existing statutes to include within the definition of *sabotage* those acts committed using radioactive, biological, and chemical agents; and a law authorizing the death penalty for peacetime espionage or sabotage. Moreover, Congress approved a witness immunity bill, although the power to grant immunity was lodged in the courts, not the attorney general. And the administration failed to win adoption of legislation allowing the use of wiretap evidence in court.[19]

Judging from the White House mail and press reaction, the frantic posturing around the Communist Control Act proved too blatantly opportunistic to pay many political dividends. The *New York Herald-Tribune* praised the ability of the politicians to arrive at a compromise, but in a more typical response, the *Louisville Courier-Journal* described the controversy as a "dismal spectacle of hundreds of grown men tumbling over one another to outlaw a ghost." Yet the administration's record during the Eighty-third Congress, along with the employee security system and its prosecution of Communist party leaders, gave the lie to any claims that President Eisenhower was soft on communism. Soon such charges would be limited almost entirely to hysterical voices on the lunatic fringe of American politics, represented most notably by Robert Welch of the John Birch Society. To be sure, the major anti-Communist initiatives of 1954 accomplished little of significance. The Communist Control Act went largely unenforced. The main purpose of the congressional witch-hunting committees had long been the exposure of Communists, not legislation. Content to force truculent witnesses to take the Fifth Amendment, HCUA made little use of the witness immunity bill. But the government had other weapons to employ against the "international communist conspiracy."[20]

Outside the halls of Congress, the federal government continued its battle to safeguard the nation's security, often in a professional, if not routine, fashion. Early in Eisenhower's first administration, two Austrians, Otto Verber and Kurt L. Ponger, pled guilty to conspiring with Yuri V. Novikov, the second secretary of the Soviet Embassy in Washington, to give American defense secrets to the Russians. It was hardly a case of domestic subversion; Verber and Ponger had been arrested in Vienna, where their conspiracy allegedly originated. Then in January 1955, Joseph S. Peterson, Jr., who had leaked classified information to the Dutch, pled guilty to the charge of espionage. He received a seven-year jail sentence.[21]

Actual cases of espionage, however, rarely surfaced. At a more prosaic level, the administration promulgated a security regimen for employees in sensitive positions with private defense contractors. Operating much like the program for government workers, the industrial security program netted no spies and few, if any, Communists, but it did expose a mixed bag of ex-party members, alcoholics, petty criminals, and invariably, homosexuals. In one of the first uses of the tax laws for essentially political purposes, the government initiated a tax-evasion case against Vincent Hallinan, the Progressive party candidate for president in 1952. The Eisenhower administration continued Truman's crackdown on alleged alien and naturalized subversives; by December 1954, the White House boasted of having deported 129 such individuals, with approximately 450 deportation and denaturalization cases pending. After securing a registration order against the Communist party from the SACB in April 1953, the Department of Justice brought 14 additional such cases against alleged Communist-front organizations in fiscal 1953. Two registration cases were filed with the SACB in the twelve months thereafter. Elaborate legal productions, SACB proceedings typically involved a cadre of government witnesses—often previously confidential informants—along with thousands of pages of testimony, months of hearings, and years of appellate review. In response to the swelling work load, the Department of Justice, in July 1954, transferred responsibility for security cases from its Criminal Division to the newly created Division of Internal Security under Assistant Attorney General William F. Tompkins. On April 25, 1956, the government filed its first sedition case in ten years, charging that John William Powell, Sylvia Campbell Powell, and Julian Schumann, as the editors of the San Francisco–based *China Monthly Review*, had made statements designed to hinder military recruitment and interfere with the prosecution of the Korean War.[22]

The case of Owen Lattimore, an Asian specialist who had served as a State Department consultant, nicely illustrates the essentially political nature of much of the anti-Communist crusade. After McCarthy's Wheeling speech came under close scrutiny from his colleagues, the senator announced that he would "stand or fall" on the case of Owen Lattimore. McCarthy labeled Lattimore "the principal architect" of America's Far Eastern policy and "the top Russian spy" in the United States. Lattimore was indeed a critic of Western imperialism in Asia, but he was neither a Communist nor an important influence on American policy. When McCarthy's interest in the case began to wane, as it often did after his allegations had received sufficient publicity, Nevada Senator Patrick A. McCarran, a Democrat, launched his own investigation of Lattimore. Pressure from McCarran led to an indictment against the professor. The government's case rested on the argument that Lattimore had lied to McCarran's Internal Security Subcommittee when he denied that he was sympathetic to communism, since he had frequently advocated positions, such as the need to reach an accommodation with the People's Republic of China, that paralleled the "alleged Communist party line." Leaving office in 1953, the Truman administration—gladly, one may presume—bequeathed the case to Eisenhower.[23]

In one of his first acts as deputy attorney general, William Rogers promised that "every possible assistance," including additional office space, personnel, and if needed, a further FBI investigation, would be given to the lawyers prosecuting Owen Lattimore. Rogers's best efforts came to naught. The case against the Asian scholar proved so flimsy that the government encountered difficulty in drafting a legally sufficient indictment or, perhaps more accurately, in finding a crime of which Lattimore could be accused. After the government failed to have reversed on appeal a trial court ruling dismissing two of the counts against him, the Department of Justice concluded that "there was no reasonable likelihood of a successful prosecution on the remaining five counts." The government withdrew the charges.[24]

Notwithstanding the failure of the case against Lattimore, charges of perjury, or the lesser offense of making false statements, became a staple of government prosecutors. Besides lying to a congressional committee, a suspected subversive might be charged with mendacity in filling out an application for a passport, government employment, or even public housing. Most notably, the Labor Management Relations Act of 1947 required that union officials file, with the National Labor Relations Board, affidavits stating that they were not Communists. Under this provision, for example, the government obtained the conviction of Ben Gold, the president of the International Fur and Leather Workers Union. One may well question the propriety of punishing an individual for lying when the conduct that gave rise to the false statement—and the action that the government actually wanted to deter— might not itself be illegal. To cite a particularly promiscuous use of the perjury statutes, Frank Cook, a Cincinnati resident, was charged with lying to a grand jury, in the course of a perjury investigation of two other men, about attending a CPUSA function. Dismissing the charges against Cook, the trial court concluded that, in light of the defendant's limited intelligence, the government had failed to demonstrate that he knew the meetings in question "to be meetings of the Communist Party."[25]

The preeminent weapon in the government's statutory arsenal, however, remained the 1940 Smith Act. First invoked against a group of Minneapolis Trotskyists in 1941, the Smith Act prohibited participation in any conspiracy to advocate the violent overthrow of the U.S. government or membership in any organization involved in such a conspiracy. During Harry Truman's presidency, the act's conspiracy section had been invoked against the top echelon of the CPUSA's leadership. Indeed, before Truman left the White House, the government, in the so-called *Flynn* case, had launched Smith Act prosecutions against second- and third-tier party leaders. In retrospect, the Smith Act defendants seem to have been a remarkably docile group of revolutionaries. So little real evidence existed of any concrete plans for a violent revolution that the trials inevitably degenerated into tendentious debates about Marxist doctrine.[26]

Smith Act prosecutions seemed to lag during the 1952 campaign and the subsequent presidential transition. Nevertheless, Attorney General Brownell believed that the party could be effectively crippled by a series of selective prosecutions in industrial centers and port cities where Communists were most numerous and where they would pose the most serious threat to national security should they elect to embark on a course of espionage and sabotage. In July 1953, federal authorities arrested several Communist leaders in Philadelphia and, shortly thereafter, another group of CPUSA officials in Cleveland. On June 26, 1954, federal prosecutors brought the first indictment, against Claude Lightfoot, under the Smith Act's membership clause. By election day 1954, Smith Act cases were under way, or only recently completed, in cities all across the nation, including Honolulu, Pittsburgh, Seattle, Detroit, and St. Louis.[27]

Yet three developments would stymie the administration's legal war against the Red menace. First, before the end of Eisenhower's first term, it became apparent that the Supreme Court, under a new chief justice, Earl Warren—whom, ironically, Ike had appointed—was experiencing second thoughts about some of the government's antisubversive tactics. In the 1951 *Dennis* case, the Court had upheld the Truman administration's first set of Smith Act convictions. But on October 17, 1955, the Court issued a writ of certiorari to review the virtually identical *Yates* case, an ominous sign to federal prosecutors.[28] Second, the government's case in trials under the Smith Act and similar statutes usually depended in large part on the testimony of paid informants and former Communists, an almost inherently unstable group that seemed to include a disproportionate number of mental patients and ex-convicts. President Eisenhower reportedly told Herbert Brownell, "[The ex-Communists are] such liars and cheats that even when they apparently recant and later testify against someone . . . my first reaction is to believe that the accused person must be a patriot."[29] Indeed, in 1955 several of the ex-Communists-turned-informants, in particular Harvey M. Matusow, began to recant their accusations. The government had relied on Matusow's testimony when it secured the conviction of Clinton E. Jencks, an official of the Mine, Mill, and Smelter Workers Union, for filing a false affidavit with the NLRB. Matusow's recantation eventually resulted in Jencks's vindication and Matusow's own conviction for perjury.[30] Brownell claimed that the whole affair had been concocted by the Communists to embarrass the government. If it was, it worked.[31] Finally, undercover informants, despite their instability, constituted the linchpin of the FBI's intelligence-gathering apparatus; the government's prosecutorial efforts had exposed over a hundred of them. Concerned about the effect of such disclosures on the FBI's intelligence network, J. Edgar Hoover apparently managed to restrain further Smith Act prosecutions from late 1954 until 1956, when William Rogers, in the heat of a presidential campaign, filed ten new cases.[32]

Hoover responded to such difficulties with a scheme designed to disrupt the Communist party through the use of covert, extralegal tactics. Begun in August 1956, the FBI's COINTELPRO (Counter-Intelligence Program) sought to capitalize on the turmoil created within the Communist world by Soviet Premier Nikita Khrushchev's repudiation of Joseph Stalin at the Twentieth Party Congress in Moscow. The FBI hoped to use its informants not simply to provide intelligence reports, but to sow discord within the party. Initially aimed only at the CPUSA, the operation grew in the 1960s to include the infiltration and disruption of a variety of non-Communist groups, especially civil rights and peace organizations, through techniques that included unauthorized wiretapping, mail opening, and burglary. Publicly exposed in the mid-1970s, the bureau's program of "harassment of innocent citizens engaged in lawful forms of political expression," a panel of Senate investigators concluded, had done "serious injury to the First Amendment guarantee of freedom of speech and the right of a free people to assemble peaceably and to petition the government for a redress of grievances."[33]

By all accounts, the FBI director initiated COINTELPRO without the consent or knowledge of either President Eisenhower or Attorney General Brownell. Not until May 1958 did Hoover advise the White House or his superiors at the Department of Justice of the existence of the secret program, and then he sketched for Robert Cutler and William Rogers only the outlines of COINTELPRO. Hoover failed to disclose, for example, the bureau's widespread use of illegal wiretaps. He revealed even less when he briefed the cabinet the following November. There Hoover emphasized the FBI's battle against Soviet espionage agents, not the agency's infiltration of the CPUSA.[34]

Nevertheless, COINTELPRO grew from the administration's policies—its crusading anticommunism, its minimal concern for civil liberties, and its decentralized management style—as inevitably as if it had been expressly approved by Dwight Eisenhower. The FBI's responsibility for policing internal security matters had evolved slowly since the beginning of World War II through an ad hoc series of presidential directives; Eisenhower reaffirmed the FBI's primary jurisdiction in subversion cases in a public statement in December 1953. Wiretapping for essentially political purposes began under Franklin D. Roosevelt, and so too, presumably, did "black bag jobs"—surreptitious entries to install microphones. In February 1952, however, J. Howard McGrath, Truman's last attorney general, ordered an end to black bag jobs that involved trespass. Shortly after Eisenhower took office, the Supreme Court delivered its decision in *Irvine v. California*, which held, as McGrath had apparently anticipated, that committing trespass to install a listening device violated the Fourth Amendment prohibition of unreasonable searches and seizures. Yet in a May 20, 1954, directive to Hoover, Attorney General Brownell lifted the McGrath ban. Arguing that the *Irvine* case did not apply to cases involving national security, Brownell authorized the FBI to make "unrestricted use . . . in the national interest" of trespass in the installation of microphones.[35] Brownell may have felt fewer reservations about the legality of FBI wiretaps than did Hoover. The FBI director, in March 1955, wrote Brownell to suggest that the attorney general ask President Eisenhower whether he approved "of the policies of the Department of Justice with respect to wiretapping." Brownell replied that since he had already discussed the issue with the president, the NSC, the cabinet, and the House and Senate judiciary committees, "he did not think it necessary to reopen the matter at this time." In fact, when Hoover revealed at a March 1956 NSC meeting that the bureau's efforts to curb the CPUSA had included break-ins, buggings, mail openings, and wiretapping, no one, including the president, objected.[36]

The White House also received ample warnings that Hoover's campaign against American Communists might broaden into a general war against political dissent. Many anti-Communists had long experienced a distinct myopia in distinguishing among Soviet spies, political cranks, and social reformers. Indeed, it was never altogether obvious just what it was about the "international communist conspiracy" that some Americans found so frightening— Russian espionage, the influence of fellow travelers within the government, or the possibility of a Communist brainwashing of the American public. Short of espionage or sabotage, what might reasonably be considered subversive? As one historian of the FBI has written, "'Security' and 'subversion' are words that are almost impossible to define . . . what is subversive to one man may, of course, be the height of patriotism to another."[37] To J. Edgar Hoover, the civil rights movement, in particular, fell far short of the "height of patriotism." Early in 1956, Hoover sent Dillon Anderson, Robert Cutler's replacement as national security adviser, a report on the possibility that violence might arise out of the troubled state of race relations in the South, an understandable fear given many white southerners' defiant reaction to the *Brown* decision. But the FBI director also used the growing concern over racial tensions as an opportunity to provide the White House with purely political intelligence about the National Association for the Advancement of Colored People (NAACP). Anderson, for example, received from Hoover a memorandum detailing the substance of a meeting between officials of the NAACP and Illinois Senators Paul H. Douglas and Everett M. Dirksen.[38]

When Hoover briefed the cabinet on "racial tension and civil rights" on March 9, 1956, he strove to maintain a professional, moderate tone. In refusing to call for decisive federal intervention to advance the cause of racial equality, Hoover was manifestly conservative. At the same time, he sounded a mildly progressive note, praising "the steady decrease of lynchings and the expansion of integrated education" throughout the South. Yet Hoover's report demonstrated the nexus between domestic politics and domestic subversion. Communist operatives from New England, he said, were attempting to infiltrate the NAACP in Alabama, Georgia, and Mississippi. They hoped, Hoover told the cabinet, to alienate the administration from its southern supporters by forcing the federal government to take "immediate action" to enforce the *Brown* decision. The Communists' goals included a federal investigation of the murder of Emmett Till in Mississippi; federal legislation to outlaw lynching, the poll tax, and employment discrimination; the ejection of the Mississippi delegation from Congress; and the termination of federal aid to segregated schools. Hoover did carefully avoid the allegation that only Communists favored such proposals. Indeed, he acknowledged the outspoken anticommunism of the NAACP leadership. Yet one implication seems obvious from his presentation: in the eyes of the bureau, Communists had seized on civil rights as an issue capable of weakening the nation, so that those non-Communists who advocated the speedy abolition of Jim Crow were, at best, doing the work of the nation's enemies. The shadow of disloyalty that Hoover's presentation cast over the civil rights movement raised no eyebrows, apparently, within the Eisenhower cabinet, but it did provide a rationale to support the administration's gradualist approach to integration.[39]

Hoover's remarks to the cabinet suggest one consideration, almost wholly unrelated to the task of exposing subversives, that helped to fuel the expansion of the national security bureaucracy. It offered the White House a vehicle for gathering essentially political intelligence. Reporting to the national security adviser, Hoover, for example, provided the White House with information on the plaintiffs, who included Norman Thomas, Linus Pauling, and Bertrand Russell, in a suit to stop nuclear testing. Through a "confidential informant," the FBI produced a report on the plans for Eleanor Roosevelt to host a reception for a prominent civil rights leader. The White House also received memoranda on the social and political contacts of the former first lady, Supreme Court Justice William O. Douglas, and financier Bernard Baruch. In addition to civil rights leaders, writers and journalists seemed especially threatening to the FBI; Hoover once sent Sherman Adams a report on Ernest Hemingway, who had criticized the agency. The White House sometimes initiated such reporting. In 1957, Adams requested that the FBI conduct a name-check on the Authors League of America, a writers' guild. By 1960, the FBI's Washington office contained over four hundred thousand files on allegedly suspicious groups and individuals. The bureau's field offices contained still more dossiers.[40]

The once proud image of J. Edgar Hoover and the FBI as incorruptible paragons of professional law enforcement has faired badly at the hands of subsequent historians and journalists. According to one recent biography, "Hoover had more to do with undermining American constitutional guarantees than any political leader before or since."[41] Peter Steinberg, a student of the Smith Act, has accused Hoover of a design for "shifting political thought in the United States to the right by eliminating a persistent 'leftist' opposition." In a similar vein, Sanford Unger has written that the bureau, under its longtime director, became "a kind of ideological security police, an arbiter of what was inside the boundaries of legitimate discourse and what was outside."[42]

Such criticisms of Hoover are perhaps overdrawn. It is at least arguable that he demonstrated considerably less distaste for legal norms and free debate than did, to give an obvious comparison, Richard Nixon. Nevertheless, Hoover and the bureau did emerge as the principal publicists for what might be called the anti-Communist creed, a series of assumptions that underlay the country's crusade against communism. This anti-Communist creed shaped the intellectual environment in which the Eisenhower presidency functioned. It may go further in explaining the administration's reaction to the Red Scare than anything else, except for Dwight Eisenhower's own attitudes about civil liberties.

First, the anti-Communists believed, the writings of the enemy had to be taken seriously. Americans might not always live up to the ideals of the Declaration of Independence, and Christians might not always abide by the teachings of Jesus, but the Communists could invariably be counted on to follow the *Communist Manifesto* like a "battle plan for conquest." Drawing an analogy between Soviet Russia and Nazi Germany, American anti-Communists assumed that any totalitarian state must inevitably be expansionistic. As part of a worldwide Communist conspiracy, one orchestrated from the Kremlin, the CPUSA could not be treated as an ordinary political party. The Communists sought to effect their conspiracy not by espionage or sabotage but by the infiltration of otherwise respectable institutions—labor unions, civil rights groups, and even veterans' organizations and parent-teacher associations. There they could agitate for various short-term Communist objectives. As identified in the FBI's 1953 report to Congress, these included the admission of the People's Republic of China to the UN, a summit meeting between the president and the Soviet premier, and increased Western trade with the Communist world. To be sure, as cold war tensions eased and U.S. presidents embraced more and more of the Soviet agenda, the FBI's list of Communist causes shrank.[43]

Next, as an article of faith, came the conviction that the FBI itself represented the nation's most formidable barrier in the CPUSA's path to a Soviet America. Yet, mindful of the relatively minuscule number of spy cases that the government uncovered, compared with the thousands of security investigations that it conducted, the anti-Communists concluded, "Since this work is primarily preventive in nature, its success cannot be measured in terms of arrests and convictions."[44]

Finally, although J. Edgar Hoover made no particular effort to popularize this view, many anti-Communists believed that the United States faced a foe so ruthless and so dangerous that traditional legal standards and ordinary notions of decency would have to be set aside. William F. Buckley and Brent Bozell ridiculed the thought that the presumption of innocence or the right to confront one's accusers should be allowed to hamstring the government's efforts to drive subversives out of the civil service.[45] A similar view received official sanction from former President Herbert C. Hoover's commission on government organization. In a September 1954 report on the activities of the Central Intelligence Agency, the commission asserted that "no rules" existed in the struggle between the Free World and "the international Communist conspiracy." It added that the American people might have to be made to understand and support the idea that "hitherto acceptable norms of human conduct" did not apply in the cold war.[46]

Beginning in February 1946, the FBI had embarked on a propaganda campaign designed to alert the American people to the alleged danger posed by domestic Communists and other political radicals. Thereafter, the bureau leaked supposedly confidential information to HCUA and to friendly journalists like Paul Harvey and Fulton Lewis, Jr. In addition to also providing FBI reports to Joseph McCarthy, Hoover helped place an ex-FBI agent, Don Surine, on the senator's staff. Before resigning as the bureau's assistant director for intelligence in 1971, veteran FBI official William C. Sullivan went so far as to accuse Hoover of manipulating the agency's imposing propaganda machine to the point that he "caused a Communist scare in the nation which was entirely unwarranted." After Eisenhower became president, the FBI director supplied the White House with a steady stream of memoranda calculated to assure the president that the Red menace remained as formidable as ever.[47]

The writer Frank Donner has noted that J. Edgar Hoover's image as "the quintessential anti-Communist" served at least two purposes for American presidents. Hoover's presence convinced conservatives of presidents' com-

Eisenhower meets with Attorney General Herbert Brownell (left) and FBI
Director J. Edgar Hoover (right). Hoover, according to one bureau official,
had Ike "wrapped around his finger." (UPI/Bettmann Archive)

mitment to anticommunism while reassuring liberals of their essential moderation and professionalism. Dwight Eisenhower sometimes disregarded Hoover—for example, the president met with Khrushchev after the FBI had declared a summit conference to be a Communist objective—but, for the most part, Eisenhower, unlike Harry Truman, warmly supported the director. When Eisenhower learned, shortly after his election, that Hoover "had been out of favor in Washington," the president-elect summoned the FBI director to a meeting to assure Hoover of the "complete support" of the new administration. "Such was my respect for him," Eisenhower recalled telling Hoover, "that I wanted him in government as long as I might be there." To ingratiate himself with the new president, Hoover advised Ike that one of his aides was a homosexual, after which the young man quietly disappeared from the presidential entourage. According to William Sullivan, Hoover soon had Eisenhower "wrapped around his finger." Eisenhower, to show his appreciation for Hoover's services, publicly honored the director on two occasions, with a

National Security Medal in 1955 and, three years later, with a medal for Distinguished Federal Civil Service.[48]

Eisenhower did not, of course, bring J. Edgar Hoover to Washington, but judging from the new president's record on most of his major appointments, he might well have done so if he had had the opportunity. In men like Richard Nixon, Herbert Brownell, and John Foster Dulles, the president surrounded himself with militant cold-warriors. When Brownell resigned, Eisenhower replaced him with another unmistakable anti-Communist, William Rogers; the new attorney general had been one of the administration's principal liaisons with Joseph McCarthy and was personally close to Hoover.[49] Undoubtedly, such appointments, along with the president's cordial relationship with the FBI director, both evidenced and reinforced Eisenhower's own anticommunism.

Criticizing a Supreme Court decision limiting his power to restrict passports, John Foster Dulles, as late as 1958, justified his actions on the basis of the "state of emergency" then facing the nation. "The idea that this was a time of normal 'peace,'" Dulles complained, "which the Supreme Court had apparently adopted, was absurd." Ike apparently agreed. In contrast with the solicitude he demonstrated toward the secretary of state, Eisenhower, in a famous remark, described his appointment of Earl Warren to the Supreme Court as "the biggest damn fool thing" he ever did. In Eisenhower's eyes, Warren's worst heresy may have been his dissent from the anti-Communist creed. According to Warren's account of a conversation he had with Eisenhower after Ike left office, the president's disappointment with Warren's performance stemmed from what Eisenhower called "those Communist cases," especially the *Yates* decision. He balked at Warren's belief that the Court was "obliged to judge Communists by the same rules . . . applied to all others." When asked by Warren how he would handle American Communists, the former president reportedly replied, "I would kill the S.O.B.s."[50]

Eisenhower readily accepted the platitudes of American constitutional folklore but never seemed fully to appreciate their implications; his concerns for the rights of federal employees involved in security investigations rarely passed beyond ensuring a minimum level of procedural safeguards, and those ranked a distant second to the interests of the government. He favored adoption of an American version of the British Official Secrets Act but recognized that public opinion would not support it. His willingness to break with American tradition and impose prior restraints on the press disturbed as sound an anti-Communist as Senator William Knowland. More common than distinctly illiberal attitudes were the president's ignorance and nonchalance. According to Earl Warren, the president never read the opinions in "those Communist cases" that he had found so offensive. Rather than rejecting the arguments against government wiretapping, Eisenhower seems initially to have been oblivious to them. When the NSC considered the proposed wiretapping legislation in November 1953, the president had to have Brownell and Dulles tell him "why American liberals were so violently opposed" to electronic surveillance, had to have it explained that when the government installed a listening device, it could not distinguish among the kinds of conversations or discriminate among the individuals that it monitored.[51]

The controversy over the Bricker Amendment, in which Eisenhower resolutely opposed a popular proposal to restrict the authority of the president to conduct foreign policy, demonstrated that he was not wholly incapable of assuming a difficult position. On more than one occasion, to be sure, Eisenhower manifested considerable moral courage. Rarely, however, did these cases involve a conflict between civil liberties and internal security. While serving as president of Columbia University, Eisenhower had opposed the passage of the McCarran Act; perhaps more significant, he had declined an opportunity to testify against the measure. On the campaign trail in 1952, the general had complained that the affidavit provision of the Taft-Hartley Act unfairly singled out union leaders, but under his administration, false affidavit prosecutions continued unabated. Moreover, there were the constant attempts throughout the first year of his presidency to conciliate Senator McCarthy, and there was Eisenhower's relative silence thereafter. Eisenhower's concept of civil liberties was too vague and his commitment to their defense too fragile to provide a basis on which the president might resist the anti-Communist crusade.[52]

★ ★ ★

The Waning of the Red Scare

On January 14, 1955, little more than a month after the censure of Joseph R. McCarthy, the U.S. Senate, without dissent, passed a resolution reaffirming its commitment "to investigate, expose, and combat" the international Communist conspiracy against "all democratic forms of government."[1] In reality, however, the censure of the Republican lawmaker marked an obvious turning point in the anti-Communist crusade, both for the Senate and for the nation as a whole. Americans, by the middle years of the Eisenhower presidency, may have been no less hostile to communism than they had been during the earlier days of the cold war, but the country did appear less fearful. If Americans had not become more tolerant of Communists, they did seem less concerned about the non-Communist Left, or at least the remnant that survived into the new age of conformity and consensus.

At the White House, Dwight Eisenhower tried neither to revive the anti-Communist crusade nor to alleviate the nation's residual paranoia. The president's foreign policy initiatives, in particular the Korean armistice of 1953 and the Geneva Conference two years later, helped to ease the international tensions on which domestic anticommunism thrived. Still, the White House continued to pay at least a perfunctory devotion to the internal security state. In a minor section of his State of the Union Address in 1956, President Eisenhower pledged that his administration would "not relax its efforts to deal forthrightly and vigorously in protection of this government and its citizens against subversion." Two years later, he signed an innocuous congressional resolution establishing a national "Loyalty Day." As late as July 1959,

Eisenhower could not tell reporters whether he had detected any slackening in Communist efforts to subvert the United States.[2]

At the same time, a few subtle signs pointed toward a waning of the Red Scare within the executive branch. The administration's public posture drifted along with changes in the political environment. Unwilling to admit that the subversive menace, if it ever existed, had largely passed, the administration nevertheless began to temper its own anticommunism. In the spring of 1956, the Atomic Energy Commission unveiled a series of new regulations designed to give greater protection to employees called before its security boards. The AEC, along with the U.S. Public Health Service, also stopped requiring that individuals receiving government grants for nonsecret scientific research first obtain a security clearance.[3] In April 1957, the White House advised FBI Director J. Edgar Hoover that reports of full-field investigations on presidential appointees could, in the future, be sent to the president in summary form only. The directive suggested a declining interest in the details of the clearance process. During Eisenhower's second term, the caseload of the Department of Justice's Internal Security Division was scarcely sufficient to justify its existence.[4] From 1957 to 1961, moreover, no one was discharged or suspended from federal employment under Executive Order No. 10450, the president's once vaunted security program.[5] Few suspicious employees, in all likelihood, remained on the government payroll.

After the censure of Joseph McCarthy, the dimming spotlights of the Communist controversy shifted from the Senate and the White House to the House Committee on Un-American Activities and the Federal Bureau of Investigation. Despite a decline in the number of HCUA hearings, and cuts in staff and budget, the committee launched a well-publicized investigation of the Fund for the Republic, a nonprofit, private foundation that had produced a steady stream of anti-anti-Communist propaganda. The committee also continued its investigation of the entertainment industry, especially Broadway; the testimony of Boris Morros, a Russian-born Hollywood composer and double agent, led to the indictment of several Americans on espionage charges. Yet HCUA investigations soon degenerated into—or, perhaps more accurately, returned to—more frivolous enterprises. By 1959, HCUA was holding hearings on the U.S. exhibition at a Moscow art fair, where the works of some allegedly left-wing American artists had been displayed. A year later, Representative Francis E. Walter found himself defending the fundamentalist author of an air force training manual that claimed Communists had infiltrated the National Council of Churches and had influenced the editing of its Revised Standard Version of the Bible. President Eisenhower took such episodes in stride. He disliked modern art, but he largely ignored chronic conservative complaints about the supposed left-wing bias of government-sponsored exhibitions. Surely mindful of the administration's brush with J. B. Matthews in 1953, the president readily endorsed a statement by the secretary of the air force repudiating attacks on the loyalty of the Protestant clergy. The small-scale student riot triggered by HCUA's appearance at San Francisco's city hall in May 1960 graphically, and embarrassingly, demonstrated the committee's fading ability, in the last part of the Eisenhower presidency, to intimidate the political nonconformist.[6]

A continent and a generation removed from the California student protestors, J. Edgar Hoover retained his anti-Communist zeal. As late as 1959, four hundred agents in the FBI's New York field office were assigned to subversive activities; only four were responsible for organized crime. In addition to initiating COINTELPRO, the FBI director, working closely with HCUA and congressional conservatives, continued to fight growing public and official complacency toward the threat of internal subversion. Hoover recalled the Communist party's resurgence following the post–World War I Palmer Raids and feared that the party might yet enjoy another revival.[7] Repeatedly, bureau publications warned that American Communists, under the cloak of "peaceful coexistence," remained "the foremost domestic threat to our national security." Year after year, Hoover claimed that the CPUSA was "as fanatically dedicated to the overthrow of our Government as ever before in its . . . history."[8]

In reality, the FBI knew by the mid-1950s that the Soviets had stopped using the CPUSA for espionage; the party was considered to be no more than a "potential" recruiting ground for spies. More important, the party's membership had fallen so precipitously as to create a real public relations dilemma for the bureau. When membership dropped to a few thousand, Hoover responded by classifying the statistics and refusing to provide them even to the attorney general.[9] Through such tactics, the nation's chief law enforcement officer succeeded in maintaining a free hand for the FBI's covert antisubversive operations, but even Hoover could not wholly arrest changes in public opinion. Although Eisenhower allowed COINTELPRO to evolve largely unfettered by presidential supervision, he no longer fully shared Hoover's obsession with the international Communist conspiracy. The president, for example, seemed indifferent at a February 1960 press conference when asked about Hoover's statement that Nikita Khrushchev's upcoming visit to the United States might somehow make Americans "more receptive to communism."[10]

By 1956, the administration felt little political need to appease the more outspoken Republican anti-Communists. Admittedly, the campaign season saw a brief flurry of Smith Act indictments, but the security question attracted scant attention as Eisenhower coasted to an impressive, personal victory in his rematch against Adlai Stevenson. The Democratic platform had pledged a "full and fair hearing," including the right of confrontation, to anyone who was the target of a loyalty or security investigation. Tagged an "issueless candidate," however, Stevenson failed to exploit any popular concerns about domestic subversion or civil liberties that might have survived McCarthy's downfall.[11] Among the Republicans, Richard Nixon may have initially hoped to press the issue on which he had built his career, but even the vice president, campaigning in Wisconsin in 1956, kept a respectable distance from Joseph McCarthy.[12]

The election returns evidenced Eisenhower's growing independence from the Republican party, if not his alienation from the GOP Right. As Stephen E. Ambrose, Ike's best-known biographer, has noted, Eisenhower, despite defeating Stevenson by ten million votes, became the first candidate in 108 years to win the presidency without carrying at least one house of Congress with him. The president explained the congressional results to Nixon as the fault of "all those damned moss-backs and hard-shell conservatives . . . in the party." Over Nixon's objections, Ike, on election night, proclaimed his victory a triumph for "Modern Republicanism," a vague concept that was nevertheless anathema to Republican conservatives.[13]

It is possible, however, that behind the scenes, the political residue of the

Communist controversy continued to be felt. Skeptical of Nixon's maturity and judgment, Eisenhower had hoped to shuffle Nixon aside to a cabinet post at the end of his first term. Eisenhower considered several replacements for the young vice president and seemed especially taken by Secretary of the Navy Robert Anderson, a Texas oilman. Nixon, understandably, wanted to remain on the Republican presidential ticket. Loath to force a confrontation, Eisenhower ultimately refused to select another running mate. According to at least one White House intimate, the president's distaste for controversy was buttressed by a sense of obligation toward Nixon because of the vice president's earlier efforts to contain McCarthy. The former California senator had served, without complaint, in the unenviable position as the administration's point man in its dealings with the Wisconsin legislator. Eisenhower, probably to his great dismay, felt indebted to the vice president.[14]

Anxiety about communism in the United States played no apparent role in the last two campaigns of the Eisenhower era—the 1958 congressional elections and the 1960 presidential race. Speaking to a Republican dinner in Minneapolis in January 1958, Sherman Adams hinted that the GOP might attempt to resurrect the Red menace. Attacking the Democrats for every foreign policy setback from Pearl Harbor to Korea, Adams also blamed them for "the scientific catastrophe of losing our atomic secrets." But Eisenhower had already told a Republican gathering in Chicago that "peace and security" should not be issues in 1958. In any event, Adams's remarks were soon overshadowed by his involvement in an alleged influence-peddling scheme with businessman Bernard Goldfine. Memories of Alger Hiss and the Truman administration's other security problems could not prevent the Democrats from gaining almost two-to-one majorities in both houses of Congress in the midterm elections of 1958.[15]

The presidential election two years later did, however, demonstrate how an anti-Communist cold war orthodoxy had encrusted itself on the American political system. Notwithstanding increasing tensions within the Sino-Soviet alliance, Richard Nixon continued to warn that the two Communist giants still shared "their long range objective of Communist domination of the world." According to a poll taken by the Nixon camp, Americans, by a 47 to 24 percent plurality, hoped that the new president would get "tougher" with the

Russians.[16] On the Democratic side, Senator John F. Kennedy chided the administration for an alleged "missile gap" and tried to exploit the "loss" of Cuba to Fidel Castro, an intractable, if exaggerated, problem. Both candidates quibbled over the depth of the American commitment to protect from the Chinese Communists two insignificant and indefensible offshore islands, Quemoy and Matsu. Yet eight years of Eisenhower had produced no single issue capable of galvanizing the electorate; Kennedy's Catholicism and his striking personal appearance, well showcased in a series of televised debates with Nixon, shaped the course of the race more than anything else.[17]

In addition to the censure of Senator McCarthy, two developments help to explain the waning of the Red Scare between 1955 and, roughly, 1958. First, there was the almost total disintegration of the already anemic American Communist party. In 1955, both FBI estimates and CPUSA propaganda placed the party's membership at approximately 20,000. Yet as early as December 1954, the party had had only 3,474 paid-up members. Thereafter, Smith Act prosecutions and FBI harassment continued to take their toll, but the party's fatal wounds were largely self-inflicted. Responding to government persecution, the party in the early 1950s had reorganized itself into five-person cells and sent its key leaders underground, a cumbersome arrangement that disrupted intraparty communications and gave the CPUSA an even more furtive appearance. Proving that a McCarthyite mentality is not unique to the radical Right, the party conducted its own internal witch-hunt, dropping loyal but inactive members and expelling others on the flimsiest evidence of disloyalty. Worse yet, the CPUSA never managed to free itself from the domination of Moscow or to develop tactics and a philosophy that would be appropriate to the situation facing it in the United States.[18]

The party's final collapse began in 1956. Khrushchev's denunciation of Stalin at the Twentieth Party Congress in February and the Soviets' brutal suppression of the Hungarian revolution that autumn deeply divided and embarrassed American party members. Hundreds began leaving the organization in the fall of 1956. When Herbert Brownell returned to private practice the following year, he could claim that he had accomplished his two main goals as attorney general—the passage of the first civil rights act since Reconstruction and the near annihilation of the CPUSA. By 1958, barely enough Reds remained in the United States to frighten even the most timid anti-Communist.[19]

While the CPUSA crumbled, the U.S. Supreme Court began to chip away at much of the legal foundation of the anti-Communist crusade. Avoiding a broad holding that governmental scrutiny of a citizen's political beliefs violated the Constitution, the Court instead entered a series of narrow, procedural rulings. In the 1955 *Peters* case, the Court overturned the dismissal of a consultant for the U.S. Public Health Service under Truman's employee loyalty order. But *Peters* seemed an uncertain harbinger of the court's future course; the government's case was so feeble that the solicitor general refused to sign the Department of Justice's brief.[20] Then in 1956, the Court reversed a registration order issued by the Subversive Activities Control Board against the CPUSA. The agency's decision, the Court said, had been tainted by the "completely untrustworthy" testimony of paid government witnesses. During the same term, the Court held that state sedition laws were preempted by federal legislation. *Slochower* v. *Board of Higher Education* (1956) overturned, on due process grounds, the dismissal, without a hearing, of a New York professor for taking the Fifth Amendment before the Senate internal security subcommittee. *Slochower* should have laid to rest the notion, often repeated by President Eisenhower, that because government employment was a privilege, not a right, constitutional considerations did not apply to security investigations. The anti-anti-Communist trend continued into 1957. The State Department was ordered to reinstate John Stewart Service, and the Court, in the *Watkins* case, reversed a contempt citation by HCUA on the grounds that the scope of the committee's investigation was unconstitutionally vague.[21]

By far the most important decisions, however, were *Cole* v. *Young* (1956), which drastically curbed the Eisenhower security program, and *Yates* v. *United States* (1957), which virtually emasculated the Smith Act. In *Cole*, the Court decided that the Summary Suspension Act of 1950, the statutory basis for Executive Order No. 10450, had not been intended to cover nonsensitive positions, about 80 percent of the federal work force. In *Yates*, a six-to-one majority determined that the government could not invoke the Smith Act against the "theoretical advocacy" of the violent overthrow of the government but would have to prove a specific intent to incite actual violence. Later

Chief Justice Earl Warren (right) visiting the White House in 1956. His relationship with Eisenhower was strained by the Supreme Court's decisions in what Ike called "those Communist cases." (Eisenhower Library/National Park Service)

decisions found both the State Department's regulations restricting the issuance of passports to suspected subversives and the administration's industrial employee security program to lack proper statutory bases. But *Yates* represented the high watermark of the Court's effort to dismantle the nation's internal security bureaucracy. In its 1959 *Barenblatt* decision, the Court upheld a HCUA contempt citation, and in the *Scales* case two years later, it affirmed a conviction under the Smith Act's membership clause, although only on a showing of the kind of intent required by *Yates*. The Supreme Court, in a relatively brief burst of activism, had, nonetheless, effectively hamstrung the legal prosecution of the CPUSA. Of 141 persons indicted under the Smith Act, only 29 served prison terms. With the exception of Junius Scales, no Communist went to jail for his or her political activities after the *Yates* decision.[22]

From the administration's perspective, the search for security, during the last two years of Eisenhower's first term and all of his second term, consisted largely of a series of responses to initiatives from Congress and the courts. This is not to suggest that President Eisenhower remained wholly passive. Although he failed to provide forceful public or, for that matter, private leadership, Dwight Eisenhower did seek, with some success, to defend the prerogatives of the executive branch from congressional and judicial assault.

Eisenhower's diffident public style ill served the administration in one of the most spectacular episodes of his second term. On March 14, 1957, the Senate internal security subcommittee released a seven-year-old intelligence report, from the Royal Canadian Mounted Police, claiming that E. Herbert Norman, then Canada's ambassador to Egypt, was a Communist. Within days, Norman committed suicide. The Canadian government, which had already cleared the career diplomat, protested vigorously, threatening to end its exchange of classified information with the United States. Eisenhower's lame response exacerbated the crisis. After expressing his "great sorrow," the president voiced his "hope that the thing" could now "be dropped." America's allies, Ike assured a reporter, understood "the privileges and rights of our

legislative branch [in] conducting investigations and making public their findings." Many Canadians were outraged at what the *Toronto Globe and Mail*
described as Eisenhower's "impudent and patronizing" suggestion that the
two countries should resume normal relations within days of Norman's death.
After passions cooled, Robert Murphy presented the Canadian ambassador
with a note assuring him that the United States would try to keep a closer rein
on intelligence data provided to it by the Canadians.[23]

More substantive, if less tragic, than the Norman affair was the continuing
debate over the appointment of a special governmental commission to study
the whole Communist controversy. Conventional wisdom among political
moderates and cold war liberals had long maintained the need for such a
panel, but the administration, from the very first, had opposed it. In 1953,
Sherman Adams claimed that the administration needed time to gain experience with its new employee security system before agreeing to a comprehensive study. Two years later, Herbert Brownell told an interviewer that a special
commission was unnecessary because the program "was operating very successfully." Writing a St. Louis businessman, President Eisenhower proposed
that a study be sponsored by a private organization; he did not want to be
accused of trying to make "political capital by any such move."[24] To be sure,
political factors and, to an extent, constitutional considerations motivated the
administration. Vice President Nixon, for one, recognized that a special investigation would be deeply resented by Senator McCarthy and other congressional anti-Communists. Moreover, although the administration routinely
sought to avoid confrontations with Capitol Hill, the White House viewed any
independent panel as another threat to executive primacy in the security area.
As William Rogers wrote Sherman Adams during the 1955 congressional
debate over the authorization of a special study, "The legislative powers
should not be permitted to impede the lawful carrying out of the executive
responsibility."[25]

Ultimately, however, the pressure for a special commission became too
great for the administration to resist. Even Gordon Gray, who had rendered
yeoman's service to the administration as chairman of the special hearing
board in the Oppenheimer case, warned Robert Cutler that the White House
might be "underestimating the depth of . . . feeling among thoughtful people"

about the need for a further review of the government's security policies.[26] In July 1955, Congress, with several prominent Republicans defecting from the administration's position, passed a much-debated resolution creating a twelve-member bipartisan commission to study "the entire Government security program." Its report was not to be released until after the 1956 elections.[27]

Bowing to the inevitable, Eisenhower raised no objections to a special commission at a press conference on June 29. "This administration," he said, "has nothing to hide." The following spring he sent his department heads a memorandum urging them to cooperate with the commission's investigation.[28] In reality, the administration's initial hostility persisted. Four of the commission members were to be appointed by the Speaker of the House and four each by the president and the vice president. The administration lingered in selecting its representatives. More important, the administration, through the commission's administrative director, FBI Assistant Director D. Milton Ladd, managed to limit the commission's investigation by restricting its access to FBI files.[29] Meanwhile, the essentially conservative Commission on Government Security, under the chairmanship of former American Bar Association President Loyd Wright, launched its review, perhaps more concerned about building a consensus behind a revised internal security policy than about uncovering any new facts.[30]

The commission released its 807-page final report on June 21, 1957. At least two of its recommendations followed the anti-Communist hard line. First, the report urged Congress to make it a crime for reporters or private citizens, as well as government employees, to disclose classified information. Second, the commission endorsed legislation to permit the use in subversion cases of evidence obtained by wiretapping, if the attorney general had specifically approved the tap. In the critical area of employee security, however, the commission adopted a more moderate stance. The report proposed a ban on the readjudication of personnel cases in the absence of new evidence. Recommending a modest expansion in the right to confrontation, it urged that an employee be allowed to face his or her accuser unless the accuser was a "regularly established confidential informant" whose anonymity was required by national security. Some of the commission's most important proposals harked back to the Truman administration. Responding to the *Cole* decision, the study suggested that all employees be subjected to a loyalty investigation but that all other personnel issues be addressed simply under the civil service's normal suitability requirements. Finally, the commission advocated the creation of an independent Central Security Office, apparently similar to the old Loyalty Review Board, which would hear appeals from departmental decisions and monitor the operation of the program.[31]

The response from the White House was at best noncommittal. At a press conference on June 26, Eisenhower said that he had reviewed the report "very hastily"; the only recommendation that raised his eyebrows, the president said, was a relatively minor proposal for transferring responsibility from the State Department to the attorney general for issuing visas. Eisenhower waffled when asked specifically about the need for an American official secrets act. Saying that he had considered the issue very "seriously," Eisenhower added, "Any man who knowingly reveals a secret that affects the security of our country is doing something for which he ought to be ashamed even if there is no law to that effect."[32] Unimpressed with a report that it had never wanted in the first place, the administration soon gave the long-awaited study a proper bureaucratic burial. As Patrick Coyne of the NSC staff wrote Robert Cutler, "It would be difficult to find very many worthwhile recommendations in the Report which have not been the subject of prior consideration."[33]

On July 23, 1957, Eisenhower instructed all agency heads to send their comments on the commission's report to the Personnel Security Advisory Committee (PSAC), an interdepartmental panel headed by William Tompkins, the chief of the Justice Department's Internal Security Division.[34] Tompkins's group was then to report to the cabinet. By January 1958, the PSAC had reached general agreement on a set of recommendations, although debate continued on the need for legislation to create a new loyalty program for employees in nonsensitive positions. Early in April, after several more weeks of interdepartmental debate, Maxwell M. Rabb, the secretary to the cabinet, advised Sherman Adams that the matter was ready for cabinet consideration and a final decision by the president. Rabb acknowledged, however, that controversy had now arisen over the proposal to create a central security office and that certain issues raised by the Commission on Government Security might best be referred to the NSC. But Rabb, pressing Adams for some kind of action, warned him that Loyd Wright and others were becoming impatient. "Individual people on the Hill are beginning to needle the Administration—with the implication that we have been 'sitting' on this Report." The cabinet secretary added, "It wouldn't take much—only the slightest incident—to break this whole basket wide open."[35]

In a series of meetings with various administration officials early in May, Rabb, joined by White House counsel Gerald Morgan, continued to press for a cabinet discussion of the commission's report. Besides his concern about the political risks of inaction, Rabb believed that legislation then pending in Congress to reform the employee security program necessitated some kind of decisive action by the administration. On the other hand, the Department of Justice, and presumably William Rogers, who had replaced Herbert Brownell as attorney general, showed no apparent interest in giving the commission's report serious consideration. The Justice Department had long exercised an informal primacy in internal security matters, and Rogers's opposition proved fatal to Rabb's efforts. The attorney general did agree, however, to advise the cabinet at a May 16 meeting that the PSAC had reviewed the Wright commission's recommendations but that final action would await a further review by the NSC.[36]

As Rabb had predicted, the House of Representatives, on July 10, 1958, passed an antisubversive bill, generally known as S. 1411. Adopted by a vote of 295 to 46, the measure would have extended the employee security program to all government employees, effectively overturning the *Cole* decision. Much to the administration's chagrin, S. 1411 would also have allowed an employee to appeal a dismissal to the Civil Service Commission. Few members of Congress seemed impressed by the Justice Department's belated plea to delay legislative action until the administration could complete its study of the rapidly aging report by the Wright commission. And within days of the House's action, the NSC staff advised the cabinet secretary's office that the much-studied report did "not appear to raise policy issues requiring consideration by the Council."[37]

During the summer of 1958, Robert Gray, who had been an aide to Sherman Adams, replaced Maxwell Rabb as cabinet secretary. As had his predecessor, Gray told Adams, "The Administration would look quite bad in case of any further delay, after all the public and congressional controversy in 1953–54 and after these years of subsequent study." Following the House's passage of S. 1411 and the NSC staff's retreat from the debate, Gray finally succeeded in having the PSAC's report circulated among members of the cabinet and in having it placed on the agenda for an August 8, 1958, cabinet meeting. Distributed as a cabinet paper, the PSAC's report contained few surprises. It expressed reservations about the Wright commission's proposals to expand an employee's right of confrontation and to restrict subsequent investigations of employees already cleared by earlier security proceedings. Rather than adopting a simple loyalty program for all federal workers, the Tompkins's group recommended retention of the existing security system for sensitive positions and new legislation subjecting employees in nonsensitive positions to a loyalty investigation. Processing security risks, as opposed to disloyal workers, under normal civil service regulations, which the Wright commission proposed to do, would, the PSAC argued, actually reduce the procedural rights of the employees involved. Consistent with long-established administration policy, the PSAC also opposed the creation of a central appeals board, partly because, in a telling commentary on the decline of the Communist controversy, "the potential caseload" appeared too small to justify its existence. Here, perhaps ironically, there was one important dissenter—former Congressman Harris Ellsworth, whom Eisenhower had appointed chairman of the Civil Service Commission in 1957.[38]

Presenting the PSAC's report to the cabinet on August 8, Attorney General Rogers conveyed the panel's disapproval of the Wright commission study, in particular its recommendation for a central security agency. The attorney general also expressed his opposition to sending any last-minute proposals to Congress so near the end of the current session. Neither the Department of Defense nor the U.S. Post Office shared Rogers's patience. The Pentagon had an understandable concern about security; Deputy Defense Secretary Donald Quarles wanted legislation declaring all positions in his department to be "sensitive." *Cole* v. *Young* had left the thousands of nonsensitive employees at the post office covered only by civil service suitability requirements. The postmaster general strongly favored remedial legislation. Arthur Summerfield had earlier demanded an executive order from the president making all postal service jobs sensitive if a bill was not soon forthcoming from Congress. But with Eisenhower showing no interest in pursuing the issue, Rogers carried the day. The cabinet agreed simply to authorize the PSAC to consider a possible legislative package for the coming year. On the written record of the cabinet's decision is the handwritten note, perhaps by Robert Gray, "buried, after this."[39]

One reason the White House, from a political standpoint at least, could afford to do nothing was the inability of Congress to do anything. On August 22, 1958, the House passed a conference committee version of S. 1411, but the measure died in the Senate during the waning days of the Eighty-fifth Congress. The next Congress proved unable to move a new loyalty-security bill past the hearing stage. Within the administration, the Civil Service Commission continued, over the dogged opposition of the attorney general, to favor the creation of an independent appeals board. Yet, if ever such a body had been needed, William Rogers advised Eisenhower, the moment had "long since passed."[40]

The PSAC dutifully drafted a package of antisubversive bills for the administration to submit to Congress, but at a White House meeting in April 1959, it was decided that remedial legislation was no longer necessary. In June, Loyd Wright wrote the president to complain about the administration's failure to act on his commission's report. Unmoved, Eisenhower replied by repeating his opposition to a central review board. With regard to the commission's other recommendations, the president referred Wright to the attorney general, who could hardly be expected to lend him a sympathetic ear.[41] Had it come earlier, the Commission on Government Security might have helped defuse some of the worst of the nation's anti-Communist hysteria, but the peak of the Red Scare had passed long before Wright and his colleagues began their work. By 1957, the commission could not muster enough political momentum to force the administration from its preferred position of handling security questions itself.

It is difficult to characterize the Eisenhower administration's approach to the Communist controversy during Dwight Eisenhower's last term in office. While Eisenhower's attorney general opposed expanding the rights of employees subjected to security investigations, the White House gave only tepid support to legislation to repair the security program in the wake of *Cole* v. *Young*. Publicly, President Eisenhower seemed committed to steering a middle course, apparently hoping above all to avoid, as much as possible, the issue that had generated so much controversy during his first two years in the Oval Office. The administration's moderation did not stem from any particular devotion to civil liberties but from the changing political realities and a desire to preserve a certain constitutional balance. However unassuming he might appear, Ike strove to maintain executive prerogatives. When the Supreme Court, in *Kent* v. *Dulles*, ruled that the secretary of state lacked authority to deny passports to suspected subversives, the president promptly responded with a special message to Congress calling for remedial legislation.[42] The administration would not, however, often endorse measures designed to enhance congressional power or to restrict the jurisdiction of the Supreme Court, even in the name of anticommunism.

Reacting to the Supreme Court's assault on the anti-Communist crusade, Senator William Jenner introduced a bill in 1957 to deprive the Court of appellate jurisdiction in cases involving contempt of Congress, the federal employee loyalty program, state antisubversive laws, subversion in academic institutions, and admission to the bar. Here, and elsewhere, the Department of Justice may have had a liberalizing effect on the president. Deeply disturbed by Earl Warren's performance on the bench, Eisenhower initially favored legislation to overturn the *Cole* decision and seems to have supported the Jenner bill, although Herbert Brownell, before leaving the government, advised the cabinet that the prospects for circumventing the Court's decisions through remedial legislation were not good.[43]

In April 1958, Senator John Marshall Butler introduced his own omnibus antisubversive package as a substitute for the Jenner bill. Butler proposed to give congressional committees sole discretion to determine if the questions they put to witnesses were pertinent to a legitimate investigation, to extend the security program to all federal employees, to require an express statement by Congress before a federal law could be held to preempt state action, to outlaw even the "theoretical advocacy" of the violent overthrow of the U.S. government, and like Jenner's bill, to prohibit the Supreme Court from reviewing state rules regulating admission to the bar. Raising constitutional questions about several of the proposals, the Department of Justice, in a public statement by Deputy Attorney General Lawrence E. Walsh, soon went on record opposing the Butler bill. Nevertheless, a coalition of southern Democrats and Republicans on the Senate Judiciary Committee, including the anti-McCarthy administration stalwart Arthur V. Watkins, recommended passage of the measure substantially intact, except for the provision expanding the personnel security program. Shortly thereafter, Attorney General Rogers, despite the president's original misgivings, came out against the Butler bill, although the administration did endorse a narrow antipreemption bill drafted simply to overturn *Pennsylvania* v. *Nelson*. Without administration support, if that would have made a difference, the Senate defeated a general preemption bill. The Butler bill was voted down 49 to 41.[44]

The following year, 1959, found the administration, through Deputy Attorney General Walsh, opposing bills to outlaw the "theoretical advocacy" of revolution, to provide for the automatic dismissal of any federal employee who refused to cooperate with a congressional investigation, and to authorize the Department of Justice to question aliens who were subject to final deportation orders. The White House continued to oppose legislation to prevent federal preemption absent an unreconcilable conflict between national and state laws or an express statement by Congress of an intent to preempt state action. The administration itself stopped pressing for restrictive passport legislation and, as noted earlier, a law to include nonsensitive workers within the employee security program. On the other hand, Walsh and others continued to lobby for legislation to permit the enforcement of state sedition laws and to define the word *organize* in the Smith Act to include the recruitment of new members to a subversive organization; *Yates* had, among other things, interpreted *organize* to refer only to the initial formation of a subject group.[45]

While Congress held hearings on various antisubversive bills, the Supreme

Court dealt its last major blow to the search for security. On June 29, 1959, in *Greene* v. *McElroy*, an eight-to-one majority held that neither Congress nor the president had ever empowered the Department of Defense to make use of confidential informants in its industrial security program. More precisely, the Court ruled that the Pentagon lacked the authority to classify an employee of a defense contractor as a "security risk" without affording the employee the right to confront and cross-examine the accusers. The administration's response was vintage Eisenhower. Forgoing an opportunity to express alarm at a July 1 press conference, the president simply reported that the Court's opinion was still under study and that reporters would have to await a substantive reaction from the administration.[46]

The administration debated its response to *Greene* for months.[47] The Civil Service Commission and some officials elsewhere in the executive branch favored remedial legislation. Others thought an executive order would satisfy the court. That group further split into opposing camps. One faction, led by Attorney General Rogers, favored a short order simply delegating to the secretary of defense the authority to establish a new industrial security program. Another bloc, including White House lawyer Phillip E. Areeda, supported a longer order expanding the procedural rights of industrial workers. A few, Areeda among them, proposed using *Greene* as an opportunity to liberalize the entire employee security system.[48] One decision came quickly. The White House, or at least the staff, would formulate the administration's position. As Areeda explained the administration's problem, "Various difficulties in the security area have arisen precisely because the responsibility for wise programs was left to others . . . and they have not exercised it wisely."[49]

Eventually, Eisenhower took the more economical course of a presidential directive. By so doing, he effectively scuttled H.R. 8121, an attempt by Francis Walter and HCUA to undo the *Greene* decision by an act of Congress. Rogers had, in the meantime, dropped his opposition to a substantive order. Executive Order No. 10685, issued in February 1960, imposed some significant limitations on the use of confidential informants in the industrial security program. The order guaranteed an employee the right of confrontation except when the informant was engaged in regular intelligence work, when the informant was physically unable to appear, or when the agency head, usually the secretary of defense, determined that "good and sufficient" reasons existed to preserve the informant's anonymity. When one of these exceptions was invoked, the accused would receive a summary of the informant's testimony. The hearing board was also to consider the denial of the right to confrontation as a mitigating circumstance in the employee's defense. Yet President Eisenhower refused to go further than the immediate circumstances seemed to demand; he did not, as he might logically have done, expand the protection of Executive Order No. 10685 to employees of the federal government.[50]

The president's order represented the administration's last significant initiative in its quest for internal security. "I don't know of anything else," Ike told reporters, ". . . any internal or procedural problem—that has more engaged my attention for these past years."[51] Although the nation retained its staunchly anti-Communist foreign policy and much of its internal security bureaucracy, Dwight Eisenhower had presided over a dramatic lessening in public anxieties about domestic subversion. He had done so, moreover, at a time when the raw materials for another Red Scare lay readily at hand.

Many of the events that had helped to trigger the anti-Communist crusade in the late 1940s had neat analogues in Eisenhower's second term. For the Soviet explosion of an atomic bomb in 1949, there was the launching of Sputnik in 1957. For the "loss" of China, there was Fidel Castro's rise to power in Cuba, although an initial uncertainty about Castro's devotion to communism considerably muddled the Cuban issue.[52] And for Alger Hiss, the Rosenbergs, and all the spies, real or imagined, of the immediate postwar era, there was a rash of dramatic espionage cases in the late 1950s. In January 1957, the FBI arrested Jack Soble, his wife, Myra, and Jack Albam, all Lithuanian immigrants, as Russian agents. Three months later, the Sobles and Albam entered guilty pleas in federal court in New York City. Arrests of supposed members of the Soble spy ring continued into late 1960. The government, in June 1957, arrested Rudolf Abel, a colonel in the Soviet secret police, who had been posing as a New York photographer. Described by the *New York Times* as "the most important Soviet spy ever caught in the United States," Abel eventually received a thirty-year prison sentence.[53] After the Soble and Abel cases broke, Attorney General Rogers warned the nation during a televised interview in May 1959 of an intensification of Soviet espionage activities.[54] To complicate matters, Bernon F. Mitchell and William H. Martin, two mathematicians who did cryptographic work for the top-secret National Security Agency, disappeared during the summer of 1960, only to reemerge, as defectors, at a Moscow press conference.[55]

But none of this could revive the Communist controversy. The stimuli were there, but the political catalyst was lacking. After eight years of Eisenhower's leadership, the Republicans could hardly complain that the government was still riddled with subversives. Admittedly, the hard core of the Republican Right remained alienated from the president, and the early 1960s witnessed a flurry of radical anti-Communist groups, but the militant conservatives clearly stood outside the political mainstream.[56] Among the Democrats, even Hubert Humphrey, who had criticized the Republicans' employee security program and spearheaded the drive for a special commission on domestic subversion, credited the waning of the Communist controversy, in large part, to the trust and affection Americans reposed in President Eisenhower.[57] More than Ike's reassuring grin and grandfatherly demeanor, however, underlay the ebbing of the Red Scare. His victories in 1952 and 1956 had spoiled the issue for the Republicans. And despite their best efforts, Democrats could never effectively play the politics of anticommunism. McCarthyism had been energized not by opposition to communism but by illiberalism, by the linkage of Marxism with liberalism. The search for security rested on the notion that a perfectly loyal American like John Paton Davies could be considered a "security risk" because he opposed aiding Chiang Kai-shek. As the ostensibly liberal party in American politics, the Democrats could not exploit the Communist issue without abandoning their own heritage—John F. Kennedy ignored the Mitchell-Martin caper in the 1960 campaign.[58] For his part, Dwight Eisenhower had not championed civil liberties as president, but by politically preempting the more vocal anti-Communists, he had robbed the search for security of much of its anger and intensity.

9

★ ★ ★

Conclusion

Surely nothing in Dwight Eisenhower's record as president has garnered more criticism than his efforts, early in his administration, to appease Senator Joseph McCarthy.[1] Ike's defenders can rightly note, however, that within a year and a half of Eisenhower's election in 1952, McCarthy found himself mortally wounded, politically and perhaps physically. The Eisenhower White House played a relatively modest role in McCarthy's downfall, but for so talented a demagogue, the Wisconsin anti-Communist demonstrated a remarkably brief shelf life once Eisenhower became president. Even some of those who, at the time, had urged the president publicly to confront McCarthy concluded in hindsight that Eisenhower's prudence may have been well-advised.[2]

Yet Eisenhower's dealings with his principal Republican adversary suggest little about his handling of the Communist controversy; McCarthy could be separated too easily from McCarthyism. Charles Potter, the lone anti-McCarthy Republican on McCarthy's Senate subcommittee, delivered a speech pounding away at the late Harry Dexter White while censure charges were pending against his Wisconsin colleague. As noted earlier, Arthur Watkins supported both Senator McCarthy's censure and Senator Jenner's proposal to overturn by legislation a number of the Supreme Court's anti-anti-Communist decisions. Of all people, Robert Stevens, one of McCarthy's most long-suffering targets, tried to have Thomas I. Emerson, a noted civil libertarian, dismissed from his position on the Yale law faculty. Emerson was not a Communist, but he had represented Smith Act defendants. Stevens belonged to the Yale board.[3] Like Potter, Watkins, Stevens, and countless others, President Eisenhower, despite his revulsion at McCarthy's "methods," found himself all too often caught up in the same kind of thoughtless hyperpatriotism.

At the outset of the cold war, General Eisenhower had demonstrated decidedly moderate instincts—defending McCarthyite targets like Philip S. Jessup, cooperating as NATO commander with European Socialist leaders, and expressing an interest in a rapprochement with Yugoslavia's maverick Communist strongman, Marshal Josip Tito. Under pressure from Republican conservatives, candidate Eisenhower moved steadily toward the Right in the heat of the 1952 presidential campaign. Once in the Oval Office, the old soldier seemed to embrace much of the agenda of the anti-Communists and to share many of their fears about the nation's internal security. Although Eisenhower eventually presided over an ebbing of the Communist controversy, it was not the result of a conscious commitment to bring the Red Scare to an end in the interest of free and unfettered political discourse.

If the president's own anticommunism contributed to McCarthy's demise, it otherwise paid few dividends, either to the nation or to the Republican party. Breaches of American security continued to occur regularly throughout the late 1950s and, for that matter, to the present day. The almost absolute security that the United States sought during the Eisenhower years remained elusive, in part because the federal employee security system contained a fundamental defect. Obsessed with ferreting out political radicals and social nonconformists, the government overlooked one salient point—the great majority of spies were generally nondescript mercenaries motivated by money, not ideology. One of the worst nightmares of the cold war security officer, the homosexual blackmailed into espionage, proved to have almost no empirical basis.[4]

Politically, the consequences of the administration's antisubversive efforts are difficult to assess. The president marveled at how conservative commentators such as George Sokolsky, David Lawrence, and Westbrook Pegler could claim that he was surrounded by "left-wing" advisers. Eisenhower believed that such charges represented a deliberate effort by the GOP Right "to smear the Eisenhower people in the party." The White House, without doubt, fully understood the basic cold war political ploy of attacking one's opponents as soft on communism.[5] All the political rhetoric aside, many in the old Taft wing of the Republican party surely appreciated the president's anticommunism, but it was not enough to make them like Ike. For example, the most popular media intellectual on the GOP Right, William F. Buckley, Jr., noted in July 1960, "Mr. Eisenhower has been pretty good where China is concerned" But Buckley added, "He tends to be pretty good on everything to which he does not turn his attention."[6]

The Communist issue may have drawn a few conservatives, especially conservative Catholics, away from the Democratic party. Such gains could not, however, arrest a general decline in Republican fortunes—the GOP held far fewer governorships and congressional seats when Eisenhower left office than it had when he had entered the White House. Not only did Eisenhower fail to transfer his popularity to the Republican party, but the moderate wing of the GOP, with which the president was identified, seemed to stagnate under his leadership.[7] Essentially, Eisenhower made an indifferent party politician—Barry Goldwater once said he had "no aptitude at all for the practical side of politics."[8] The administration's anti-Communist crusading could not have attracted many moderates or liberals to the Republican party.

Although Eisenhower largely failed as a party builder, he proved quite adept at preserving his own reputation through the vicissitudes of cold war politics. As the diplomatic historian Henry Brands has observed, "Popularity was the cloak that concealed Eisenhower's ambition from himself." It was public acclaim that allowed Ike to rationalize in his own mind his decision to enter politics—not necessarily an easy step for a supposedly apolitical career soldier. Throughout his presidency, Eisenhower sought mainly to protect, not exploit, the esteem in which millions of his fellow citizens held him.[9] By subtly distancing himself from Senator McCarthy while otherwise subscribing to an anti-Communist cold war orthodoxy, Eisenhower managed to offer something to liberals and conservatives alike. More important, he successfully appealed to the broad, if indifferent, middle range of public opinion. By delegating authority—appearing to reign but not rule—Eisenhower minimized, in the public mind, his culpability for both the excesses and the lapses of his employee security program.[10] In the course of the administration's quest for internal security, Eisenhower's ability to survive the Communist controversy with his popularity intact may have been his most impressive accomplishment.

The nation, nevertheless, paid a price for Eisenhower's commitment to what one historian has called "holding the line."[11] Emmet Hughes, for one, later dismissed the Eisenhower years as a "waste" in terms of improving relations with the Soviets and "in terms of establishing a mentality in the Republican party for dealing with the world of today."[12] The administration had helped to exorcise Joseph McCarthy from the body politic, but the nation's postwar traumas left permanent scars. The principal crises of that generation of Americans who came after Eisenhower—the war in Vietnam and the Watergate scandal—had their roots in the 1950s. The growth of government secrecy, the abuse of intelligence agencies, and above all, a reflexive anticommunism all stemmed, at least in part, from the search for internal security. President Eisenhower scarcely thought of trying to arrest the dominant trends of his era. His was a thoroughly conventional mind, projected onto a global stage by a first-class temperament, administrative ability, and the vagaries of a world war. The controversy over domestic communism, along with the question of civil rights for American blacks, represented the great moral issues of the day. On neither did Dwight Eisenhower demonstrate any particular sensitivity. He was a manager, not a moral leader.[13]

Notes

Chapter 1

1. Latham, *Communist Controversy*, pp. 359–62; Cochran, *Harry Truman and the Crisis Presidency*, pp. 357–58. For a useful collection of basic documents on the Communist controversy, see Matusow, *Joseph R. McCarthy*. Fried provides a sound overview of the topic in *Nightmare in Red*.

2. On the antiradical tradition in the United States, see generally Higham, *Strangers in the Land*. See also Bennett, *Party of Fear*.

3. Harper, *Politics of Loyalty*, pp. 12–14; Fried, *Men against McCarthy*, pp. 7–9; Cook, *Nightmare Decade*, pp. 34–47; Latham, *Communist Controversy*, p. 347.

4. Latham, *Communist Controversy*, p. 395; Gaddis, *Origins of the Cold War*, pp. 42–46; Levering, *American Foreign Policy*, pp. 85–86.

5. Matusow, *Joseph R. McCarthy*, pp. 4–9; Harper, *Politics of Loyalty*, pp. 20–23; Gaddis, *Origins of the Cold War*, pp. 552–58; Latham, *Communist Controversy*, p. 9.

6. Stouffer, *Communism, Conformity, and Civil Liberties*, p. 158ff.

7. The authorship of *America's Retreat from Victory* has long been debated. See Oshinsky, *A Conspiracy So Immense*, p. 200. Theoharis, in *Seeds of Repression*, pp. 69ff, provides a useful summary of the Yalta accords.

8. Theoharis, *Seeds of Repression*, pp. 60, 75ff.

9. In addition to Theoharis's *Seeds of Repression*, the revisionists' arguments can be found in his "Rhetoric of Politics"; in Sitkoff, "Years of the Locust"; and in Freeland, *Truman Doctrine*.

10. Hamby, *Beyond the New Deal*, p. 401. For similar criticisms of the revisionist position, see Fried, *Men against McCarthy*, pp. 13–32, and Gosnell, *Truman's Crises*, p. 506.

11. On press accounts of Russian brutality in Eastern Europe, see *Time*, August 6, 1945, p. 34; Heinz Elaus, "Democracy versus Tyranny in Bulgaria," *New Republic*, September 3, 1945, pp. 273–74; *New York Times*, September 16, 1945, p. E-5; and *Atlanta Constitution*, September 9, 1945, p. 5-D. For examples of the congressional reaction, see *Congressional Record*: 79th Cong., 2d sess., app., 1946, pp. 3702, 4523;

80th Cong., 1st sess., 1947, pp. 1073–75; 79th Cong., 1st sess., app., 1946, pp. A2147–49, A3263; 79th Cong., 2d sess., app., 1946, p. A3972.

12. On concern for Poland, see "Remarks of Thad F. Waslelewski" and "Remarks of Noah M. Mason," both in *Congressional Record*, 79th Cong., 2d sess., app., 1946, pp. A1777–78, A2230–31, and Vandenberg, *Private Papers*, p. 155–56.

13. On Hopkins's meeting with Stalin, see Bohlen, *Witness to History*, pp. 217–19, and "Bohlen Memo on Stalin-Hopkins Meeting," in Bernstein and Matusow, *Truman Administration*, p. 166ff. In reality, considerable confusion existed as to the actual situation in Eastern Europe. The *New Republic*'s Polish correspondent, Irving Brant, called reports of political oppression there exaggerated. *New Republic*, January 7, 1946, pp. 15–18. Likewise, Richard C. Hottelett reported that there was "no question of any totalitarian system being set up" in Czechoslovakia. George F. Kennan later wrote that the Soviets were then "laying the groundwork for establishment of a Communist monopoly of power." *Christian Science Monitor*, September 20, 1945, p. 11; Kennan, *Memoirs, 1925–1950*, p. 254.

14. Vandenberg, *Private Papers*, pp. 256, 353–58; Acheson, *Present at the Creation*, pp. 161–62; Hartmann, *Truman and the 80th Congress*, pp. 32–35.

15. Gallup, *Gallup Poll* 1:523, 565, 587, 594–95; Cook, *Nightmare Decade*, pp. 57–61.

16. Bernstein and Matusow, *Truman Administration*, pp. 231–56; Vandenberg, *Private Papers*, pp. 342–43.

17. *Time*, March 10, 1947, p. 17; *Newsweek*, March 10, 1947, pp. 23–24; *Atlanta Constitution*, March 2, 1947, p. 2-D; *Christian Science Monitor*, March 1, 1947, p. 18.

18. Gallup, *Gallup Poll* 1:623, 636; *Time*, March 24, 1947, pp. 17–18.

19. Thompson, *Frustration of Politics*, pp. 18–20; Byrnes, *All in One Lifetime*, pp. 320–25.

20. Donovan, *Conflict and Crisis*, pp. 292–93. See also Freeland, *Truman Doctrine*, pp. 122–28; Theoharis, *Seeds of Repression*, p. 105; and Harper, *Politics of Loyalty*, pp. 20–44. For Truman's views on the Temporary Commission, see his *Memoirs: Years of Trial and Hope*, pp. 278–81.

21. Hartmann, *Truman and the 80th Congress*, p. 18; Thompson, *Frustration of Politics*, pp. 30–34. In later years, Truman minimized the danger that the country would "be upset from within," a statement that seems to reflect his views for much of his presidency. Truman, *Memoirs: Years of Trial and Hope*, pp. 269–70. Shortly after taking office, however, he confessed that although he was "not afraid of Russia," his "only trouble" was "the crazy American communist." Truman, *Off the Record*, pp. 44–45.

22. Bernstein and Matusow, *Truman Administration*, pp. 357–63; Thompson, *Frus-*

tration of Politics, p. 31; McCoy, *Presidency of Harry S. Truman*, pp. 274–76. According to Robert J. Donovan, the Canadian spy case involved the blackmail of homosexuals. *Conflict and Crisis*, p. 293.

23. Bontecou, *Federal Loyalty-Security Program*, pp. 104–56; McCoy, *Presidency of Harry S. Truman*, pp. 216–17. Bontecou puts the number of dismissals under the Truman order as of March 1952 at 378, McCoy at 384.

24. Freeland, *Truman Doctrine*, pp. 147, 208–19; Theoharis, *Seeds of Repression*, pp. 123–46; Bernstein and Matusow, *Truman Administration*, pp. 391–401.

25. Bernstein and Matusow, *Truman Administration*, pp. 363–71. For criticism of Truman from historians and journalists of varying ideological backgrounds, see Cochran, *Harry Truman and the Crisis Presidency*, pp. 353–77; Cook, *Nightmare Decade*, pp. 62–70; Donovan, *Conflict and Crisis*, p. 298; Freeland, *Truman Doctrine*, pp. 241, 358ff; Hartmann, *Truman and the 80th Congress*, p. 28; McCoy, *Presidency of Harry S. Truman*, p. 319; and Theoharis, *Seeds of Repression*, pp. 101, 169ff.

26. Truman, *Memoirs: Years of Trial and Hope*, pp. 269–85; Bernstein and Matusow, *Truman Administration*, pp. 385–91. The description of Truman's veto is from Hamby, *Liberalism and Its Challengers*, pp. 89–90.

27. Goldman, *Crucial Decade*, p. 112.

28. Harper, *Politics of Loyalty*, pp. 72–73; Thompson, *Frustration of Politics*, pp. 94–95.

29. The events of 1949 are described in detail in Goldman, *Crucial Decade*, pp. 91–112; Donovan, *Tumultuous Years*, pp. 95–127; Cook, *Nightmare Decade*, pp. 68–70; and Matusow, *Joseph R. McCarthy*, pp. 5–9. On the weakness of the KMT, see Harper, *Politics of Loyalty*, pp. 107–14.

30. Harper, *Politics of Loyalty*, pp. 20–23; Hamby, *Beyond the New Deal*, p. 381.

31. Acheson, *Present at the Creation*, pp. 250–52.

32. Nixon, *Memoirs*, pp. 47–48.

33. Nixon gives his version of the Hiss case in his *Six Crises*, pp. 1–72, and *Memoirs*, pp. 47–71. For a skeptical view, see Cook, *Story of Alger Hiss*. Debate over Hiss's guilt or innocence continues with two relatively recent and thorough studies coming to opposite conclusions. John Cabot Smith argues that Hiss "wasn't a Communist and he didn't give Chambers any of the incriminating documents," in *Alger Hiss*, p. 438. However, Allen Weinstein concludes, "The jurors in the second trial made no mistake in finding Alger Hiss guilty as charged." *Perjury*, p. 565. Hiss maintains his innocence in *Recollections of a Life*. On Truman's "red herring" remark, see Bernstein and Matusow, *Truman Administration*, pp. 385–86.

34. Matusow, *Joseph R. McCarthy*, p. 7. The devastating impact of the Hiss case on American liberals is discussed in Hamby, *Beyond the New Deal*, pp. 383–86.

35. The role of the press in inciting concern about subversion is discussed in Bayley, *Joe McCarthy and the Press*, p. 3ff.

36. Rovere, *Senator Joe McCarthy*, pp. 123–34; Bernstein and Matusow, *Truman Administration*, pp. 401–7. McCarthy later claimed that he had said at Wheeling that there were "only" fifty-seven Communists in the State Department. Some evidence exists to support his version of the speech. See Buckley and Bozell, *McCarthy and His Enemies*, p. 401ff.

37. Rovere, *Senator Joe McCarthy*, pp. 168–77; Matusow, *Joseph R. McCarthy*, pp. 54–60; Griffith, *Politics of Fear*, pp. 133–35.

38. Rovere, *Senator Joe McCarthy*, pp. 267–69; Oshinsky, *A Conspiracy So Immense*, p. 184; Kutler, *American Inquisition*, p. 192ff; Acheson, *Present at the Creation*, pp. 369–70. On Senate opposition to McCarthy during the Truman administration, see Griffith, *Politics of Fear*, pp. 52–185. On Lattimore, see chapter 6, infra.

39. Fried, *Nightmare in Red*, pp. 8–9; Rogin, *Intellectuals and McCarthy*, pp. 2–5, 103, 216–60. See also Markowitz, "The McCarthy Phenomenon"; Griffith, "The Politics of Anti-Communism"; Hofstadter, *Paranoid Style*, chapter 2; and Bell, *Radical Right*.

40. Martin, *My First Fifty Years*, pp. 197–98; White, *Taft Story*, pp. 84–92. For a somewhat more sophisticated analysis of the role of the 1948 election in the emergence of McCarthyism, see Latham, *Communist Controversy*, p. 394ff.

41. Russell, "Looking Backward to the 1950s"; Lubell, *Revolt of the Moderates*, pp. 72–74.

42. Bayley, *Joe McCarthy and the Press*, pp. 29–30, 51, 71ff; Rovere, *Senator Joe McCarthy*, p. 138.

43. Gallup, *Gallup Poll* 2:1003; Stouffer, *Communism, Conformity, and Civil Liberties*, p. 86; Rogin, *Intellectuals and McCarthy*, p. 243. Writing in 1954, Stouffer warned future historians against the temptation "from isolated and dramatic events in the news to portray too vividly the emotional climate of America." *Communism, Conformity, and Civil Liberties*, p. 72.

44. The Communist controversy as a conflict between elites is discussed in Rogin, *Intellectuals and McCarthy*, pp. 216–60, and is noted in Cochran, *Harry Truman and the Crisis Presidency*, pp. 371–73.

45. Stouffer, *Communism, Conformity, and Civil Liberties*, pp. 40–43, 59; Rogin, *Intellectuals and McCarthy*, p. 245. The effect of the defeats of Tydings and Lucas on McCarthy's status in the Senate is examined in Griffith, *Politics of Fear*, pp. 122–31.

46. Brendon, *Ike*, p. 22.

47. Eisenhower, *At Ease*, pp. 36, 68. On the religious life of the Eisenhower family, see Lyon, *Eisenhower*, pp. 37–42, and Ambrose, *Eisenhower: Soldier*, pp. 14–22.

48. Eisenhower, *At Ease*, p. 79.

49. Ibid., pp. 39–43.

50. Ibid., pp. 7–16; Brendon, *Ike*, pp. 32–37; Ambrose, *Eisenhower: Soldier*, p. 53. For Eisenhower's early life, I have also drawn generously from Burk, *Eisenhower*, pp. 3–21.

51. Merson, *Private Diary*, p. 74.

52. Dwight D. Eisenhower (hereafter cited as DDE) to Swede Hazlett, February 24, 1950, in Eisenhower, *Letters to a Friend*, pp. 68–75.

53. Diary entry, July 14, 1953, Emmet J. Hughes Papers, Box 1, Sealy G. Mudd Library, Princeton University; Eisenhower, *Diaries*, ed. Ferrell, pp. 226–27. When quoted in his memoirs, the passage from Eisenhower's diary was sanitized to read "business failures, political hacks, and New Deal lawyers." See Eisenhower, *White House Years: Mandate for Change*, p. 111.

54. DDE to Meade Alcorn, August 30, 1957, Ann Whitman File, Dwight D. Eisenhower Diary Series, Box 25, Eisenhower Library. Unless otherwise indicated, all manuscript collections cited herein are from the Eisenhower Library.

55. DDE to Swede Hazlett, October 23, 1954, in Eisenhower, *Letters to a Friend*, pp. 134–35.

56. Eisenhower, *White House Years: Waging Peace*, pp. 654–55.

57. Ambrose, *Eisenhower: The President*, pp. 16–17, 26–27, 616–17. For insights into Eisenhower's relationship with his father, see Eisenhower, *At Ease*, pp. 29–38.

58. See Griffith, "Dwight D. Eisenhower and the Corporate Commonwealth." See also Burk, *Eisenhower*, chapter 10.

59. DDE to Henry Luce, August 8, 1960, Ann Whitman File, Dwight D. Eisenhower Diary Series, Box 52; Griffith, "Dwight D. Eisenhower and the Corporate Commonwealth," p. 110; Greenstein, *Hidden-Hand Presidency*.

60. See Schlesinger, *Cycles of American History*, p. 389; and Richardson, *Presidency of Dwight D. Eisenhower*, chapter 3.

61. Immerman, "Confessions of an Eisenhower Revisionist."

62. McCann, *Man from Abilene*, p. 85.

63. Lyon, *Eisenhower*, pp. 54–75. See generally Davis, *Soldier of Democracy*.

64. Butcher, *My Three Years with Eisenhower*, pp. 854–55; Eisenhower, *Crusade in Europe*, pp. 436–47, 474–76.

65. Eisenhower, *Crusade in Europe*, pp. 438–39, 474–78. For more on Eisenhower's views of the Soviets and his relationship with Zhukov, whom he once called "the greatest military strategist of our time," see Gunther, *Eisenhower*, p. 88.

66. Caute, *The Great Fear*, pp. 406–407, 415; DDE to Louis Graham Smith, May 25, 1948, and DDE to Richard Lloyd Jones, October 14, 1949, both in Eisenhower,

Papers 10:84–86, 779–80. Eisenhower recalls his Columbia years in *At Ease*, pp. 336–62.

67. DDE to Arthur Hayes Sulzberger, July 27, 1948, and DDE to Henry Steel Commager, July 29, 1949, both in Eisenhower, *Papers* 10:162–66, 170–72.

68. DDE to William H. Burnham, November 4, 1948, DDE to Henry Steele Commager, June 16, 1949, and DDE to John Stephens Wood, June 20, 1949, all in Eisenhower, *Papers* 10:285–86, 638–39, 464–49.

69. Lyon, *Eisenhower*, pp. 398–99; DDE to Alger Hiss, September 10, 1948, DDE to William Wallace Chapin, September 17, 1948, DDE to James Thomson Shotwell, September 21, 1948, and DDE to Richard B. Russell, December 14, 1950, all in Eisenhower, *Papers* 10:185–86, 203–4, 214–15, 11:1482–83; Griffith, *Politics of Fear*, pp. 134–39; Gunther, *Eisenhower*, p. 128.

70. DDE to Albert Charles Jacobs, August 9, 1949, DDE to Philip C. Jessup, March 18, 1950, DDE to Francis Joseph Toohey, March 27, 1950, and DDE to H. L. Hunt, September 22, 1950, all in Eisenhower, *Papers* 10:713–14, 11:1014, 1033–34. The McCarthyites held up Jessup's nomination until the Senate adjourned, after which Jessup received a recess appointment. See Griffith, *Politics of Fear*, pp. 146–51.

71. Griffith, *Politics of Fear*, pp. 115–16; Gunther, *Eisenhower*, p. 15.

72. Lyon, *Eisenhower*, p. 421; Ambrose, *Eisenhower: Soldier*, pp. 502–5.

73. DDE to Swede Hazlett, June 21, 1951, and November 14, 1951, both in Eisenhower, *Letters to a Friend*, pp. 86–88, 92–93; Gunther, *Eisenhower*, p. 131; DDE to Robert A. Lovett, July 10, 1948, diary entry, April 29, 1950, DDE to John Stephens Wood, March 23, 1950, and DDE to Godfrey Lowell Cabot, November 3, 1950, all in Eisenhower, *Papers* 10:132–33, 11:1091–93, 1028–30, 1400–1401; Eisenhower, *Diaries*, ed. Ferrell, pp. 189–90. See also Ambrose, *Eisenhower: Soldier*, p. 512. McCarthy wrote Eisenhower in March 1951 to deny Pearson's charges, but given his reputation for verisimilitude, that could hardly have been reassuring to Eisenhower. See Oshinsky, *A Conspiracy So Immense*, pp. 234–36.

Chapter 2

1. Parmet, *Eisenhower and the American Crusades*, pp. 54–55; Gallup, *Gallup Poll* 2:1041, 1045. Adams's role in the New Hampshire primary is discussed in Rovere, "Boss of the White House."

2. Research Services, "Presidential Choices of Republican Party Members, New Hampshire, December, 1951," and Research Services, "Weekly Report," March 10, 1952, Henry Cabot Lodge Papers, Box 23, Massachusetts Historical Society (hereafter cited as MHS); Alexander, *Holding the Line*, p. 2.

3. *Time*, May 5, 1952, pp. 23–24; E. Stewart to Hugh Scott, July 16, 1951, Arthur E. Summerfield Papers, Box 2; memorandum by Gabriel Hague, May 2, 1952, Lodge Papers, Box 19, MHS. Some of the ugliest of the anti-Eisenhower propaganda is collected in the folder "Examples of Anti-Eisenhower Smear Campaign (with explanatory notes)," Thomas E. Stephens Records, Box 16.

4. *Denver Post* clippings, June 15, June 29, 1952, Stephens Records, Box 16; *Time*, May 5, 1952, pp. 23–24; Parmet, *Eisenhower*, pp. 58–60, 76–78; Ambrose, *Eisenhower: Soldier*, p. 536; Snyder, *My Friend Ike*, pp. 16–18.

5. Parmet, *Eisenhower*, pp. 68–69; interview with William F. Knowland, Columbia University Oral History Project (hereafter cited as COHP), June 20, 1967, vol. 2, p. 9; Gallup, *Gallup Poll* 2:1060, 1069–70.

6. Interview with Lucius D. Clay, COHP, 1970–1971, p. 857; interview with Sinclair Weeks, COHP, February 2, 1967, vol. 1, p. 11.

7. Alexander, *Holding the Line*, pp. 3–6; Oshinsky, *A Conspiracy So Immense*, pp. 228–29; Ricks, "'Mr. Integrity' and McCarthyism."

8. Nixon, *Memoirs*, pp. 82–83. For a sympathetic view of Taft from a revisionist perspective, see Barton J. Bernstein, "Election of 1952," in Schlesinger and Israel, *American Presidential Elections* 4:3215–337. Patterson provides an excellent analysis of Taft's foreign policy views in *Mr. Republican*, pp. 474–96.

9. On Dewey and the eastern wing of the GOP, see generally Smith, *Thomas E. Dewey*.

10. Lloyd H. Hall Co., "A Measurement of the Strength of Feeling for Eisenhower among Those Who Currently Favor Him for President," March 17, 1952, Sherman Adams Papers, Box 5, Baker Memorial Library, Dartmouth College; Research Services to Ed Bermingham, October 27, 1951, Lodge Papers, Box 19, MHS; Gallup, *Gallup Poll* 2:1038, 1041, 1060–73 passim.

11. Memorandum to file, December 13, 1951, and Herbert Hukriede to Barak T. Mattingly, April 16, 1952, Lodge Papers, Box 18, MHS.

12. Parmet, *Eisenhower*, pp. 58–60; Ambrose, *Eisenhower: Soldier*, pp. 530–31.

13. *New York Times*, June 27, 1952, pp. 1, 10.

14. Interview with Charles A. Halleck, Dwight D. Eisenhower Oral History Project (hereafter cited as DEOHP), April 26, 1977, p. 4; *Official Report of the Proceedings of the Twenty-Fifth Republican National Convention*, pp. 162, 400; Parmet, *Eisenhower*, pp. 75–100; Bernstein, "Election of 1952," pp. 3230–34.

15. *Official Report of the Proceedings of the Twenty-Fifth Republican National Convention*, pp. 67–76, 80ff, 102–11, 136–39, 300–307, 326.

16. Ibid., pp. 142–47; Oshinsky, *A Conspiracy So Immense*, pp. 230–31.

17. *Official Report of the Proceedings of the Twenty-Fifth Republican National Convention*, pp. 309–24.

18. Ibid., pp. 347ff, 386ff.

19. Nixon, *Memoirs*, pp. 88–91; interview with Herbert Brownell, DEOHP, February 24, 1977, pp. 16–17; Adams, *Firsthand Report*, p. 34.

20. Slater, *The Ike I Knew*, p. 55; Nixon, *Memoirs*, pp. 80–81; Eisenhower, *White House Years: Mandate for Change*, pp. 46–47.

21. Quoted in Mazo and Hess, *Nixon*, pp. 76–78.

22. Nixon, *Memoirs*, pp. 83–84; Smith, *Thomas E. Dewey*, pp. 583–97. Ambrose details Nixon's "campaign" for the vice-presidential nomination in *Nixon*, p. 249–70.

23. Smith, *Thomas E. Dewey*, pp. 583–97; Adams, *Firsthand Report*, pp. 34–36; Herbert Brownell to Sherman Adams, December 23, 1958, Adams Papers, Box 14, Baker Library, Dartmouth; Brownell interview, DEOHP, February 24, 1977, pp. 16–17.

24. Nixon, *Memoirs*, pp. 90–91.

25. Research Division, Citizens for Eisenhower, "The Case for Eisenhower," March 19, 1952, Lodge Papers, Box 23, MHS.

26. Henry Cabot Lodge to DDE, undated, Lodge Papers, Box 13, MHS. Contrary to Lodge's advice, Brownell and Dewey also recommended that Eisenhower make use of the corruption issue. Memorandum to file, July 22, 1952, Lodge Papers, Box 13, MHS.

27. Memorandum to file, undated, and "Campaign Plan," undated, Robert Humphreys Papers, Box 8.

28. On the strategy committee's influence on the 1952 campaign, see the material contained in the file "1952 Campaign & Election—Document X," Humphreys Papers, Box 8. See also Robert Humphreys to Sherman Adams, undated, Adams Papers, Box 5, Baker Library, Dartmouth.

29. Martin, *Stevenson*, pp. 524–92 passim; Sievers, *Last Puritan*, pp. 46–49.

30. Alexander, *Holding the Line*, pp. 21–22; Martin, *Stevenson*, pp. 450–71, 642–45; Stevenson, *Papers* 4:11–19.

31. Martin, *Stevenson*, pp. 404–7.

32. AES to Wilson Wyatt, August 4, 1952, in Stevenson, *Papers* 4:34–35; Martin, *Stevenson*, p. 646. Stevenson had reason to believe that the Republicans, because of the ties Eisenhower and his chief foreign policy adviser, John Foster Dulles, themselves had to Hiss, might not seek to use the affair against the governor. In fact, later in the campaign, Sherman Adams, who was then managing Eisenhower's staff, initiated a frantic, and fruitless, search for a letter Dulles had supposedly written to Eisenhower asking him to write a letter in Hiss's defense. See Bernard M. Shanley Diaries, Box 1, pp. 533–34.

33. Paul Hoffman to DDE, August 21, 1952, Ann Whitman File, Administration

Series, Box 19. See also Henry Cabot Lodge to DDE, August 21, 1952, White House Central Files, Preinaugural File, Box 6.

34. *New York Times*, August 23, 1952, pp. 1, 8; *Newsweek*, September 1, 1952, p. 16; *Time*, September 1, 1952, pp. 10–11.

35. *New York Times*, August 23, 1953, pp. 1, 8. For another view that Summerfield was pivotal in preventing Eisenhower from breaking with McCarthy, see interview with Bernard M. Shanley, DEOHP, May 16, 1975, pp. 28–29.

36. Shanley Diaries, Box 1, p. 494ff; Eugene C. Pulliam to Henry Cabot Lodge, July 29, 1952, Lodge Papers, Box 13, MHS.

37. *New York Times*, September 10, 1952, pp. 1, 9; Shanley interview, DEOHP, May 16, 1975, pp. 28–29.

38. Hughes, *Ordeal of Power*, pp. 41–44; interview with Gabriel Hague, COHP, March 10, 1967, vol. 1, pp. 15–16.

39. *New York Times*, September 10, 1952, pp. 1, 16; Bayley, *Joe McCarthy and the Press*, p. 88ff; Thomas E. Stephens to Sherman Adams, September 13, 1952, Adams Records, Box 36.

40. Crossley, Inc., Report, January 1952, Lodge Papers, Box 18, MHS; interview with Walter Kohler, COHP, December 2, 1970, pp. 16–17; Oshinsky, *A Conspiracy So Immense*, pp. 234–36; Reeves, *Joe McCarthy*, pp. 437–40.

41. Martin, *Stevenson*, pp. 655–56; Eisenhower-Nixon Research Service Report, September 10, 1952, Adams Records, Box 37. Stevenson's American Legion address appears in Stevenson, *Papers* 4:49–54.

42. George Creel to Richard M. Nixon, September 7, 1952, Talbot T. Speers to Sherman Adams, September 16, 1952, Ralph I. Strauss to DDE, August 22, 1952, and Bradley L. Morrison to John Cowles, September 13, 1952, all in Ann Whitman File, Campaign Series, Box 6; DDE to Edward M. Earle, September 2, 1952, in Eisenhower, *Strictly Personal*, pp. 392–94.

43. Eisenhower-Nixon Research Service Report, September 18, 1952, Adams Records, Box 37; Sherman Adams to Gerald Lambert, September 5, 1952, and Mr. Batchelder to Sherman Adams, September 20, 1952, Adams Papers, Box 5, Baker Library, Dartmouth. The cities surveyed were New York, Boston, Detroit, and San Francisco.

44. "Address to State Convention of New York Liberal Party," August 28, 1952, in Stevenson, *Papers* 4:60–64.

45. Adams, *Firsthand Report*, pp. 30–33; Hughes, *Ordeal of Power*, pp. 41–44; C. D. Jackson to Sherman Adams, February 16, 1959, Adams Papers, Box 5, Baker Library, Dartmouth; "Communism and Freedom," sixth draft, Stephen Benedict Papers, Box 3.

46. Hughes, *Ordeal of Power*, pp. 41–44; Adams, *Firsthand Report*, pp. 30–33; Oshinsky, *A Consiracy So Immense*, pp. 234–38; Ewald, *Eisenhower, the President*, pp. 60–61; Kohler interview, COHP, December 2, 1970, pp. 18–23.

47. Adams, *Firsthand Report*, pp. 30–33; Eisenhower, *White House Years: Mandate for Change*, pp. 317–18.

48. Adams, *Firsthand Report*, pp. 30–33; Kohler interview, COHP, December 2, 1970, pp. 23–27; Walter Kohler to Sherman Adams, April 27, 1959, Adams Papers, Box 5, Baker Library, Dartmouth; Cutler, *No Time for Rest*, pp. 286–88; Pusey, *Eisenhower*, pp. 28–32; Hague interview, COHP, March 10, 1967, vol. 1, pp. 16–18.

49. *New York Times*, October 4, 1952, pp. 1–8; Walter Kohler to Sherman Adams, April 27, 1959, Adams Papers, Box 5, Baker Library, Dartmouth; Kohler interview, COHP, December 2, 1970, pp. 18–23; Shanley Diaries, Box 1, p. 524ff; Reeves, *Joe McCarthy*, pp. 437–40.

50. Ewald, *Eisenhower, the President*, pp. 61–63; Ambrose, *Eisenhower: Soldier*, p. 565.

51. Alexander, *Holding the Line*, pp. 17–19; Arthur H. Sulzberger to Sherman Adams, October 8, 1952, Adams Papers, Box 5, Baker Library, Dartmouth.

52. *New York Times*, October 4, 1952, pp. 1, 8; Robert Humphreys to Sherman Adams, February 19, 1959, Humphreys Papers, Box 1; Shanley Diaries, Box 1, p. 524ff; Ewald, *Eisenhower, the President*, p. 58.

53. *Newsweek*, October 13, 1952, p. 30; Edward J. Bermingham to C. D. Jackson, October 3, 1952, C. E. McCarthy to C. D. Jackson, October 6, 1952, and F. D. Gurley to DDE, October 16, 1952, all in Ann Whitman File, Campaign Series, Box 6.

54. Eisenhower-Nixon Research Service Report, September 23, 1952, Adams Records, Box 37; Gerald Lambert to DDE, October 9, 1952, Adams Papers, Box 5, Baker Library, Dartmouth; Gallup, *Gallup Poll* 2:1094, 1100. See also Divine, *Foreign Policy*, pp. 80–85.

55. Eisenhower-Nixon Research Service, October 29, 1952, Adams Records, Box 37; Nixon, *Memoirs*, p. 110; Martin, *Stevenson*, p. 722.

56. *New York Times*, October 6, 1952, pp. 1, 14, and November 1, 1952, pp. 1, 10; *Newsweek*, October 27, 1952, pp. 26–27; *Time*, November 3, 1952, p. 22.

57. Shanley Diaries, Box 1, pp. 536–38, 582; Martin, *Stevenson*, pp. 618, 681–83. See generally Crosby, "Politics of Religion."

58. Robert Cutler to Sherman Adams and Fred Seaton, September 28, 1952, Lodge Papers, Box 13, MHS; Robert E. Bradford to Sherman Adams, October 15, 1952, Adams Papers, Box 5, Baker Library, Dartmouth; Frederick Ayer, Jr., to Sinclair Weeks, October 16, 1952, Ann Whitman File, Campaign Series, Box 6.

59. Oshinsky, *A Conspiracy So Immense*, pp. 239–42; Reeves, *Joe McCarthy*, pp. 442–44; Henry Cabot Lodge to Herbert Brownell, August 22, 1953, Lodge Pa-

pers, Box 13, MHS; Henry Cabot Lodge to John Fox, October 20, 1952, Lodge Papers, Box 12, MHS.

60. *Christian Science Monitor*, October 21, 1952, p. 1, and November 4, 1952, p. 1; *New York Times*, October 22, 1952, pp. 1, 16; "Final Draft of Street Corner Speech," October 22, 1952, Lodge Papers, Box 9, MHS; undated, unsigned memorandum, Lodge Papers, Box 20, MHS; *Time*, November 3, 1952, p. 26.

61. Anderson, "China Policy"; Harris, *Republican Majority*, pp. 22–32, 87–94, 164–69, 203–4.

62. Goldwater, *With No Apologies*, pp. 55, 64; Leuchtenburg, *Papers of the Republican Party*, Reel 2:001; Reichard, *Reaffirmation of Republicanism*, pp. 14–24.

63. Reeves, *Joe McCarthy*, pp. 453–54.

64. Bernstein, "Election of 1952," pp. 3259–66; *Newsweek*, October 20, 1952, p. 37; *Time*, November 10, 1952, p. 21.

65. Gallup, *Gallup Poll* 2:1050–52, 1066, 1068.

66. For insight into Eisenhower's relative lack of political sophistication, which should not be minimized in evaluating his response to the Communist controversy in the 1952 campaign and in the first months of his presidency, see Pearson, *Diaries*, pp. 219–20, and Sulzberger, *A Long Row of Candles*, p. 779.

Chapter 3

1. *Public Papers*, 1953, pp. 24–25.

2. *Christian Science Monitor*, February 5, 1953, p. 11.

3. Parmet, *Eisenhower*, p. 230.

4. Martin, *My First Fifty Years*, pp. 235–37; *Newsweek*, November 3, 1952, p. 36; Reinhard, *Republican Right*, pp. 117–19; Patterson, *Mr. Republican*, p. 589.

5. Ambrose, *Nixon*, pp. 302–13; Griffith, *Politics of Fear*, pp. 200–201; Ambrose, *Eisenhower: The President*, p. 59; Ewald, *Who Killed Joe McCarthy?*, p. 55. On the origins of McCarthy's letter protesting the Conant nomination, see Buckley, "For the Record."

6. Ewald notes the tendency of McCarthy's charges to overshadow serious discussion of national security in *Who Killed Joe McCarthy?*, p. 65.

7. In a February 7, 1953, diary entry, Eisenhower expressed surprise and satisfaction at the degree of cooperation he was receiving from "Senators Bridges, Capehart, Dirksen, and others of this general group." Eisenhower, *Diaries*, ed. Ferrell, p. 227. On his desire to ignore McCarthy, see ibid., pp. 233–34, and Eisenhower, *White House Years: Mandate for Change*, pp. 319–20.

8. Interview with Homer H. Gruenther, COHP, January 11, 1972, p. 13.

9. Reinhard, *Republican Right*, p. 90.

10. Arthur Summerfield to Joseph R. McCarthy, July 5, 1951, Box 5, Joseph R. McCarthy to Arthur Summerfield, May 23, 1950, Box 5, and Arthur Summerfield to Sam Rayburn, February 29, 1952, Box 2, all in Summerfield Papers. For biographical information on key administration figures, see Schoenebaum, *Political Profiles*.

11. Sinclair Weeks to Lawrence G. Brooks, April 20, 1950, Summerfield Papers, Box 5; "Transcript of Hall's Remarks on 'Youth Wants to Know' Radio and TV Program," May 24, 1953, Humphreys Papers, Box 2. Many of the younger GOP House members had apparently pressured the White House to select Hall as national chairman. See Bryce N. Harlow to DDE, April 3, 1953, Harlow Records, Box 13.

12. See chapter 5 infra.

13. Interview with Wilton B. Persons, COHP, June 24, 1970, pp. 21–25.

14. Eisenhower, *White House Years: Mandate for Change*, p. 87; Eisenhower, *Diaries*, ed. Ferrell, p. 237. On Humphrey's years in the cabinet, see Humphrey, *Papers*. On Humphrey and the censure of McCarthy, see chapter 5 infra.

15. Ambrose, *Nixon*, pp. 311–12; Mazo and Hess, *Nixon*, pp. 128–35; Nixon, *Memoirs*, pp. 139–40, 149; Griffith, *Politics of Fear*, p. 131.

16. Eisenhower, *Diaries*, ed. Ferrell, p. 238; Eisenhower, *The President Is Calling*, pp. 316–18; interview with Milton Eisenhower, COHP, June 21, 1967, pp. 65–66.

17. Interview with Gerald D. Morgan, COHP, April 29, 1968, pp. 85–88; Ewald, *Who Killed Joe McCarthy?*, p. 45. Cutler recounts his White House years in *No Time for Rest*, p. 293ff.

18. Brands, *Cold Warriors*, p. 164. See also Eisenhower, *Diaries*, ed. Ferrell, pp. 238–39, and Lodge, *As It Was*, pp. 131–33.

19. *Time*, February 16, 1953, pp. 23–26. See also *U.S. News and World Report*, February 6, 1953, pp. 16–17.

20. Interview with Herbert Brownell, COHP, April 12, 1968, p. 300ff. See also U.S. Congress, Senate, 83d Cong., 1st sess., *Hearings before the Committee on the Judiciary on Herbert Brownell, Jr.*, and "Suggested Statement," undated, Ann Whitman File, Administration Series, Box 7.

21. Shanley Diaries, Box 1, pp. 666–67, 735, Box 2, pp. 1037, 1307, 1330; Brands, *Cold Warriors*, pp. 117–37; Ambrose, *Nixon*, pp. 311–15. Like Shanley, Jackson and Paul Hoffman lamented the administration's inability to develop a coherent response to McCarthy. See Paul Hoffman to C. D. Jackson, May 10, 1954, and memorandum to the president, undated and unsigned, Jackson Papers, Box 49. Nevertheless, Greenstein argues that Eisenhower had a covert anti-McCarthy strategy during "his first months in office," which included the use of the employee security program to seize the initiative from McCarthy. *Hidden-Hand Presidency*, p. 169–227. On the other hand, Donovan, in one of the first serious studies of the Eisenhower

presidency, reported, "Most, although not all, of those who were closest to the problem in the White House do not believe that the President followed any carefully planned, deliberate strategy toward McCarthy." In Donovan's opinion, an "attitude" of "disdain" for the Republican from Wisconsin, not a comprehensive plan, guided Ike's behavior. *Eisenhower*, p. 257.

22. Eisenhower, *Diaries*, ed. Ferrell, pp. 226–27, 270, 291; White, *Taft Story*, p. 198; Nixon, *Memoirs*, pp. 139–40; interview with William F. Knowland, COHP, June 20, 1967, pp. 9–13. For more on the ideological leanings of Republicans in the Eighty-third Congress, see Reichard, *Reaffirmation of Republicanism*, pp. 32–50.

23. Bohlen, *Witness to History*, p. 309.

24. Ruddy, *Cautious Diplomat*, p. 112.

25. Eisenhower, *White House Years: Mandate for Change*, pp. 211–13; Bohlen, *Witness to History*, pp. 313–21; Rosenau, *"Chip" Bohlen*, pp. 2–3.

26. John Foster Dulles to DDE, February 24, 1953, White House Central Files, Official File, Box 159. See also Bohlen, *Witness to History*, pp. 313–23, and Hughes, *Ordeal of Power*, p. 93.

27. Eisenhower, *White House Years: Mandate for Change*, pp. 211–13.

28. Bohlen, *Witness to History*, pp. 313–21; U.S. Congress, Senate, 83d Cong., 1st sess., *Hearings before the Committee on Foreign Relations on the Nomination of Charles E. Bohlen*, p. 1ff (hereafter cited as *Bohlen Hearings*).

29. Bohlen, *Witness to History*, pp. 313–24; Hoopes, *John Foster Dulles*, 158–60; telephone conversation with William F. Knowland, March 7, 1953, in Kesaris and Gibson, *Telephone Conversations*, reel 1; Pearson, *Diaries*, pp. 254–55. On McLeod, see chapter 5 infra.

30. Rosenau, *"Chip" Bohlen*, pp. 4–5. See also Adams, *Firsthand Report*, pp. 93–96; Patterson, *Mr. Republican*, pp. 596–97; and White, *Taft Story*, pp. 233–38.

31. Conversation with Sherman Adams, March 13, 1953, in Kesaris and Gibson, *Telephone Conversations*, reel 8.

32. Rosenau, *"Chip" Bohlen*, p. 5; conversation with Robert Taft, March 16, 1953, and conversation with Charles Bohlen, March 16, 1953, both in Kesaris and Gibson, *Telephone Conversations*, reel 1; memorandum of conference with DDE, March 16, 1953, in ibid., reel 8.

33. Conversation with Donald Lourie, March 16, 1953, and conversation with DDE, March 17, 1953, both in Kesaris and Gibson, *Telephone Conversations*, reel 2, reel 8.

34. Bohlen, *Witness to History*, pp. 324–31; *Bohlen Hearings*, p. 101ff.

35. Rosenau, *"Chip" Bohlen*, p. 7; *Public Papers*, 1953, p. 109; *Congressional Record*, 83d Cong., 1st sess., 1953, 99, pt. 2:2156; Bohlen, *Witness to History*, pp. 324–31.

36. Ewald, *Who Killed Joe McCarthy?* p. 58; memorandum by L. A. Minnich, April 7, 1953, Adams Papers, Box 8, Baker Library, Dartmouth; Shanley Diaries, Box 1, p. 737; conversations with Sherman Adams, March 19, 1953, and conversations with Sherman Adams, James Hagerty, and DDE, March 20, 1953, all in Kesaris and Gibson, *Telephone Conversations*, reel 8; Adams, *Firsthand Report*, pp. 93–96. See also Emmet J. Hughes Diary, March 20, 1953, Hughes Papers, Box 1, Sealy G. Mudd Library, Princeton University. Dulles considered McLeod sufficiently contrite, but the secretary of state confessed to Adams that, with regard to an explanation for his behavior, the security officer "didn't have a very good one." Conversations with Donald Lourie and Sherman Adams, March 20, 1953, in Kesaris and Gibson, *Telephone Conversations*, reel 8. Nevertheless, McLeod's apology motivated Eisenhower to ask Dulles to convey to McLeod the president's deep appreciation for his "attitude." Scott McLeod to John Foster Dulles, March 20, 1953, and DDE to John Foster Dulles, March 23, 1953, in Dulles, *Papers*, reel 5.

37. *Congressional Record*, 83d Cong., 1st sess., 1953, 99, pt. 2:2187–2208.

38. Shanley Diaries, Box 1, pp. 668, 704–5; conversation with Herbert Brownell, March 21, 1953, and conversations with Alexander Wiley and Herbert Brownell, March 23, 1953, all in Kesaris and Gibson, *Telephone Conversations*, reel 1.

39. Conversation with Robert Taft, March 23, 1953, and conversations with Herbert Brownell and Alexander Wiley, March 24, 1953, all in Kesaris and Gibson, *Telephone Conversations*, reel 1; Eisenhower, *White House Years: Mandate for Change*, pp. 211–13; White, *Taft Story*, pp. 233–38. In reality, Taft agreed, at the insistence of J. Edgar Hoover, to review only a summary of the FBI file on Bohlen. See conversations with J. Edgar Hoover and Herbert Brownell, March 24, 1953, both in Kesaris and Gibson, *Telephone Conversations*, reel 1.

40. *Congressional Record*, 83d Cong., 1st sess., 99, 1953, pt. 2:2277–2300, 2374–92; *Public Papers*, 1953, pp. 130–32; Ambrose, *Nixon*, p. 313.

41. Adams, *Firsthand Report*, pp. 93–96; Eisenhower, *Diaries*, ed. Ferrell, pp. 234–35; Bohlen, *Witness to History*, pp. 323–31; White, *Taft Story*, pp. 238–39; Patterson, *Mr. Republican*, pp. 596–97. For a further analysis of the vote, see Reichard, *Reaffirmation of Republicanism*, pp. 56–58.

42. Henderson, *United States Information Agency*, pp. 236–38; Caute, *Great Fear*, p. 321; Cook, *Nightmare Decade*, pp. 398–402; Ambrose, *Eisenhower: The President*, p. 61.

43. Henderson, *United States Information Agency*, pp. 21–52, 240–42; Ewald, *Who Killed Joe McCarthy?*, p. 60; Pearson, *Diaries*, p. 259; Patterson, *Mr. Republican*, pp. 394–95; interview with James C. Hagerty, COHP, 1967–68, pp. 383–86. The Jackson group eventually made dozens of recommendations for changes in the IIA.

See "The Report of the President's Committee on International Information Activities," June 30, 1953, in Slany, *Foreign Relations of the United States* 2:1795–899.

44. U.S. Congress, Senate, 83d Cong., 1st sess., *Hearings before the Permanent Subcommittee on Investigations of the Committee on Government Operations on State Department Information Program—Voice of America* and *Hearings before the Permanent Subcommittee on Investigations of the Committee on Government Operations on State Department Information Program—Information Centers.*

45. Merson, *Private Diary*, p. 14; C. D. Jackson to John Foster Dulles, February 19, 1953, Jackson Records, Box 3; *Public Papers*, 1953, pp. 61–62. Eisenhower again refused to take a stand on the IIA controversy at a later press conference on March 5. *Public Papers*, 1953, p. 88.

46. Caute, *Great Fear*, pp. 322–23; Merson, *Private Diary*, pp. 68, 72–74; Ambrose, *Nixon*, pp. 311–15.

47. "Memorandum by the Assistant Secretary of State for Public Affairs to the Acting Administrator of the United States Information Administration," March 17, 1953, in Slany, *Foreign Relations of the United States* 2:1685–86.

48. Merson, *Private Diary*, p. 42ff; Caute, *Great Fear*, p. 324. Cohn gives his account of his "investigation" of the IIA libraries in *McCarthy*, pp. 75–92, where he concedes that the book purge was "an error in judgment," at least with regard to nonpolitical literature, and that his activities in Europe were poorly received because many people there saw McCarthy as an "anti-European isolationist." For documents detailing the Cohn-Schine trip to Europe, see Slany, *Foreign Relations of the United States* 1:1437–57.

49. IIA press release, July 18, 1953, statement of IIA's book policy, undated, IIA press release, July 9, 1953, Joseph R. McCarthy to Robert L. Johnson, July 9, 1953, all in Jackson Records, Box 4; Henderson, *United States Information Agency*, pp. 48–52, 236–38. The House Appropriations Committee eventually found IIA libraries to contain thirty-nine books by eight pro-Communist authors. Henderson, *United States Information Agency*, pp. 236–38.

50. Quoted in Ambrose, *Eisenhower: The President*, p. 81. For Bullis's advice to Eisenhower during the presidential campaign, see Harry A. Bullis to DDE, October 2, 1952, and Harry A. Bullis to DDE, October 26, 1952, both in White House Central Files, Preinaugural File, Box 7. Bullis was chairman of the board of General Mills, Inc.

51. *Public Papers*, 1953, pp. 414–15; Pusey, *Eisenhower*, pp. 264–66; Pearson, *Diaries*, pp. 299–300.

52. Conversation with DDE, June 15, in Dulles, *Papers*, reel 1; *Public Papers*, 1953, pp. 426–38, 465–67.

53. *Minutes and Documents of the Cabinet*, June 26, 1953, reel 1; "Memorandum to the President by the Secretary of State," June 27, 1953, in Slany, *Foreign Relations of the United States* 2:1715–16. Like Eisenhower, the president's Psychological Strategy Board concluded that in light of "the serious effects on world opinion produced by reports of 'book-burning,'" IIA libraries should be allowed to select books on at least as liberal a basis as that followed by libraries in the United States. "Memorandum by the Acting Director of the Psychological Strategy Board to the Under-secretary of State," July 6, 1953, in Slany, *Foreign Relations of the United States* 2:1722.

54. Roderick L. O'Connor to John Foster Dulles, July 8, 1953, and John Foster Dulles to Robert Johnson, July 8, 1953, John Foster Dulles Papers, Subject Series, Box 1. The July 8 directive notwithstanding, the State Department still felt the need to assure Congress that books by Communist authors and by those who had taken the Fifth Amendment before congressional committees had been removed from circulation. State Department Release, July 15, 1953, ibid.

55. *Minutes and Documents of the Cabinet*, July 10, 1953, reel 1. See also Donovan, *Eisenhower*, pp. 91–93.

56. C. D. Jackson to DDE, July 3, 1953, and DDE to James B. Conant, July 20, 1953, both in Jackson Papers, Box 41; conversations with Carl McCardle and C. D. Jackson, July 18, 1953, in Kesaris and Gibson, *Telephone Conversations*, reel 1.

57. Interview with Theodore C. Streibert, COHP, December 10, 1970, pp. 1–23; interview with Andrew H. Berding, COHP, June 13, 1967, p. 9; Henderson, *United States Information Agency*, pp. 52–57; "Supplemental Cabinet Notes," November 2, 1953, Adams Papers, Box 8, Baker Library, Dartmouth. For more on Eisenhower's subsequent support for the USIA, see Eisenhower, *White House Years: Waging Peace*, pp. 136–38; *Public Papers*, 1957, p. 27; and L. A. Minnich, Jr., to Mr. Hughes, May 10, 1954, Ann Whitman File, Legislative Meetings Series, Box 1.

58. Bryce N. Harlow to Sherman Adams, March 4, 1954, Box 10, Adams Papers, Baker Library, Dartmouth. One of the ironies of the massive force reductions suffered by the USIA was the dismissal of many of McCarthy's informers within the organization. See Cook, *Nightmare Decade*, p. 415.

59. Both quoted in Cook, *Nightmare Decade*, pp. 402–3.

60. Berding interview, COHP, June 13, 1967, p. 9; interview with Sigurd S. Larmon, COHP, November 10, 1970, p. 49; Kretzman, "Voice of America."

61. Merson, *Private Diary*, p. 7; Reinhard, *Republican Right*, p. 121ff; diary entry, February 20, 1953, Hughes Papers, Box 1, Sealy G. Mudd Library, Princeton University.

62. *Public Papers*, 1953, pp. 63–67; Hughes, *Ordeal of Power*, pp. 94–97; memorandum by L. A. Minnich, July 29, 1953, Adams Papers, Box 10, Baker Library, Dartmouth; "Minnich Notes," July 29, 1953, White House Office, Office of the Staff

Secretary, L. A. Minnich Series, Subseries A, Box 1; diary entry, July 15, 1953, Hughes Papers, Box 1, Sealy G. Mudd Library, Princeton University.

63. Memorandum by Robert Cutler, April 30, 1953, White House Office, Office of the Special Assistant for National Security Affairs (hereafter cited as OSANSA), Special Assistant Series, Name Subseries, Box 3.

64. Joseph R. McCarthy to Allen Dulles, July 16, 1953, Richard M. Nixon Vice-Presidential Papers, Box 490, National Archives and Record Service (hereafter cited as NARS), Laguna Nigel, Calif.; Ambrose, *Nixon*, p. 315; Nixon, *Memoirs*, pp. 139–40.

65. Smith, *OSS*, pp. 369–72; Allen W. Dulles to Joseph R. McCarthy, October 23, 1953, and July 7, 1954, White House Office, Office of the Staff Secretary, Box 9; Allen W. Dulles to Joseph R. McCarthy, July 23, 1953, Nixon Papers, Box 490, NARS. See also folder, "McCarthy, Joe 1953," Allen W. Dulles Papers, Box 58, Sealy G. Mudd Library, Princeton University.

66. *New York Times*, March 29, 1953, p. 34; Shanley Diaries, Box 1, p. 784; *Public Papers, 1953*, pp. 149–55.

67. Conversation with James C. Hagerty, April 2, 1953, in Kesaris and Gibson, *Telephone Conversations*, reel 8; memorandum by John W. Hanes, April 13, 1953, in ibid., reel 2; Joseph R. McCarthy to John Foster Dulles, April 2, 1953, and John Foster Dulles to Joseph R. McCarthy, May 6, 1953, and May 7, 1953, all in Dulles Papers, General Correspondence Series, Box 3.

68. Joseph R. McCarthy to DDE, May 20, 1953, Nixon Papers, Box 108, NARS; memorandum by L. A. Minnich, May 22, 1953, Adams Papers, Box 20, Baker Library, Dartmouth; Adams, *Firsthand Report*, pp. 139–41; Mazo and Hess, *Nixon*, pp. 133–34; diary entry, March 2, 1953, Hughes Papers, Box 1, Sealy G. Mudd Library, Princeton University. In reality, the State Department advised the White House that the "free world members of the UN" had already embargoed the shipment to China of most items that the United States considered to be of strategic importance. The department also recognized that a total ban on commerce with the People's Republic would deprive the West of valuable Chinese goods. Carl W. McCardle to James C. Hagerty, Carl W. McCardle Papers, Box 9.

69. Quoted in von Hoffman, *Citizen Cohn*, p. 170. Concerns in a key state about Eisenhower's weak public posture were reported to the White House in "Survey of California Opinion Poll," September 30, 1953, in Eisenhower, *Diaries*, ed. Lester, reel 3.

70. Quoted in Schlesinger, *Imperial Presidency*, p. 152.

71. Larson, *Eisenhower*, pp. 13–14; Eisenhower, *Diaries*, ed. Ferrell, pp. 233–34; Slater, *The Ike I Knew*, p. 53; Eisenhower, *Letters to a Friend*, pp. 107–11; William E. Robinson to DDE, July 22, 1953, and DDE to William E. Robinson, July 27, 1953, both in William E. Robinson Papers, Box 6.

72. Cohn, *McCarthy*, pp. 112–13.

73. *Public Papers*, 1953, pp. 63–67.

74. Shanley Diaries, Box 1, pp. 625–625e; Shanley interview, DEOHP, May 16, 1975, p. 79; J. Edgar Hoover to Robert Cutler, March 18, 1953, White House Office, OSANSA, FBI Series, Current Intelligence Estimates Subseries, Box 6; *Public Papers*, 1953, pp. 40–41, 466–47. Eisenhower defended his action in the Rosenberg case in *White House Years: Mandate for Change*, pp. 223–25. Indicative of the spirit of the time was the attitude of C. D. Jackson. Although he wanted to delay the execution so that further attempts could be made at "cracking" the Rosenbergs, even Jackson believed they deserved "to fry a hundred times" for what they had done. C. D. Jackson to Herbert Brownell, February 23, 1953, Jackson Records, Box 2. Fuchs, who was tried in England, received a fourteen-year prison sentence. In the United States, Gold received thirty years and Greenglass fifteen.

75. DDE to John Foster Dulles, June 23, 1953, in Dulles, *Papers*, reel 1; Radosh and Milton, *Rosenberg File*, pp. 373–80, 450–52. See also Parrish, "Cold War Justice."

76. Tom Coleman to Leonard Hall, June 15, 1953, Hall Papers, Box 177; H. J. Burdinshaw to Leonard Hall, October 1953, Hall Papers, Box 5; Mrs. Loyd R. Haight to Leonard Hall, November 17, 1953, Hall Papers, Box 50. For relevant correspondence with RNC headquarters, see the following folders, all in the Hall Papers: "Mail Summary 1953," Box 1; "Campaign 1953 (Wisconsin Election)," Box 5; and "Communism 1953 12," Box 50.

77. Harris, *Republican Majority*, pp. 205–8; Central Surveys, "Opinion Survey, 9th Congressional District, Wis., October 27–November 5, 1953," Hall Papers, Box 126.

78. Quoted in Reinhard, *Republican Right*, p. 119.

79. Richard M. Nixon to DDE, undated, Nixon Papers, Box 344, NARS; Ambrose, *Nixon*, p. 310.

80. *New York Times*, November 7, 1953, p. 11; Pearson, *Diaries*, p. 284; DDE to Alfred M. Gruenther, November 23, 1953, in Eisenhower, *Diaries*, ed. Lester, reel 2; Adams, *Firsthand Report*, pp. 133–39; Henry Cabot Lodge to DDE, November 16, 1953, Ann Whitman File, Administration Series, Box 23.

81. *Public Papers, 1953*, pp. 757–65; entry by Ann Whitman, November 27, 1953, Ann Whitman File, Ann Whitman Diary Series, Box 1; Eisenhower, *White House Years: Mandate for Change*, pp. 314–15. In *The Bureau*, p. 38, William C. Sullivan, a former assistant director of the FBI, concluded that Truman correctly dismissed the charges against White as a "red herring." For Truman's reaction to the charges, see Truman, *Off the Record*, pp. 300–301.

82. *New York Times*, November 25, 1953, pp. 1, 5. Davies had been transferred by this time to the American mission in Peru. See chapter 5 infra.

83. C. D. Jackson to Sherman Adams, November 25, 1953, Jackson Papers, Box 23; Stanley M. Rumbough, Jr., and Charles Masterson to Murry Snyder, December 1, 1953, Adams Papers, Box 10, Baker Library, Dartmouth; Hagerty, *Diary*, pp. 127–29.

Chapter 4

1. Branyon and Larsen, *Eisenhower Administration* 1:135–36. Eisenhower had hoped to make Flemming, then president of Ohio Wesleyan University, chairman of the Civil Service Commission, but since Flemming had a reputation on Capitol Hill as a "bit of a New Dealer," Eisenhower instead made him director of the Office of Defense Mobilization, a position not requiring Senate confirmation. Eisenhower, *Diaries*, ed. Ferrell, pp. 226–27.

2. Unsigned memorandum, January 7, 1953, in Eisenhower, *Diaries*, ed. Lester, reel 2; Milt Hall to Wilton B. Persons, January 12, 1953, Box 481, and Sherman Adams to Herbert Brownell, January 5, 1953, Box 438, both in White House Central Files, Official File.

3. Lodge, *As It Was*, pp. 53–54. See also chapter 5 infra.

4. *New York Times*, February 1, 1953, p. 13; Donovan, *Eisenhower*, p. 287.

5. "132nd Meeting of the NSC," February 18, 1953, Ann Whitman File, National Security Council Series, Box 5. For more on security problems at the Joint Committee, see Strauss, *Men and Decisions*, pp. 269–70, and Green, "The Oppenheimer Case."

6. Ambrose, *Nixon*, pp. 316–17; Brownell interview, COHP, April 12, 1968, p. 30ff; "Cabinet Meeting Notes," January 23, 1953, White House Office, Office of the Staff Secretary, LAM Series, Box 1.

7. "Legislative Meetings—1953 (January) (2)," Ann Whitman File, Legislative Meetings Series, Box 1; Edward H. Rees to Gerald D. Morgan, January 22, 1953, Gerald D. Morgan Papers, Box 22; *Minutes and Documents of the Cabinet*, January 23, 1953, reel 2; Eisenhower, *White House Years: Mandate for Change*, pp. 308–10.

8. *Christian Science Monitor*, February 4, 1953, p. 1. See also ibid., February 11, 1953, p. E; *New York Times*, February 8, 1953, Section IV, p. 7; and *U.S. News and World Report*, February 6, 1953, pp. 16–17.

9. Walter Lippmann, "The New Loyalty Policy," February 5, 1953, White House Office, Office of the Staff Secretary, LAM Series, Box 1.

10. *Christian Science Monitor*, February 5, 1953, p. 11; von Hoffman, *Citizen Cohn*, pp. 127–30; *New Republic*, February 16, 1953, pp. 5–6. According to von

Hoffman, a turning point in the persecution of homosexuals came in 1954 with the suicide of Democratic Senator Lester Hunt of Wyoming. Styles Bridges had told Hunt that if he refused to withdraw from his race for reelection, the Republicans would publicize the arrest of Hunt's son by Washington, D.C., police in October 1953 on a "morals charge." *Citizen Cohn*, pp. 227–33.

11. Hiram Bingham to DDE, February 12, 1953, White House Central Files, Official File, Box 481; *New York Times*, February 15, 1953, p. 1; *Christian Science Monitor*, February 18, 1953, p. E.

12. Charlie Willis to Sherman Adams, March 11, 1953, White House Central Files, Official File, Box 481.

13. Morgan interview, COHP, April 29, 1968, p. 94ff; Robert Cutler to DDE, January 21, 1953, Robert Cutler to Herbert Brownell, March 9, 1953, and James S. Lay, Jr., to Joseph M. Dodge, March 16, 1953, all in White House Office, OSANSA Papers, NSC Series, Administrative Subseries, Box 7; *New York Times*, March 1, 1953, Section IV, p. 10, March 18, 1953, p. 36, April 18, 1953, p. 10. Brownell's attack on the LRB drew a sharp rebuke from the *New York Times* columnist Arthur Krock, who was relatively sympathetic to Eisenhower: "Considering the distinguished personnel of the L.R.B. . . . its remarkable record of arduous and intelligent labor, and the executive restraints on its scope, it is strange that Brownell did not exempt this group from his remarks." *New York Times*, April 23, 1953, p. 28.

14. Herbert Brownell to DDE, April 17, 1953, White House Central Files, Official File, Box 481; Branyon and Larsen, *Eisenhower Administration* 1:136–42; Fund for the Republic, *Digest of the Public Record*, pp. 51–63.

15. Fund for the Republic, *Digest of the Public Record*, pp. 51–63.

16. Eisenhower, *White House Years: Mandate for Change*, pp. 308–20; Fund for the Republic, *Digest of the Public Record*, pp. 54–63.

17. *Minutes and Documents of the Cabinet*, April 24, 1953, reel 1; Sherman Adams to Joseph Dodge, April 27, 1953, and "Supplementary Notes" by L. A. Minnich, Jr., April 27, 1953, both in Ann Whitman File, Legislative Meetings Series, Box 1.

18. *New York Times*, April 28, 1953, p. 20; *Christian Science Monitor*, April 29, 1953, p. 1.

19. *Public Papers*, 1953, pp. 373–76, 404–5.

20. Ibid., p. 841; *Public Papers*, 1954, pp. 6–22, 50–62, 225–34.

21. U.S. Congress, Senate, 84th Cong., 2d sess., Report No. 2750; U.S. Congress, Senate, 84th Cong., 1st sess., *Hearings before a Subcommittee to Investigate the Administration of the Federal Employees' Security Program of the Senate Committee on Post Office and Civil Service*, pp. 1309–13 (hereafter cited as *Johnston Subcommittee Hearings*). On practices in two representative agencies, the Treasury Department and the Post Office, see Philip Young to Sherman Adams, October 28, 1953,

White House Central Files, Confidential File, Box 66, and Elbert Tuttle to Gerald D. Morgan, February 3, 1954, Morgan Papers, Box 7.

22. Marilu to Gerald D. Morgan, February 6, 1954, Morgan Papers, Box 7; Eisenhower, *White House Years: Mandate for Change*, p. 315.

23. Robert Cutler to Philip Young, September 22, 1953, White House Office, OSANSA, NSC Series, Administrative Subseries, Box 7; Ambrose, *Nixon*, pp. 316–17; Henry Cabot Lodge to Paul T. Carroll, October 26, 1953, White House Central Files, Confidential File, Box 66. Tuttle later recalled that, at a meeting of department security officers, Nixon was told that with the exception of a tiny handful of security risks, there was "no real problem." Nixon supposedly replied: "God damn it, I want numbers! I want numbers!" In his efforts to prove that the administration stood vigilant against communism, the vice president, Tuttle concluded, "was playing McCarthy's game." Interview with Elbert Tuttle, COHP, June 26, 1970, pp. 84–85.

24. Philip Young to Sherman Adams, October 28, 1953, White House Central Files, Confidential File, Box 66; Edward H. Rees to DDE, February 10, 1954, Gerald D. Morgan to Edward H. Rees, February 17, 1954, Edward H. Rees to DDE, March 5, 1954, Philip Young to Sherman Adams, June 7, 1954, and Philip Young to Sherman Adams, September 30, 1954, all in Adams Papers, Box 8, Baker Library, Dartmouth; interview with Maxwell Rabb, DEOHP, May 13, 1975, p. 15; Robert Cutler to Herbert Brownell, September 25, 1953, and memorandum by Pat Coyne, September 18, 1953, both in White House Office, OSANSA, NSC Series, Adm. Subseries, Box 7.

25. Benson, *Cross Fire*, pp. 226–29; Hagerty, *Diary*, pp. 153–54; Shanley Diaries, Box 2, pp. 1705–7; *Public Papers*, 1955, pp. 54–66.

26. Robert Cutler to Philip Young, August 8, 1953, Philip Young to Robert Cutler, October 15, 1953, Robert Cutler to Philip Young, October 9, 1953, and Robert Cutler to Joseph M. Dodge, October 1, 1953, all in White House Office, OSANSA, NSC Series, Adm. Subseries, Box 7; press release, October 14, 1953, White House Central Files, Official File, Box 481; William P. Rogers Papers, Box 16; U.S. Congress, Senate, 84th Cong., 1st sess., *Hearings before a Subcommittee on Reorganization of the Committee on Government Operations on SJ Resolution 21*, pp. 135–36 (hereafter cited as *Humphrey Subcommittee Hearings*).

27. Philip Young to NSC, October 21, 1953, White House Office, OSANSA, Special Assistant Series, Presidential Subseries, Box 1; DDE to Henry Cabot Lodge, November 30, 1953, Henry Cabot Lodge to DDE, December 2, 1953, and DDE to Herbert Brownell, December 9, 1953, all in Eisenhower, *Diaries*, ed. Lester, reel 2; Henry Cabot Lodge to DDE, February 5, 1955, in ibid., reel 5; Herbert Brownell to DDE, March 5, 1955, in ibid., reel 6.

28. Cabinet Notes, January 15, 1954, Adams Papers, Box 8, Baker Library, Dartmouth; "228th Meeting of the NSC," December 9, 1954, Ann Whitman File,

National Security Council Series, Box 6; Maxwell M. Rabb to Thomas J. Donegan, May 17, 1956, White House Office, Cabinet Secretariat Records, 1953–60, Series I, Subseries B, Box 10.

29. Johnson, "Eisenhower Personnel Security Program," p. 625.

30. Kunetka, *Oppenheimer*, pp. 32–41, 114–17; Goodchild, *J. Robert Oppenheimer*, pp. 86–99, 174–90. Useful on the physicist's early life and wartime experiences is Oppenheimer, *Letters*. Haakon Chevalier gives his account of his relationship with the physicist in *Oppenheimer*.

31. Stern, *Oppenheimer Case*, pp. 168–211 passim; Goodchild, *J. Robert Oppenheimer*, pp. 195–211; Pearson, *Diaries*, p. 305; Lilienthal, *Journals* 3:521–23.

32. Goodchild, *J. Robert Oppenheimer*, pp. 217–18; Oshinsky, *A Conspiracy So Immense*, p. 360.

33. William L. Borden to J. Edgar Hoover, November 7, 1953, in Atomic Energy Commission, *J. Robert Oppenheimer*, pp. 837–38.

34. According to the journalist Warren W. Unna, Brownell and Hoover visited the White House shortly after receiving Borden's letter to demand that Oppenheimer's clearance be revoked. See "Dissension in the AEC." Hoover's response to Unna's story was to claim that he had not gone to Eisenhower to demand such action, an answer that leaves in question whether Hoover was denying a visit to the White House or an attempt to have Oppenheimer dismissed. J. Edgar Hoover to Editor, undated, in *Atlantic Monthly*, August 1957, pp. 24–25. Cf. Stern, *Oppenheimer Case*, p. 220. The tone of Eisenhower's diary entries for December 2 and 3, admittedly an impressionistic matter, seems to suggest, however, that he had not had an extensive or detailed briefing on the charges against Oppenheimer until the first of December.

35. Borden to Hoover, November 7, 1953, in Atomic Energy Commission, *J. Robert Oppenheimer*, pp. 837–38.

36. Donovan, *Eisenhower*, p. 294–95; memorandum, December 2, 1953, in Eisenhower, *Diaries*, ed. Lester, reel 3; Eisenhower, *Diaries*, ed. Ferrell, pp. 259–60; Eisenhower, *White House Years: Mandate for Change*, pp. 310–11. Notwithstanding Eisenhower's disclaimer, the political implications of the Oppenheimer affair were, of course, obvious, and they were heightened by the rumor that William Jenner's internal security subcommittee intended to conduct its own review. See Strauss, *Men and Decisions*, p. 276.

37. Eisenhower, *Diaries*, ed. Ferrell, pp. 260–61; Strauss, *Men and Decisions*, pp. 267–69; Eisenhower, *White House Years: Mandate for Change*, pp. 310–15; DDE to Herbert Brownell, December 3, 1953, in Eisenhower, *Diaries*, ed. Lester, reel 2.

38. Kenneth D. Nichols to Robert Oppenheimer, December 23, 1953, in Atomic Energy Commission, *J. Robert Oppenheimer*, pp. 3–7; Goodchild, *J. Robert Op-*

penheimer, pp. 234–35; Stern, *Oppenheimer Case*, pp. 258–62; Strauss, *Men and Decisions*, p. 279. Eisenhower possessed a high regard for Gray's character and judgment but once confided to a friend, "I do not suppose you would class him as an intellectual giant." DDE to Swede Hazlett, February 24, 1950, in Eisenhower, *Letters to a Friend*, pp. 68–75.

39. Goodchild, *J. Robert Oppenheimer*, pp. 224–35; Kunekta, *Oppenheimer*, p. 205; Stern, *Oppenheimer Case*, pp. 238–56, 369. To be sure, Lloyd Garrison, lead counsel for Oppenheimer, refused an offer from the AEC to seek a security clearance. The agency did not, however, offer the possibility of clearance to Garrison's co-counsel, and more important, such clearance would not have ensured Garrison access to all relevant classified information or have wholly solved the problem of the panel's use of material outside the record. Garrison, by not pursuing a security clearance for himself, apparently hoped to pressure the panel to minimize its use of classified information.

40. Hagerty, *Diary*, pp. 42–44; *Public Papers*, 1954, pp. 381–90; Lilienthal, *Journals* 3:499–501. Despite the allegedly confidential nature of the commission proceedings, James Reston of the *New York Times* knew of the charges against Oppenheimer in January, and the syndicated columnists Joseph and Stewart Alsop learned of them a short time thereafter. Kunekta, *Oppenheimer*, p. 219.

41. Atomic Energy Commission, *J. Robert Oppenheimer*, pp. 160–80, 372–82, 384–94, 398–425, 560–68, 731–42, 909–15. See also Green, "Oppenheimer Case," pp. 12–16, 56–61.

42. Interview with Gordon Gray, COHP, 1966–67, pp. 188–216; Atomic Energy Commission, *J. Robert Oppenheimer*, pp. 1ff, 44ff, 51ff.

43. Hagerty, *Diaries*, pp. 58–59, 61, 80–81; *Public Papers*, 1954, pp. 434–35, 530; DDE to Lewis Strauss, June 10, 1954, in Eisenhower, *Diaries*, ed. Lester, reel 4.

44. Gordon Gray to Ward V. Evans, June 9, 1954, and Gordon Gray to Ernest M. Eller, June 8, 1954, Gordon Gray Papers, Box 4; Lilienthal, *Journals* 3:519–21; Kunekta, *Oppenheimer*, pp. 252–54; Strout, "Oppenheimer Case," pp. 268–80.

45. Memorandum by Paul T. Carroll, July 9, 1953, White House Central Files, Official File, Box 66; Shanley Diaries, Box 2, p. 1589; unsigned memorandum, April 26, 1954, in Eisenhower, *Diaries*, ed. Lester, reel 3; DDE to James B. Conant, April 26, 1954 (unsent), in ibid., reel 4; Eisenhower, *White House Years: Mandate for Change*, pp. 310–15. The Oppenheimer case, to be sure, created a reciprocal animosity. Eisenhower, in a rare public display of anger, described Strauss's defeat as "one of the most depressing official disappointments" of his presidency. He attributed the Senate's action to "the maneuverings of jealous, vindictive and little men," among

whom he expressly included Margaret Chase Smith, an anti-McCarthy Republican liberal. Eisenhower, *White House Years: Waging Peace*, pp. 392–96.

46. Stern, *Oppenheimer Case*, p. 498; Anderson, *Outsider in the Senate*, pp. 184–221; Kennan, *Memoirs, 1950–1963*, p. 20; Green, "Oppenheimer Case," p. 12ff.

47. Eisenhower, *White House Years: Mandate for Change*, p. 308; *Minutes and Documents of the Cabinet*, March 5, 1954, reel 1; DDE to Cabinet, March 5, 1954, in Eisenhower, *Diaries*, ed. Lester, reel 3.

48. Eisenhower, *White House Years: Mandate for Change*, p. 301ff; Hagerty, *Diary*, p. 156.

49. Eisenhower, *Diaries*, ed. Ferrell, p. 256ff; *Minutes and Documents of the Cabinet*, October 30, 1953, reel 1.

50. DDE to Herbert Brownell, July 2, 1953, Ann Whitman File, Administration Series, Box 8; DDE to Herbert Brownell, November 5, 1953, in Eisenhower, *Diaries*, ed. Lester, reel 2; *Minutes and Documents of the Cabinet*, January 7, 1953, reel 2, and May 16, 1956, reel 5; interview with Dwight D. Eisenhower, COHP, July 23, 1967, p. 99; Philip Young to Sherman Adams, May 14, 1956, White House Central Files, Confidential File, Box 66.

51. *Minutes and Documents of the Cabinet*, September 25, 1953, reel 1, and July 2, 1954, reel 2; "189th Meeting of the National Security Council," March 19, 1954, Ann Whitman File, National Security Council Series, Box 5.

52. Memorandum by DDE, March 18, 1953, in Eisenhower, *Diaries*, ed. Lester, reel 2. See also DDE to Aaron W. Berg, March 28, 1953, in ibid., reel 6, and *Minutes and Documents of the Cabinet*, March 20, 1953, reel 1. Interestingly, administration officials did not consider the departmental security officers to be entirely reliable. Many of them were holdovers from the Truman administration. *Minutes and Documents of the Cabinet*, February 16, 1954, reel 1; Roger Steffan to Sherman Adams, February 16, 1954, White House Central Files, Confidential File, Box 66. For more on Eisenhower and the patronage issue, see Brendon, *Ike*, pp. 241–43, and Ambrose, *Eisenhower: The President*, pp. 151–52.

53. Memorandum by L. A. Minnich, April 10, 1953, Adams Papers, Box 9, Baker Library, Dartmouth; *U.S. News and World Report*, May 1, 1953, pp. 22–24; Gray, *Eighteen Acres*, pp. 77–78; Knowland interview, COHP, June 20, 1967, pp. 9–10, 130–36.

54. *Minutes and Documents of the Cabinet*, May 8, 1953, reel 1, and October 30, 1953, reel 1; "Supplementary Notes" by L. A. Minnich, March 30, 1953, in Eisenhower, *Diaries*, ed. Lester, reel 2; Morgan interview, COHP, April 29, 1968, pp. 42–46; unsigned memorandum, February 8, 1955, Ann Whitman File, Ann Whit-

man Diary Series, Box 4; interview with Roger W. Jones, COHP, July 13, 1967, p. 45; Gray, *Eighteen Acres*, pp. 61–64, 77–78.

55. Bontecou quoted in *New York Times*, September 13, 1954, p. 10; Anthony Lewis to Bernard M. Shanley, January 4, 1954, and Walter P. Reuther to DDE, January 18, 1955, both in White House Central Files, Official File, Box 481.

56. *Johnston Subcommittee Hearings*, pp. 1299–301; *Humphrey Subcommittee Hearings*, pp. 437ff, 478ff.

57. Donovan, *Eisenhower*, pp. 287, 297–98; Pusey, *Eisenhower*, pp. 274–83; *New York Times*, November 16, 1954, p. 28; *Minutes and Documents of the Cabinet*, November 19, 1954, reel 2.

58. On Cain's break with the administration, see *New York Times*, January 16, 1955, p. 71, and June 3, 1955, pp. 1, 14. See also Harry Cain to Sherman Adams, June 30, 1955, Rogers Papers, Box 47.

58. *Humphrey Subcommittee Hearings*, pp. 66–67; Stern, *Oppenheimer Case*, pp. 490–91; Association of the Bar of the City of New York, *Federal Loyalty-Security Program*, pp. 114–24. A leading student of the subject concluded, "We find no responsible claims that the loyalty-security programs have caught a single known spy." Brown, *Loyalty and Security*, p. 36 n. 21.

59. von Hoffman, *Citizen Cohn*, p. 187ff. On McCarthy's private life, see Oshinsky, *A Conspiracy So Immense*, pp. 17, 28–29, 56, 59, 231–32, 465, 503–5; Reeves, *Joe McCarthy*, pp. 637–72 passim; and Rovere, *McCarthy*, pp. 52, 44–47. On Cohn, see von Hoffman, *Citizen Cohn*, pp. 3–40, and Zion, *Autobiography of Roy Cohn*, pp. 235–46. A leading biographer of Hoover concludes that it is uncertain whether Hoover and Tolson actually consummated a homosexual union but writes that they at least enjoyed a "spousal relationship." Powers, *Secrecy and Power*, pp. 169–73. Cf. von Hoffman, *Citizen Cohn*, pp. 338–39.

60. *Public Papers*, 1954, pp. 336–37; *Minutes and Documents of the Cabinet*, June 11, 1954, reel 2.

61. Rosenbloom, *Federal Service and the Constitution*, p. 169; McCloskey, *American Supreme Court*, pp. 203–204; Murphy, *Constitution in Crisis Times*, p. 30.

62. *New York Times*, June 3, 1953, p. 1, June 14, 1953, Section IV, p. 2, and September 12, 1953, p. 11; October 12, 1954, press release, Herbert Brownell to DDE, July 30, 1954, and William Hopkins to James S. Lay, August 5, 1954, all in White House Central Files, Official File, Box 481.

63. *Minutes and Documents of the Cabinet*, October 23, 1953, reel 1; Philip Young to Sherman Adams, January 13, 1955, White House Central Files, Confidential File, Box 66.

Chapter 5

1. Memorandum, *Minutes and Documents of the Cabinet*, January 12, 1953, reel 1.

2. Murphy, *Diplomat among Warriors*, pp. 364–65. See also interview with John W. Hanes, Jr., COHP, December 30, 1970, pp. 15–18.

3. See Kennan, *Memoirs, 1950–1963*, pp. 190–93.

4. "Secretary Dulles' Message to His New Associates," January 21, 1953, in *Department of State Bulletin*, February 2, 1953, pp. 170–71; *Minutes and Documents of the Cabinet*, March 27, 2953, reel 1; *Time*, March 23, 1953, p. 21.

5. Hoopes, *John Foster Dulles*, pp. 135–41; Drummond and Coblentz, *Duel at the Brink*, pp. 20–35; Eisenhower, *Diaries*, ed. Ferrell, p. 237; Hanes interview, COHP, December 30, 1970, pp. 8–21; interview with Andrew H. Berding, COHP, October 19, 1972, pp. 8–9.

6. Interview with Dwight D. Eisenhower, COHP, July 28, 1964, p. 12ff. On the development of the relationship between Eisenhower and Dulles, see interview with Emmet J. Hughes, John Foster Dulles Oral History Project, Princeton University (hereafter cited as JFDOHP), April 22, 1965, p. 10ff, and interview with Gabriel Hague, JFDOHP, January 25, 1966, pp. 19–21.

7. Quoted in Hoopes, *John Foster Dulles*, p. 141.

8. Interview with George V. Allen, COHP, March 1967, p. 34ff; interview with Eleanor Lansing Dulles, COHP, May 4, 1964, pp. 523–24. See also Guhin, *John Foster Dulles*, pp. 186–93, and interview with Robert D. Murphy, JFDOHP, May 19, 1965, pp. 22–23. For a revisionist view of Dulles, suggesting that his notion of a monolithic communism bent on world conquest was more subtle and sophisticated than long imagined, see Gaddis, "John Foster Dulles."

9. Kennan, *Memoirs, 1950–1963*, p. 184. See also interview with Robinson McIlvaine, DEOHP, July 7, 1978, p. 7ff. For a contrary view, see interview with Donald B. Lourie, JFDOHP, April 8, 1965, p. 24ff. Apparently sensitive to Dulles's brusque demeanor, even Eisenhower privately felt doubts about the secretary of state "in the general field of personality." Eisenhower, *Diaries*, ed. Ferrell, p. 236.

10. Drummond and Coblentz, *Duel at the Brink*, p. 65; "Effect of Security Program on Foreign Service," *Department of State Bulletin*, February 1, 1954, p. 169; John Foster Dulles (hereafter cited as JFD) to Henry P. Van Dusen, May 27, 1958, Dulles Papers, Chron. Series, Box 16.

11. Kennan, *Memoirs, 1950–1963*, vol. 2, pp. 180–81; diary entry, June 24, 1953, Hughes Papers, Box 1, Sealy G. Mudd Library, Princeton University. See also Hughes, *Ordeal of Power*, pp. 88–94; Murphy, *Diplomat among Warriors*, p. 448; and Lilienthal, *Journals* 3:376.

12. "Memorandum of Telephone Conversation," February 19, 1953, in Slany, *Foreign Relations of the United States* 1:1436–37. See also Parmet, *Eisenhower*, p. 233. Dulles had, in fact, once written, "There is no reason to doubt Mr. Hiss' complete loyalty to our American institutions." JFD to Mr. Davidow, December 26, 1946, Dulles Papers, Box 70, Sealy G. Mudd Library, Princeton University.

13. Dulles was willing, however, to let the IIA director defend the organization on his own. See John J. McCloy to JFD, undated, and JFD to John J. McCloy, July 20, 1953, Dulles Papers, Gen. Corp. Series, Box 3.

14. Interview with Charles E. Bohlen, COHP, December 17, 1970, pp. 1–7; Hoopes, *John Foster Dulles*, pp. 141–43; JFD to Maude Pellegrino, December 10, 1953, Dulles Papers, Box 70, Sealy G. Mudd Library, Princeton University.

15. "Press Conference Statement by Secretary Dulles," February 27, 1953, in *Department of State Bulletin*, March 9, 1953, pp. 390–91.

16. "Memorandum of Telephone Conversation," February 12, 1953, in Slany, *Foreign Relations of the United States* 2:1670–71. In a similar vein, when McCarthy told Dulles that he planned to begin a review of the State Department's filing system, Dulles readily conceded that "he knew from previous experience that once anything was filed here it was lost." "Memorandum of Telephone Conversation," January 28, 1953, in ibid. 1:1433–34.

17. JFD to Reuben B. Robertson, December 1, 1952, Dulles Papers, Subject Series, Box 8.

18. Interview with Walter S. Robertson, COHP, April 18, 1967, pp. 1–34 passim; Hoopes, *John Foster Dulles*, pp. 146–47. For a sample of Robertson's substantive views on foreign policy, which included optimism regarding the ability of the French to defeat the Viet Minh and the belief that Vietnam was one of the "gateways" to Communist domination of all Asia, see "The Communist Campaign in the Far East," October 14, 1953, in *Department of State Bulletin*, November 2, 1953, pp. 59295.

19. "Office of the Under Secretary for Administration Established," *Department of State Bulletin*, March 30, 1953, p. 487; Donald B. Lourie to JFD, December 23, 1952, and Thurston Morton to JFD, January 8, 1953, both in Dulles Papers, Subject Series, Box 8.

20. Hoopes, *John Foster Dulles*, pp. 151–58; Hughes, *Ordeal of Power*, pp. 84–85; Hill interview, COHP, October 19, 1972, pp. 8–9.

21. Conversation with Sherman Adams, March 19, 1953, in Kesaris and Gibson, *Telephone Conversations*, reel 8.

22. "Interview with R. W. Scott McLeod," *U.S. News and World Report*, February 12, 1954, pp. 62–73.

23. "Address by Mr. Scott McLeod, American Legion Convention, Topeka, KS,

August 18, 1953," in Dulles, *Papers*, reel 5; Mr. English to Mr. McCardle, December 31, 1953, and memorandum by Ward Cameron, February 1954, both in John W. Hanes, Jr., Papers, Box 5. See also Hoopes, *John Foster Dulles*, pp. 158–60.

24. Bohlen interview, COHP, December 17, 1970, pp. 1–7. See also Bohlen, *Witness to History*, pp. 335–36. Excellent on McLeod's career is Purdum, "Politics of Security."

25. Philip D. Reed to DDE, June 8, 1953, and DDE to JFD, June 17, 1953, both in Dulles, *Papers*, reel 1; interview with Francis O. Wilcox, COHP, April 3, 1972, pp. 25–26.

26. "Memorandum and Discussion of the 153rd meeting of the National Security Council," July 9, 1953, in Slany, *Foreign Relations of the United States* 1:1462–63.

27. "Memorandum by the Secretary of State to the President," July 23, 1953, in ibid., p. 1464; "The Secretary of State to Certain Diplomatic Missions," July 23, 1953, in ibid., p. 1465; "Memorandum of Discussion at the 157th Meeting of the National Security Council," July 30, 1953, in ibid., pp. 1466–68.

28. "Draft Memorandum Prepared in the Bureau of European Affairs," undated, in ibid., pp. 1469–80.

29. "Special Report Prepared by the Psychological Strategy Board," September 11, 1953, in ibid., pp. 1480–525.

30. "Memorandum of Discussion at the 164th Meeting of the National Security Council," October 1, 1953, in ibid., pp. 1545–48. See also "Memorandum by the Executive Secretary of the National Security Council to the NSC," September 24, 1953, in ibid., pp. 1527–43.

31. William Clark to JFD, December 2, 1953, Dulles Papers, Gen. Corp. Series, Box 2; "The Ambassador in the United Kingdom to the Department of States," March 4, 1954, in Slany, *Foreign Relations of the United States* 1:1548–51; "The Ambassador in France to the Department of State," March 31, 1954, in ibid., pp. 1552–56; "Memorandum Prepared in the International Exchange Service of the Bureau of Public Affairs," undated, in ibid., pp. 1557–59.

32. U.S. Congress, Senate, 84th Cong., 2d sess., Report No. 2750, pp. 508–13; Paul Gordon Lauren, "The China Hands: An Introduction," in Lauren, *China Hands' Legacy*, pp. 1–36; Kahn, *China Hands*, p. 35. The Sevareid quote is from ibid.

33. Ernest R. May, "The China Hands in Perspective: Ethics, Diplomacy, and Statecraft," in Lauren, *China Hands' Legacy*, pp. 97–123; Kahn, *China Hands*, pp. 1–22.

34. "Davies, Vincent Loyalty Cases: Loyalty Review Board's Findings," *Department of State Bulletin*, January 19, 1953, p. 121. See also Koen, *China Lobby*, pp. 163–64.

35. "President Authorizes New Review of Vincent Case," *Department of State*

Bulletin, January 19, 1953, pp. 122–23; Acheson, *Present at the Creation*, pp. 710–13.

36. "Secretary Dulles to Examine Case of John Carter Vincent," *Department of State Bulletin*, February 9, 1953, p. 241; Acheson, *Present at the Creation*, pp. 711–14; May, *China Scapegoat*, p. 264ff.

37. "Secretary Dulles' Memorandum on John Carter Vincent," *Department of State Bulletin*, March 23, 1953, pp. 454–55; May, *China Scapegoat*, p. 264ff; John Carter Vincent to JFD, February 28, 1953; Herman Phleger to JFD, February 24, 1953, both in Dulles Papers, Subject Series, Box 7.

38. Acheson, *Present at the Creation*, p. 713.

39. May, *China Scapegoat*, p. 275.

40. "Davies, Vincent Loyalty Cases," *Department of State Bulletin*, p. 121.

41. William P. Rogers to William E. Jenner, July 6, 1953, Rogers Papers, Box 15; Kennan, *Memoirs, 1950–1963*, pp. 200–214; *U.S. News and World Report*, December 11, 1953, p. 26ff; Kahn, *China Hands*, p. 258. With customary inaccuracy, McCarthy's speech identified Davies as serving in Germany, when in fact he had, by that time, been assigned to Peru.

42. "Memorandum of the Conversation between Scott McLeod and John Paton Davies, Jr.," January 19, 1954, in Dulles Papers, Subject Series, Box 3. See also Kahn, *China Hands*, p. 246.

43. Security Hearing Board to JFD, August 30, 1954, and "Memorandum of Security Hearing Board," August 30, 1954, both in Dulles Papers, Subject Series, Box 3. See also "Press Conference Statement by Secretary Dulles," March 23, 1954, in *Department of State Bulletin*, April 5, 1954, p. 528. It is interesting to note at least two similarities between the Davies case and that of J. Robert Oppenheimer, in addition to the fact that both men were ultimately condemned on old charges of which they had previously been exonerated. First, in both instances, the adverse decisions rested in part on their allegedly evasive testimony, a subjective factor that suggests that the hearings were not simply investigations into the evidence but were tests of the suspects' character. Second, both men were found guilty of the rather Orwellian crime of independent thinking. Davies was allegedly "prone to place his judgment above that of any person or group with whom" he was "not in accord." Compare this with the charge that Oppenheimer was guilty of "the arrogance of his own judgment." "Findings and Recommendations of the Personnel Security Board," in Atomic Energy Commission, *J. Robert Oppenheimer*, p. 20.

44. "Determination in the Case of John Paton Davies, Jr.," November 5, 1954, in *Department of State Bulletin*, November 15, 1954, pp. 752–54.

45. News clipping, November 17, 1954, Dulles Papers, Box 80, Sealy G. Mudd Library, Princeton University; *Foreign Service Journal*, May 1954, p. 38. See also

New York Times, November 16, 1954, p. 28; *Foreign Service Journal*, December 1954, pp. 34–35, and January 1954, pp. 36–38, 42.

46. JFD to William Phillips, November 22, 1954, Dulles Papers, Subject Series, Box 3. See also *New York Times*, November 16, 1954, p. 28.

47. *Minutes and Documents of the Cabinet*, November 19, 1954, reel 2.

48. "228th Meeting of the National Security Council," December 10, 1954, Ann Whitman File, National Security Council Series, Box 6; John W. Hanes to R. L. O'Connor, December 8, 1954, Henry Cabot Lodge to JFD, December 7, 1954, and JFD to Henry Cabot Lodge, December 9, 1954, all in Dulles Papers, Subject Series, Box 3. See also interview with Charles E. Saltzman, JFDOHP, March 1, 1967, pp. 12–18.

49. *Minutes and Documents of the Cabinet*, November 19, 1954, reel 2; JFD to William Phillips, November 20, 1954, Dulles Papers, Subject Series, Box 3.

50. John W. Hanes, Jr., to JFD, January 8, 1954, Dulles Papers, Special Assistant Chronological Series, Box 4; *Minutes and Documents of the Cabinet*, November 19, 1954, reel 2; *Public Papers*, 1954, p. 1065.

51. Cohen, *America's Response to China*, pp. 212–13. For a conventional liberal assessment of the eventual impact of the purge of the China Hands, see Kahn, *China Hands*, p. 275. See also Davies, *Foreign and Other Affairs*. For a reassessment of the consequences of the controversy, see May, "China Hands in Perspective," and John F. Melby, "The China Hands: An Overview," in Lauren, *China Hands' Legacy*, pp. 124–38.

52. Murphy, *Diplomat among Warriors*, p. 365; Caute, *Great Fear*, pp. 325–30; *Time*, November 24, 1952, p. 32; "Presentment of the Federal Grand Jury on Disloyalty of Certain United States Citizens at the United Nations," December 2, 1952, in *U.S. News and World Report*, December 12, 1952, p. 88ff. See also ibid., pp. 32, 34. For examples of coverage of the Communist controversy by *U.S. News and World Report*, see its editions of December 20, 1953, p. 128, and November 27, 1953, p. 21ff.

53. Acheson, *Present at the Creation*, pp. 713–14; "Statement by John D. Hickerson," December 31, 1952, in *Department of State Bulletin*, January 12, 1953, pp. 58–61; "Executive Order No. 10422," ibid., pp. 62–63.

54. Wilcox interview, COHP, April 3, 1972, p. 28ff. See also Huss and Carpozi, *Red Spies*, pp. 50ff, 111ff.

55. U.S. Congress, Senate, 83d Cong., 1st sess., *Hearings before the Committee on Foreign Relations on the Nomination of Henry Cabot Lodge to be United States Representative to the United Nations*, p. 1ff; U.S. Congress, House, 83d Cong., 2d sess., *Hearings before the Subcommittee on International Organizations and Movements of the Committee on Foreign Affairs*, p. 2ff; Henry Cabot Lodge (hereafter cited

as HCL) to William Henry Harrison, March 10, 1953, Lodge Papers, Box 95, MHS. See also Fedder, "United States Loyalty Procedures."

56. Lodge, *As It Was*, pp. 53–54.

57. See HCL to Donald B. Lourie, April 7, 1953, Lodge Papers, Box 79, MHS, and Murphy, *Diplomat among Warriors*, pp. 366–68.

58. "HCL to J. Edgar Hoover," January 25, 1953, in *Department of State Bulletin*, February 9, 1953, p. 229; HCL to Trygve Lie, January 29, 1953, Lodge Papers, Box 79, MHS. For Lodge's correspondence with key legislators, see Lodge Papers, Box 79, MHS.

59. Scott McLeod to HCL, April 7, 1953, Lodge Papers, Box 79, MHS. See also HCL to Scott McLeod, April 9, 1953, ibid.

60. Lodge, *As It Was*, pp. 53–54; HCL to Herbert Brownell, February 7, 1953, Herbert Brownell to HCL, February 13, 1953, HCL to Scott McLeod, April 9, 1953, Herbert Brownell to HCL, July 9, 1953, and HCL to Herbert Brownell, July 13, 1953, all in Lodge Papers, Box 79, MHS; HCL to Herbert Brownell, June 30, 1954, Ann Whitman File, Administration Series, Box 7.

61. HCL to Philip Young, April 15, 1953, Lodge Papers, Box 79, MHS. See also Philip Young to HCL, April 13, 1953, ibid.; *New York Times*, June 3, 1953, p. 1; and "Investigation of U.S. Citizens on the U.N. Secretariat," *Department of State Bulletin*, June 1953, pp. 882–83.

62. *New York Times*, June 30, 1954, pp. 1, 2; HCL to Herbert Brownell, June 30, 1954, Ann Whitman File, Administration Series, Box 7; memorandum re International Organizations Employees Loyalty Program, September 4, 1956, Louis S. Rothschild Papers, Box 8.

63. Fedder, "United States Loyalty Procedures"; Dag Hammarskjöld to HCL, August 13, 1953, in Slany, *Foreign Relations of the United States* 3:346–47; HCL to Dag Hammarskjöld, August 14, 1953, in ibid., p. 347. President Eisenhower experienced firsthand the problems presented by the quest for security at the UN. Early in his presidency, he had hoped to appoint Mildred McAfee Horton, the former WAVES commander, to represent the United States at a meeting of the UN's Social Commission, but she failed to receive a security clearance in time. DDE to Mildred McAfee Horton, June 8, 1953, in Eisenhower, *Diaries*, ed. Lester, reel 2.

64. James J. Wadsworth to HCL, August 7, 1953, in Slany, *Foreign Relations of the United States* 3:342; Dag Hammarskjöld to HCL, August 20, 1953, in ibid., pp. 348–50; James J. Wadsworth to Donald Lourie, August 28, 1953, in ibid., p. 348; memorandum of conversation by William O. Hall, October 23, 1953, in ibid., pp. 360–61.

65. Memorandum to Philip Young, June 8, 1954, Adams Papers, Box 8, Baker Library, Dartmouth; Robert Murphy to the Embassy in Switzerland, June 1, 1954, in Slany, *Foreign Relations of the United States* 3:390–91; JFD to the Embassy in

Switzerland, June 11, 1954, in ibid., pp. 394–95; Frances E. Willis to Department of State, June 16, 1954, in ibid., pp. 392–94. At one point, the American ambassador to Switzerland recommended that the hearings scheduled for Geneva be moved to Paris. Fearful of "unfavorable local publicity," John Foster Dulles initially opposed the overseas hearings but then decided that if Philip Young went along as Eisenhower's personal representative, foreign observers would be sufficiently reassured. Francis E. Willis to Department of State, July 2, 1954, in ibid., pp. 396–98; JFD to Sherman Adams, June 7, 1954, Adams Papers, Box 8, Baker Library, Dartmouth.

66. "Statement by Henry Cabot Lodge," March 28, 1953, in *Department of State Bulletin*, April 27, 1953, pp. 260–23; "JFD to Certain Diplomatic and Consular Offices," October 5, 1953, in Slany, *Foreign Relations of the United States* 3:352–56.

67. "Memorandum of Conversation by Robert Murphy," September 2, 1953, in Slany, *Foreign Relations of the United States* 3:350; *U.S. News and World Report*, October 16, 1953, p. 27; *New York Times*, June 14, 1953, p. 2. See also U.S. Congress, Senate, 83d Cong., 1st sess., Report No. 223, and U.S. Congress, Senate, 83d Cong., 2d sess., *Hearings before the Subcommittee to Investigate the Administration of the Internal Security Act and Other Internal Security Laws*. By fall 1953, William Jenner was suggesting to the White House that the Soviet Union be expelled from the UN if it failed to terminate its "fifth column" there. Eisenhower politely dismissed the notion. See William E. Jenner to DDE, September 16, 1953; Gerald D. Morgan to William E. Jenner, November 16, 1953; and DDE to William E. Jenner, November 30, 1953, all in White House Central Files, Official File, Box 659.

68. "Memorandum of Conversation by Robert Murphy," September 11, 1953, in Slany, *Foreign Relations of the United States* 3:351–52.

69. "JFD to the Embassy in France," October 21, 1953, in ibid., pp. 359–60. See also "JFD to the Embassy in the United Kingdom," November 3, 1953, in ibid., pp. 361–63.

70. "Memorandum of Conversation by James J. Wadsworth," November 4, 1953, in ibid., pp. 365–66.

71. "JFD to the Mission at the United Nations," November 30, 1953, in ibid., pp. 376–77. See also "The Ambassador in the United Kingdom to the Department of State," November 12, 1953, in ibid., p. 368; "Memorandum of Conversation by Douglas MacArthur, Jr.," November 19, 1953, in ibid., pp. 370–71; "The Chargé in France to the Department of State," November 23, 1953, in ibid., p. 371; and "The Ambassador in Belgium to the Department of State," November 27, 1953, in ibid., pp. 372–73.

72. "The Chargé in the United Kingdom to the Department of State," November 9, 1953, in ibid. 3:366; "Memorandum of conversation by Douglas MacArthur, Jr.," November 19, 1953, in ibid., pp. 370–71; "JFD to the Embassy in the United King-

dom," November 25, 1953, in ibid., pp. 374–75; "HCL to the Department of State," November 30, 1953, in ibid., p. 376.

73. "The Acting Secretary of State to Certain Diplomatic Missions," January 22, 1954, in ibid., pp. 377–82.

74. "The Ambassador in the Netherlands to the Department of State," July 13, 1954, in ibid., p. 398. See also "JFD to the Mission at the United Nations," November 25, 1953, in ibid., pp. 375–76.

75. H. R. Gross to HCL, December 7, 1954, and HCL to H. R. Gross, December 10, 1954, both in Lodge Papers, Box 95, MHS; William E. Jenner to HCL, July 16, 1954, in Slany, *Foreign Relations of the United States* 3:400–402.

76. HCL to H. R. Gross, December 22, 1954, Lodge Papers, Box 95, MHS; "Position Paper Prepared in the Department of State for the United States Delegation to the Ninth Regular Session of the General Assembly," September 9, 1954, in Slany, *Foreign Relations of the United States* 3:403–407. See also editorial note in ibid., p. 409.

77. Kahn, *China Lobby*, p. 7. On State Department morale, see generally Allen interview, COHP, March 1967, p. 34ff; Hanes interview, COHP, December 30, 1970, pp. 15–18; and McIlvanie interview, DEOHP, July 7, 1978, p. 7.

78. Morgenthau, "Loyalty-Security Measures," p. 139. See also Paul D. Tillet, "The Social Costs of the Loyalty Programs," (1964), p. 35ff, Paul D. Tillet, Jr., Papers, Box 1, Sealy G. Mudd Library, Princeton University.

79. "Rededication of Memorial to Foreign Service Officers," October 11, 1954, in *Department of State Bulletin*, November 1, 1954, pp. 437–38; interview with Loy W. Henderson, COHP, December 14, 1970, pp. 29–34; *Public Papers*, 1954, pp. 288–97; *Public Papers*, 1957, pp. 281–83. See also interview with Loy W. Henderson, JFDOHP, November 7, 1964, pp. 47–51.

80. Interview with Charles E. Bohlen, JFDOHP, June 23, 1964, pp. 12–15; interview with Herbert Brownell, JFDOHP, March 5, 1965, pp. 38–39.

81. See, for example, State Department Press Release No. 347, June 23, 1958, Dulles Papers, Box 135, Sealy G. Mudd Library, Princeton University.

82. Interview with Judd, December 11, 1965, in Judd, *Chronicles*, pp. 339–60. See also interview with Walter H. Judd, COHP, December 18, 1970, pp. 110–15.

83. See, for example, Divine's laudatory *Eisenhower and the Cold War*. But compare Brands's "Age of Vulnerability."

Chapter 6

1. Adams, *Without Precedent*, pp. 46–49, 70–74; Straight, *Trial by Television*, p. 52; memorandum by John L. Saltonstall, Jr., October 6, 1953, memorandum by C.

A. Haskins, October 9, 1953, and John G. Adams to Secretary of the Army, November 19, 1953, all in Fred A. Seaton Papers, FAS Eyes Only Series, Box 4. On McCarthy's investigation of Fort Monmouth, see U.S. Congress, Senate, 83d Cong., 1st sess., *Hearings before the Permanent Subcommittee on Investigations of the Committee on Government Operations on the Army Signal Corps—Subversion and Espionage*. All of the employees who had been suspended by the army were ultimately cleared. Adams, *Without Precedent*, pp. 70–74.

2. See Hensel's statement in "Recollections of HSH re Connection with Congressional Investigating Committee Problems and Particularly the McCarthy Subcommittee's Investigation of the Army," April 23, 1954, pp. 1–2, John G. Adams to Secretary of the Army, December 10, 1953, memorandum by John G. Adams, December 14, 1953, and John G. Adams to Attorney General, November 14 and December 4, 1953, all in Seaton Papers, FAS Eyes Only Series, Box 4; memorandum by Joseph W. Bishop, Jr., October 23, 1953, Seaton Papers, FAS Eyes Only Series, Box 6; Adams, *Without Precedent*, p. 95ff. Truman's letter to Acheson appears in *Public Papers*, 1952–53, pp. 235–36.

3. Straight, *Trial by Television*, pp. 22–23; John G. Adams to Secretary of the Army, December 29, 1953, Seaton Papers, FAS Eyes Only Series, Box 5. The army did not attempt to substantiate the rumor that Cohn was in love with Schine. In the words of one army lawyer, "We didn't try very hard, we didn't bug him." von Hoffman, *Citizen Cohn*, pp. 188–91. In the opinion of Senator Ralph E. Flanders of Vermont, however, Cohn and Schine enjoyed "an unsavory kind of relationship." According to Flanders, who played a critical role in McCarthy's political demise, "Anybody with half an eye could see what was going on." Interview with Ralph E. Flanders, COHP, February 4, 1967, pp. 7–8.

4. Ambrose, *Nixon*, pp. 132–35; Nixon, *Memoirs*, pp. 140–41.

5. Memorandum by John G. Adams, February 12, 1954, Seaton Papers, FAS Eyes Only Series, Box 6; Adams, *Without Precedent*, p. 11.

6. Memorandum by John G. Adams, February 12, 1954, Seaton Papers, FAS Eyes Only Series, Box 6; Adams, *Without Precedent*, pp. 112–13; Adams, *Firsthand Report*, pp. 133–34.

7. John G. Adams to General Trudeau, January 4, 1954, Seaton Papers, FAS Eyes Only Series, Box 5; Adams, *Firsthand Report*, pp. 145–56. On McCarthy's investigation of the Peress case, see U.S. Congress, Senate, 83d Cong., 2d sess., *Hearings before the Permanent Subcommittee on Investigations of the Committee on Government Operations—Communist Infiltration in the Army* (hereafter cited as *Peress Hearings*), p. 107ff. On Peress's military career, see "Chronology of the Military Record of Doctor Irving Peress," Seaton Papers, FAS Eyes Only Series, Box 4.

8. Eisenhower, *White House Years: Mandate for Change*, pp. 322–23; Straight, *Trial by Television*, p. 58.

9. *Peress Hearings*, p. 145ff; Straight, *Trial by Television*, p. 58; Adams, *Without Precedent*, pp. 126–27.

10. Nixon, *Memoirs*, pp. 141–42; Eisenhower, *Diaries*, ed. Ferrell, p. 245; Adams, *Without Precedent*, p. 130ff. On the administration's fading hopes for reconciliation with McCarthy during this period, see Shanley interview, DEOHP, May 16, 1975, pp. 66–70.

11. Nixon, *Memoirs*, pp. 141–42; Adams, *Firsthand Report*, pp. 146–48; "Memo of Understanding," February 24, 1953, in Adams, *Without Precedent*, p. 135.

12. Hagerty, *Diary*, p. 19; Nixon, *Memoirs*, pp. 141–42; Eisenhower, *White House Years: Mandate for Change*, p. 324; Shanley Diaries, p. 1453, Box 2; memorandum of telephone call to Lucius Clay, February 25, 1954, in Eisenhower, *Diaries*, ed. Lester, reel 3.

13. Hagerty, *Diary*, p. 20; Nixon, *Memoirs*, pp. 142–44; Adams, *Firsthand Report*, pp. 146–48; Shanley Diaries, pp. 1453–54, Box 2.

14. "Legislative Leadership Meeting," March 1, 1954, Ann Whitman File, Legislative Meetings Series, Box 1; Eisenhower, *White House Years: Mandate for Change*, p. 324ff.

15. Memorandum of telephone conversation with William F. Knowland, March 10, 1954, and diary entries of February 26, 1954, and March 5, 1954, all in Eisenhower, *Diaries*, ed. Lester, reel 3. See also Hagerty, *Diary*, pp. 20–25.

16. DDE to Paul Helms, March 9, 1954, in Eisenhower, *Diaries*, ed. Lester, reel 3; Hagerty, *Diary*, pp. 24–25, 28; *Public Papers*, 1954, pp. 288–97.

17. Stevenson's speech, entitled "Crusades, Communism, and Corruption," appears in Stevenson, *Papers* 4:327–34. See also Hagerty, *Diary*, pp. 30–36; Eisenhower, *White House Years: Mandate for Change*, p. 326; and telephone notes from Congressman Hillings, March 11, 1954, Nixon Papers, Box 18, NARS. Nixon gives his account of the speech in *Memoirs*, pp. 144–47. His address received a generally favorable response. See the material collected in folder 10 in Box 18 and in folders 1 and 2 in Box 19, Nixon Papers, NARS.

As late as March 1954, the administration lacked a united front against McCarthy. Nixon, fearful of the possible consequences for his popularity and for his efforts to conciliate McCarthy, had told Leonard Hall that he did not want to deliver the party's response to Stevenson. At about the same time, Defense Secretary Charles E. Wilson, in what Eisenhower regarded as an act of political naiveté, not insubordination, invited McCarthy to lunch at the Pentagon, thus throwing a "monkey wrench in carefully prepared plans" to ostracize him. Hagerty, *Diary*, pp. 28–29. See also Mazo, *Nixon*, pp. 136–39.

18. Lodge, *As It Was*, p. 132; C. D. Jackson to Richard M. Nixon, March 9, 1954, Jackson Records, Box 66; Ewald, *Who Killed Joe McCarthy?*, p. 214.

19. DDE to William E. Robinson, March 12, 1954, Robinson Papers, Box 2; Reinhard, *Republican Right*, pp. 121–23; Cohn, *McCarthy*, p. 110ff.

20. Gallup, *Gallup Poll* 2:1201–4, 1220.

21. William E. Robinson to DDE, March 17, 1954, in Eisenhower, *Diaries*, ed. Lester, reel 3; clipping from *Minneapolis Tribune*, May 2, 1954, and J. C. Cornelius to Robert Humphreys, February 11, 1954, both in Hall Papers, Box 126; John H. Crider to Sherman Adams, March 5, 1954, Adams Papers, Box 10, Baker Library, Dartmouth.

22. Reeves, *Joe McCarthy*, pp. 575–76. Good on the exposure of the bogus memoranda is Oshinsky, *A Conspiracy So Immense*, pp. 446–56.

23. Reeves, *Joe McCarthy*, pp. 574–80; Oshinsky, *A Conspiracy So Immense*, pp. 406–407; Griffith, *Politics of Fear*, pp. 249–50.

24. *Public Papers*, 1954, pp. 320–32; DDE to Swede Hazlett, March 18, 1954, in Eisenhower, *Letters to a Friend*, pp. 120–21.

25. Ewald, *Eisenhower*, p. 134; memorandum of telephone conversation with Karl Mundt, March 18, 1954, and memorandum of telephone conversation with William Knowland, March 20, 1954, both in Eisenhower, *Diaries*, ed. Lester, reel 3; Hagerty, *Diary*, pp. 33–34. According to John Adams, Postmaster General Arthur Summerfield, an Old Guard Republican and McCarthy ally within the administration, suggested a similar settlement—the dismissal of Cohn and Adams—to Secretary of Defense Charles Wilson. Adams, *Without Precedent*, p. 151.

26. Oshinsky, *A Conspiracy So Immense*, pp. 406–8; Adams, *Without Precedent*, pp. 152–57; Hagerty, *Diary*, pp. 32–33. Descriptions of the subcommittee members are drawn largely from Straight, *Trial by Television*, pp. 9ff, 115ff, 151ff, and 211ff, and U.S. Congress, Senate, 83d Cong., 2d sess., *Hearings before the Special Subcommittee on Investigations of the Committee on Government Operations: Special Senate Investigation* (hereafter cited as *Army-McCarthy Hearings*).

27. Oshinsky, *A Conspiracy So Immense*, pp. 408–9; Griffith, *Politics of Fear*, pp. 251–52; memorandum of telephone conversation with Karl Mundt, March 18, 1954, in Eisenhower, *Diaries*, ed. Lester, reel 3; Adams, *Without Precedent*, pp. 152–57. The candidates Mundt considered were clearly not selected for their objectivity. Morris, for example, had served as counsel to the Senate's internal security subcommittee; when the Republican lawyer was elected to a New York judgeship in November 1953, McCarthy boasted that Morris's victory demonstrated the popularity of the Communist issue. See Bean, *1954 Mid-Term Elections*, p. 8.

28. Milton Eisenhower to DDE, April 1, 1954, in Eisenhower, *Diaries*, ed. Lester,

reel 4; Oshinsky, *A Conspiracy So Immense*, pp. 409–10; Ewald, *Who Killed Joe McCarthy?* pp. 297–301.

29. Reeves, *Joe McCarthy*, pp. 581–86, 612–13; Gallup, *Gallup Poll* 2:1225. Increasingly fearful of his political future and physical safety, McCarthy began carrying a gun; on at least one occasion, he answered the door at his Washington home with a pistol in hand. The caller was Leonard Hall. See Nixon, *Memoirs*, pp. 147–49.

30. Oshinsky, *A Conspiracy So Immense*, pp. 416–17.

31. *Army-McCarthy Hearings*, p. 646ff; Straight, *Trial by Television*, pp. 234–55; Pearson, *Diaries*, p. 311.

32. DDE to Aaron W. Berg, April 7, 1954, and DDE to Dr. Milton Katz, April 8, 1954, both in Eisenhower, *Diaries*, ed. Lester, reel 4.

33. *Public Papers*, 1954, pp. 377–78, 450–59; Potter, *Days of Shame*, pp. 13–23, 182–90; DDE to Swede Hazlett, April 27, 1954, in Eisenhower, *Letters to a Friend*, pp. 124–26. Eisenhower apparently rebuffed Stevens's suggestion, at a May 29 meeting, that J. Edgar Hoover be instructed to testify and repudiate the "purloined letter." The president told Stevens that he wanted to avoid the hearings, "to keep the poison out of his system." Diary entry, May 29, 1954, Ann Whitman File, Ann Whitman Diary Series, Box 2.

34. Leonard W. Hall to William J. Morris, May 8, 1954, Hall Papers, Box 2. See also Pearson, *Diaries*, p. 311.

35. Griffith, *Politics of Fear*, p. 261; *Army-McCarthy Hearings*, p. 969ff; Adams, *Without Precedent*, pp. 185–86; Ewald, *Who Killed Joe McCarthy?*, pp. 332–34; Hagerty, *Diary*, pp. 51–52; Cohn, *McCarthy*, pp. 149–64.

36. *Army-McCarthy Hearings*, pp. 644ff, 822–23, 1038ff; *Time*, May 24, 1954, pp. 25–26.

37. *Army-McCarthy Hearings*, p. 1136ff; Attorney General to Sherman Adams, May 3, 1954, and William P. Rogers to DDE, May 2, 1954, both in Ann Whitman File, Administration Series, Box 8.

38. Ewald, *Who Killed Joe McCarthy?*, pp. 349–50; DDE to Henry Cabot Lodge, May 10, 1954, in Eisenhower, *Diaries*, ed. Lester, reel 4; Eisenhower, *Diaries*, ed. Ferrell, pp. 280–81.

39. Robert B. Anderson to Robert T. Stevens, May 13, 1954, Seaton Papers, FAS Eyes Only Series, Box 4; DDE to Charles Wilson, May 13, 1954, in Eisenhower, *Diaries*, ed. Lester, reel 4.

40. *Army-McCarthy Hearings*, pp. 1136ff, 1169ff.

41. Ibid., pp. 1249ff, 1263ff, 1280ff; Shanley Diaries, p. 1548, Box 2. The most accessible version of Eisenhower's letter to Wilson appears in *Public Papers*, 1954, pp. 483–85.

42. "Lawrence A. Minnich Notes," May 17, 1954, White House Office, Office of the Staff Secretary, LAM Series, Subseries A, Box 1; "Legislative Supplement," May 17, 1954, Adams Papers, Box 10, Baker Library, Dartmouth. Eisenhower denied at his press conference that responsibility for the army's actions passed to officials above Stevens after the January meeting. *Public Papers*, 1954, pp. 489–97. On Dirksen's efforts to limit the ban on executive testimony, see Adams, *Firsthand Report*, pp. 149–50, and Cohn, *McCarthy*, p. 176.

43. Hagerty, *Diary*, pp. 52–53. Eisenhower had previously promised that he would pardon any "Army witness" who was held in contempt of Congress for refusing to submit to abuse from Senator McCarthy. Cutler, *No Time for Rest*, p. 406 n. 3.

44. Ewald, *Eisenhower*, pp. 139–40; *New York Times*, May 18, 1954, p. 24; Berger, *Executive Privilege*, pp. 1, 213–14. On the origins of the modern doctrine of executive privilege, which lay in the Truman administration, see Schlesinger, *Imperial Presidency*, pp. 155–59, and *New York Times*, September 3, 1948, p. 5. When a later president attempted to invoke executive privilege during a criminal prosecution, a unanimous Supreme Court disposed of the claim of "uncontrolled discretion" on the elementary ground that it conflicted with the high court's duty, articulated in *Marbury v. Madison* (1803), to say what the law was. See Friedman, *United States v. Nixon*, p. 612.

45. Straight, *Trial by Television*, pp. 122, 143–44; *Time*, May 24, 1954, pp. 25–26.

46. *Army-McCarthy Hearings*, p. 1263ff; Gallup, *Gallup Poll* 2:1225, 1236, 1241, 1247, 1263; Oshinsky, *A Conspiracy So Immense*, p. 465. By the summer of 1954, Gallup had concluded that even if it had been "known that McCarthy had killed five innocent children," his remaining supporters would probably have chosen to "still go along with him." George Gallup to Gerald B. Lambert, June 14, 1954, Dulles Papers, Box 84, Sealy G. Mudd Library, Princeton University.

47. *New York Times*, June 22, 1954, pp. 1, 16; Potter, *Days of Shame*, pp. 153–61; Smith, *Declaration of Conscience*, pp. 52–58. Bean's major work on McCarthy's popularity and influence is *1954 Mid-Term Elections*. C. D. Jackson circulated a copy within the White House. C. D. Jackson to Sherman Adams, May 4, 1954, Adams Papers, Box 8, Baker Library, Dartmouth.

48. DDE to Paul Helms, March 9, 1954, in Eisenhower, *Diaries*, ed. Lester, reel 3; *Public Papers*, 1954, pp. 517–25; Hagerty, *Diary*, pp. 57–59, 71. Potter claimed that he had voted with the other Republicans against calling Struve Hensel and Frank Carr as witnesses—which was widely seen as a pro-McCarthy attempt to squelch unfavorable testimony—only because Dirksen had wrongly informed him that the White House supported the effort. Hagerty, *Diary*, p. 71.

49. Griffith, "Ralph Flanders"; Flanders, *Senator from Vermont*, pp. 253–68; Flanders interview, pp. 2–6. On the investigation of McCarthy by the Subcommittee on Privileges and Elections, see Griffith, *Politics of Fear*, pp. 152–87. For a profile of Flanders, see Pearse, "Unexpected Senator."

50. Flanders interview, COHP, February 4, 1967, pp. 10–25; Watkins, *Enough Rope*, pp. 24–25.

51. Flanders interview, COHP, February 4, 1967, pp. 12–12; Flanders, *Senator from Vermont*, p. 253ff; Donovan, *Eisenhower*, p. 258.

52. Eisenhower, for example, evaded questions about the Flanders resolution at an August 4, 1954, press conference. See *Public Papers*, 1954, p. 678ff. On the president's noninvolvement in the censure proceedings, see Ewald, *Eisenhower*, pp. 141–43; Shanley interview, DEOHP, May 16, 1975, pp. 66–70; and Gruenther interview, COHP, January 11, 1972, pp. 78–81.

53. Donovan, *Eisenhower*, p. 257. See also Greenstein, *Hidden-Hand Presidency*, pp. 155–227, and Yarnell, "Eisenhower and McCarthy."

54. Flanders interview, COHP, February 4, 1967, pp. 12, 25–38; Flanders, *Senator from Vermont*, p. 262ff; interview with William F. Knowland, COHP, November 16, 1970, p. 157.

55. Paul Hoffman to Sherman Adams, November 26, 1954, and Charles F. Willis, Jr., to Sherman Adams, July 27, 1954, both in Adams Papers, Box 10, Baker Library, Dartmouth. Griffith discusses the role of the National Committee for an Effective Congress in the censure proceedings in *Politics of Fear*, pp. 274–91.

56. Interview with Arthur Watkins, COHP, January 4, 1968, pp. 8ff, 77–78; Watkins, *Enough Rope*, pp. 223–35. For the testimony before the Watkins committee, see U.S. Congress, Senate, 83d Cong., 2d sess., *Hearings before the Select Committee to Study Censure Charges*.

57. *Public Papers*, 1953, pp. 779–91; Lodge, *As It Was*, pp. 125–26. At subsequent press conferences in December 1953 and April 1954, Eisenhower repeated his wish that the issue of subversion would be a "matter of history" by the 1954 elections. *Public Papers*, 1953, pp. 801–2, and 1954, pp. 427–38.

58. Memorandum by Earle D. Chesney, May 19, 1954, Ann Whitman File, Ann Whitman Diary Series, Box 2; W. C. Voskuil to RNC, July 13, 1954, Hall Papers, Box 126; Summary of Mail-1954, Hall Papers, Box 50; O. K. Armstrong to Leonard Hall, September 1, 1954, Hall Papers, Box 126; Henry Cabot Lodge to DDE, July 30, 1954, in Eisenhower, *Diaries*, ed. Lester, reel 4. One poll taken for the RNC indicated that 19 percent of the respondents, a relatively high percentage, believed that domestic communism was a major problem, whereas less than 5 percent thought that either curbing or supporting McCarthy was a serious issue. "Public Opinion Survey on Political Issues," Hall Papers, Box 126.

59. *Public Papers*, 1954, pp. 555–62, 779–87, 88ff; Ewald, *Eisenhower*, p. 151; entry for April 27, 1954, Ann Whitman File, Ann Whitman Diary Series, Box 2. Republican campaign literature ignored the army-McCarthy hearings and stressed the administration's record on subversion. See "Straight from the Shoulder," June and July 1954, Hall Papers, Box 8.

60. Mazo, *Nixon*, pp. 139–43; Preston Wolfe to Robert Humphreys, December 12, 1953, Humphreys Papers, Box 7; *Public Papers*, 1954, pp. 963–75; Nixon, *Memoirs*, p. 160.

61. Eisenhower, *Diaries*, ed. Ferrell, pp. 288–91; DDE to Swede Hazlett, December 8, 1954, in Eisenhower, *Letters to a Friend*, pp. 136–41; DDE to Gabriel Hague, September 30, 1954, in Eisenhower, *Diaries*, ed. Lester, reel 5.

62. Hagerty interview, COHP, 1967–68, pp. 388–89; Shanley Diaries, pp. 1691–92, Box 2; Griffith, *Politics of Fear*, p. 306; *Congress and the Nation* 4:20–21, 1657.

63. Flanders interview, COHP, February 4, 1967, pp. 15–17; Watkins interview, COHP, January 4, 1968, p. 73; Watkins, *Enough Rope*, pp. 186–87; interview with Frank G. Carlson, DEOHP, March 7, 1975, pp. 96–102.

64. *New York Times*, November 21, 1954, p. E3. See also Watkins, *Enough Rope*, pp. 80–83, 115–22.

65. C. F. Moore to Frank Carlson, November 11, 1954, and Preston Dunn to Frank Carlson, November 13, 1954, both in Frank Carlson Papers, Box 13, Kansas State Historical Society. Carlson, a member of the Watkins committee, received hundreds of letters on the censure controversy, a majority of which supported McCarthy. See generally Carlson Papers, Box 13. For more on the relationship between conservatism and McCarthyism, see Miles, *American Right*, pp. 3ff, 123–47.

66. Hagerty, *Diary*, pp. 119–20; Griffith, *Politics of Fear*, pp. 311–14.

67. *Public Papers*, 1954, pp. 1077–79; "Conference with Alexander Smith," Ann Whitman File, Ann Whitman Diary Series, Box 2.

68. Williams, *One Man's Freedom*, pp. 67–68; Goldwater, *With No Apologies*, p. 61; *Congressional Record*, 83d Cong., 2d sess., December 1, 1954, p. 16329ff.

69. "Interview with Senator Watkins," December 4, 1954, Ann Whitman File, Ann Whitman Diary Series, Box 3; Hagerty, *Diary*, pp. 125–26; Watkins, *Enough Rope*, pp. 152–54, 169–78. Connecticut Senator Prescott Bush later claimed credit for initiating the meeting between Eisenhower and Watkins. See interview with Prescott Bush, COHP, July 1, 1966, p. 105.

70. Hughes, *Ordeal of Power*, p. 132.

71. See Reichard, *Reaffirmation of Republicanism*, pp. 204–5, and "How Senators Voted on Censure of McCarthy," *Washington Star*, December 5, 1954, p. A-36, in Ann Whitman File, Ann Whitman Diary Series, Box 3.

72. DDE to Cliff Roberts, December 7, 1954, in Eisenhower, *Diaries*, ed. Lester,

reel 5; Reichard, *Reaffirmation of Republicanism*, pp. vii–viii. The Republican commitment to McCarthy may have been more widespread than the censure vote suggested. According to a December 1954 survey, Republicans opposed McCarthy's censure by 46 to 35 percent. Gallup, *Gallup Poll* 2:1296.

Chapter 7

1. Admittedly, few programmatic differences existed between Democrats and Republicans, but one must concede the stark contrast between Harry Truman's veto of the Internal Security Act of 1950 and the Eisenhower administration's support for a whole host of anti-Communist bills during the Eighty-third Congress.

2. Earl Latham notes the argument, made by some conservatives, that the popular image of McCarthyism had been invented by "anti-anti-Communists" to discredit efforts to expose subversives. Latham, *Communist Controversy*, p. 414.

3. See, for example, the editorial entitled "The McCarthy Era" in the *Nation*, August 27, 1955, pp. 165–66, in which the editors lamented that, although McCarthyism had ebbed, it was "clear that the institutional supports of the witch hunt" were "still in place and unimpaired." Among these "institutional supports," they listed HCUA, the Smith Act, and the Subversive Activities Control Board.

4. By 1954, even HCUA had started to curtail its activities, holding only 80 days of hearings, as compared with 178 days of hearings in 1953. Goodman, *The Committee*, pp. 321–50. For more on HCUA, see also Bentley, *Thirty Years of Treason*.

5. *Minutes and Documents of the Cabinet*, March 27, 1953, reel 1.

6. U.S. Congress, House, 83d Cong., 1st sess., *Hearings before Subcommittee No. 3 of the Committee on the Judiciary*, p. 27ff; Herbert Brownell to Speaker of the House, May 7, 1953, in ibid., pp. 13–14.

7. "162nd meeting of the NSC, September 17, 1953," Ann Whitman File, National Security Council Series, Box 4.

8. Herbert Brownell to Bryce Harlow, October 15, 1953, Harlow Records, Box 12; Goodman, *The Committee*, p. 351ff; *Congress and the Nation* 4:1661. See also "178th Meeting of the NSC, December 30, 1953," Ann Whitman File, National Security Council Series, Box 5.

9. "172nd Meeting of the NSC, November 24, 1953," Ann Whitman File, National Security Council Series, Box 5.

10. *Minutes and Documents of the Cabinet*, December 15, 1953, reel 1.

11. "Legislative Leadership Conference, December 19, 1953," Ann Whitman File, Legislative Meetings Series, Box 1; *Congress and the Nation* 4:1661; Shanley Diaries, p. 1344, Box 2.

12. *Public Papers*, 1954, pp. 12–13; Eisenhower, *White House Years: Mandate for Change*, p. 287; Shanley Diaries, pp. 1016, 1037, 1330, 1337, Box 2. In his memoirs, Eisenhower defended the witness immunity bill by pointing to similar laws in Great Britain and Canada; Nixon had made the same argument to the cabinet. See *Minutes and Documents of the Cabinet*, December 15, 1953, reel 1. Shanley saw the expatriation bill as a way for the administration to make good on its campaign promise to rid the government of subversives. When asked during congressional hearings on the proposal just where the administration would send native-born Americans who had been stripped of their citizenship, Brownell defended expatriation as essentially a propaganda device. Pennsylvania Democrat Francis E. Walter, who would soon become the chairman of HCUA, told Brownell, "In my mind it is no problem at all to deprive a person of his rights as a citizen." But Walter expressed skepticism that the administration would be able to deport many nonnaturalized citizens. See U.S. Congress, House, 83d Cong., 2d sess., *Hearings before Subcommittee No. 1 of the Committee on the Judiciary on Internal Security Legislation* (hereafter cited as *Subcommittee No. 1 Hearings*), pp. 144–47.

13. "Internal Security—Action in the Current Congress," *Congressional Digest* (May 1954), pp. 136–39, 160. See also *Congress and the Nation* 4:1657, and *Subcommittee No. 1 Hearings*, p. 133ff. As we shall see, a security program for employees in sensitive positions in private industry was already in place.

The administration elected against seeking a legislative solution to one supposed threat—the importation of Communist propaganda. Brownell and George Humphrey supported a law requiring the labeling of such material, presumably as hazardous to national security. Fearful of the charge of censorship, Eisenhower and Nixon dissuaded them from taking any such action. In any event, Postmaster General Arthur Summerfield reassured Eisenhower and the others that the U.S. Post Office was monitoring the situation. He added, "You'd be surprised how much of the stuff gets lost and ends up in the dead letter office." Hagerty, *Diary*, p. 52; "197th Meeting of the NSC, May 13, 1954," Ann Whitman File, National Security Council Series, Box 5.

14. *Congressional Digest*, May 1954, pp. 152, 160; "172nd Meeting of the NSC, November 24, 1953," Ann Whitman File, National Security Council Series, Box 5; *Minutes and Documents of the Cabinet*, December 15, 1953, reel 1.

15. *Subcommittee No. 1 Hearings*, p. 136; Herbert Brownell to DDE, April 9, 1954, Ann Whitman File, Administration Series, Box 7.

16. Ambrose, *Nixon*, pp. 160–64; Nixon, *Memoirs*, pp. 46–47; *Minutes and Documents of the Cabinet*, April 2, 1954, reel 1; *Subcommittee No. 1 Hearings*, p. 136ff. Not only were the administration's motives not liberal, but as Mary S. McAuliffe has pointed out in a perceptive article, proposals to outlaw the Communist party had their libertarian side—they would allow suspected party members to avail themselves of the

superior procedural safeguards of the criminal justice system. See her "Communist Control Act."

17. McAuliffe, "Communist Control Act," p. 354ff; *New York Times*, August 14, 1954, pp. 1, 5.

18. Shanley Diaries, pp. 1643–44, Box 2; McAuliffe, "Communist Control Act," pp. 357–60; *New York Times*, August 14, 1954, pp. 1, 5, and August 15, 1954, pp. 1, 32; *Public Papers*, 1954, pp. 717–18. On the adoption of the Communist Control Act, see generally *Congressional Record*, 83d Cong., 2d sess., pp. 14192–235, 14639.

19. *Public Papers*, 1954, pp. 756–60. On antisubversive legislation in the Eighty-third Congress, see generally *Congressional Digest*, May 1954, p. 136ff, and Fund for the Republic, *Digest of the Public Record*, p. 693ff. The administration also secured tougher penalties for harboring fugitives and jumping bail—five Smith Act defendants were, at the time, evading federal authorities. Two of the more petulant bills passed by Congress required "Communist-action" and "Communist-front organizations" to register their printing presses and duplicating machines with the SACB and, in a swipe at Irving Peress, amended the Doctors' Draft Law to provide that a doctor could be ordered to serve as an enlisted man.

20. McAuliffe, "Communist Control Act," pp. 361–67; Belknap, *Cold War Political Justice*, p. 160ff; Goodman, *The Committee*, pp. 351–66; O'Reilly, *Hoover and the Un-Americans*, pp. 196–97. A sample of press opinion on the Communist Control Act appears in the *New York Times*, August 21, 1954, p. 6. Robert Welch's magnum opus on Eisenhower, in which he suggests Ike was an unwitting dupe, if not a conscious agent, of the Kremlin, is *The Politician*. For more such analysis, see John Birch Society, *The Blue Book*.

21. *Annual Report of the Attorney General for the Fiscal Year Ending June 30, 1953*, pp. 6–19; *Annual Report of the Attorney General for the Fiscal Year Ending June 30, 1955*, pp. 44–66.

22. U.S. Department of Defense, *Industrial Personnel Security Review Program: First Annual Report*, pp. 3–5, 36ff; *Minutes and Documents of the Cabinet*, March 27, 1953, reel 1; *Public Papers*, 1954, pp. 533–34; *Report of the Attorney General* (1955), pp. 44–66; *Annual Report of the Attorney General for the Fiscal Year Ending June 30, 1956*, pp. 64–66. After months of litigation, the Powell case ended in a mistrial, upon which the prosecutors immediately filed treason charges against the defendants. The trial judge dismissed the charges. See *Annual Report of the Attorney General for the Fiscal Year Ending June 30, 1959*, p. 248.

23. Kutler, *American Inquisition*, pp. 183–214.

24. William Rogers to Leo Rover, February 7, 1953, Rogers Papers, Box 15; *Report of the Attorney General* (1953), p. 13ff; *Annual Report of the Attorney General*

for the Fiscal Year Ending June 30, 1954, p. 6ff; *Annual Report of the Attorney General* (1955), p. 49.

25. *Annual Report of the Attorney General* (1953), p. 16ff; ibid. (1954), p. 6ff; ibid. (1955), pp. 44–66; ibid. (1956), p. 57ff.

26. Belknap, *Cold War Political Justice*, p. 160ff. On the enforcement of the Smith Act during the Truman years, see Steinberg, *Great "Red Menace."*

27. Memorandum for the President, October 6, 1956, Ann Whitman File, Administration Series, Box 8; Belknap, *Cold War Political Justice*, pp. 152ff, 174–76; *Annual Report of the Attorney General* (1954), p. 6ff; Shannon, *Decline of American Communism*, pp. 201–3.

28. Powers, *Secrecy and Power*, p. 337. For other decisions indicating the start of a judicial backlash against cold war justice, see O'Reilly, *Hoover and the Un-Americans*, p. 197 and related notes.

29. Quoted in O'Reilly, *Hoover and the Un-Americans*, p. 239. For more on the background of the government informants, see Kahn, *Matusow Affair*, pp. 8–10. Brownell conceded the "personality traits and emotional disturbances associated with ex-Communists." *Minutes and Documents of the Cabinet*, March 4, 1955, reel 3.

30. Belknap, *Cold War Political Justice*, pp. 215–19. In a bizarre and unsettling case, the government attempted to supress the publication of Matusow's memoirs and secured his conviction for perjury not for his initial testimony against Jencks, but for recanting. Matusow's publisher presents his version of the episode in Kahn, *Matusow Affair*. Matusow's book is *False Witness*. To be sure, Matusow had lied somewhere, perhaps in his original story and in the particulars of his confession.

31. *Minutes and Documents of the Cabinet*, March 18, 1955, reel 3; *U.S. News and World Report*, April 29, 1955, pp. 54–66. Amid the controversy over the Matusow affair, Brownell announced that informants were being dropped from the government payroll and would be treated like all other witnesses. The Department of Defense also announced that workers covered by the industrial security program would no longer be required to disclose the identities of friends and relatives who belonged to "Communist-front organizations." *Public Papers*, 1955, p. 435.

32. Belknap, *Cold War Political Justice*, p. 152ff; U.S. Congress, Senate, 94th Cong., 2d sess., *Final Report of the Select Committee to Study Government Operations with Respect to Intelligence Activities* (hereafter cited as *Final Report*): Book III, *Supplementary Detailed Staff Reports on Intelligence Activities and the Rights of Americans*, pp. 16–17.

33. *Final Report*, Book II: *Intelligence Activities and the Rights of Americans*, p. 139. See also Powers, *Secrecy and Power*, pp. 338–40, and L. V. Boardman to A. H. Belmont, August 28, 1956, in U.S. Congress, Senate, 94th Cong., 1st sess., *Hearings before the Select Committee to Study Government Operations With Respect*

to Intelligence Activities (hereafter cited as *Church Committee Hearings*): vol. 6, *The Federal Bureau of Investigation*, pp. 372–753.

34. *Final Report*, Book III, p. 65; O'Reilly, *Hoover and the Un-Americans*, p. 198ff; *Minutes and Documents of the Cabinet*, November 6, 1958, reel 8; Theoharis, *Spying on Americans*, pp. 137–38.

35. *Church Committee Hearings*, vol. 5, *National Security Agencies and Fourth Amendment Rights*, pp. 85–87; *Final Report*, Book II, pp. 60–61; Theoharis, *Spying on Americans*, pp. 108–10. Under this general grant of authority, the FBI placed twelve bugs in hotel rooms occupied by Martin Luther King, Jr. *Final Report*, Book II, p. 199. On the expansion of FBI jurisdiction, see *Public Papers*, 1953, p. 830; *Final Report*, Book II, p. 22ff; Theoharis, *Spying on Americans*, pp. 81–83; and Donner, *Age of Surveillance*, p. 57.

36. *Final Report*, Book III, pp. 284–85; Theoharis and Cox, *The Boss*, p. 312.

37. Unger, *FBI*, pp. 123–24.

38. *Final Report*, Book II, pp. 232–33.

39. *Minutes and Documents of the Cabinet*, March 9, 1956, reel 4; J. Edgar Hoover, "Racial Tension and Civil Rights," in ibid., March 1, 1956, reel 4; *Church Committee Hearings*, vol. 6, pp. 158–60; Burk, *Eisenhower Administration*, pp. 160–61. Interestingly, Hoover seemed to accept a basic premise of the Communist strategy, as he described it—that greater governmental action on behalf of racial equality in American society was not in the nation's best interest. He apparently assumed that his listeners would view any cause supported by Communists as dangerous, regardless of its intrinsic value. Such thinking could confer on the tiny CPUSA an inordinate significance in the shaping of public policy. Many Americans would oppose any cause, however laudable, if the Communists endorsed it.

40. *Final Report*, Book II, pp. 9, 47–53; Mitgang, *Dangerous Dossiers*, pp. 69–245 passim. Two observations should be made to place the preceding discussion in context. First, such political intelligence gathering was not unique to the Eisenhower presidency but began under Roosevelt and continued at least into the Nixon administration. Second, the FBI focused primarily on left-wing groups, but it did not ignore right-wing extremists. Hoover provided the White House with reports on Robert Welch and, at the request of a presidential aide, on the fundamentalist minister Carl McIntyre of the International Council of Christian Churches. *Final Report*, Book II, p. 152.

41. Theoharis and Cox, *The Boss*, p. 17.

42. Steinberg, *Great "Red Menace,"* p. 289; Unger, *FBI*, p. 125. For one of the first of the "anti-FBI" books, see Cook, *The FBI Nobody Knows*.

43. *Annual Report of the Attorney General* (1953), p. 25. After Eisenhower met with Khrushchev in 1955, the FBI deleted an East-West summit meeting from its list of Communist causes, but it did find some new ones—"peaceful coexistence" between

the superpowers and a nuclear test ban treaty. See *Annual Report of the Attorney General* (1956), p. 213, and *Annual Report of the Attorney General for the Fiscal Year Ending June 30, 1957*, p. 198ff.

44. *Annual Report of the Attorney General* (1953), pp. 24–26. My version of the anti-Communist creed is pieced together from ibid., p. 24ff, ibid. (1954), p. 17ff, ibid. (1956), p. 211ff, and ibid. (1957), p. 198ff, which are in the sections dealing with the FBI. I have also drawn on Whitehead's semiofficial *FBI Story*, pp. 267–69, and on the standard text of American anticommunism, Hoover's *Masters of Deceit*. See also Paterson, *Meeting the Communist Threat*, pp. 3–17.

I do not mean to suggest that all the elements of the anti-Communist creed derived from a conservative enmity toward reform or from popular political mythology. Commentators on the Left have, for example, lamented the CPUSA's subservience to the Soviet Union and the inability of the American party to fashion a program responsive to its unique situation. Cf. Chapter 8 infra.

45. Buckley and Bozell, *McCarthy and His Enemies*, p. 280ff.

46. Quoted in *Final Report*, Book I: *Foreign and Military Intelligence*, p. 9. This conflicted with the FBI's announced position. J. Edgar Hoover was much too shrewd to ask the American people to embrace what President Hoover's Commission had called a "fundamentally repugnant philosophy." By contrast, the FBI director claimed that "*the fundamental premise of any attack against communism*" was that Americans should "be absolutely certain" that the fight was being waged "with full regard for the historic liberties of this great nation." Hoover, *Masters of Deceit*, p. 312 (emphasis in the original). On the other hand, William Sullivan, who held several key positions within the bureau, later said of COINTELPRO that "no holds were barred" in the FBI's efforts to disrupt the CPUSA. Powers, *Secrecy and Power*, pp. 338–40.

47. William C. Sullivan to J. Edgar Hoover, October 6, 1971, in Sullivan, *The Bureau*, pp. 265–77; O'Reilly, *Hoover and the Un-Americans*, p. 4ff; Powers, *Secrecy and Power*, pp. 336–39. Director Hoover and Senator McCarthy became friends soon after the latter's arrival in Washington. In 1948, for example, Hoover invited the senator to address the graduating class of the national FBI academy. Hoover began to distance himself from McCarthy in the summer of 1953. McCarthy's penchant for hiring ex-FBI agents, in particular Frank Carr, apparently led Hoover to fear that the Wisconsin Republican was learning too much about the FBI and that his relationship with the bureau was becoming too obvious. See Theoharis and Cox, *The Boss*, p. 280ff.

48. Eisenhower, *White House Years: Mandate for Change*, p. 90; Sullivan, *The Bureau*, p. 45; Donner, *Age of Surveillance*, pp. 80, 118. Hoover considered Eisenhower's tenure in the White House as "the best and happiest years he ever had." He rated Ike as the only president under whom he had served who was both "a great

man" and "a great president." Powers, *Secrecy and Power*, pp. 312–13. Hoover had supported Eisenhower in 1952 only after the collapse of Douglas MacArthur's campaign. And the later development of a cordial relationship between Ike and the director did not exempt the president from FBI surveillance. Hoover ordered an investigation of Eisenhower's supposed extramarital affairs, in particular the continuation of his wartime relationship with Kay Summersby. See Sullivan, *The Bureau*, p. 45, and Theoharis and Cox, *The Boss*, pp. 273–75.

49. On the relationship between Rogers and Hoover, see Powers, *Secrecy and Power*, pp. 316–19. In a less visible appointment, Eisenhower appointed J. Edward Lumbard, the federal prosecutor in the *Flynn* case, to a federal appeals court even after it was revealed that Lumbard had known but failed to advise the trial court that Harvey Matusow had been diagnosed as emotionally unstable and might not be a reliable witness. Kahn, *Matusow Affair*, pp. 224–26.

50. "Memorandum of Conversation with the Attorney General," June 19, 1958, Gen. Cor. Series, Dulles Papers, Box 1; Warren, *Memoirs*, pp. 5–7.

51. "Legislative Leadership Conference, December 19, 1953," Ann Whitman File, Legislative Meetings Series, Box 1; *Minutes and Documents of the Cabinet*, December 15, 1953, reel 1; Warren, *Memoirs*, pp. 3–5; "172nd Meeting of the NSC," November 23, 1953, Ann Whitman File, National Security Council Series, Box 5.

52. Ewald, *Eisenhower*, pp. 128–32; DDE to John Stephens Wood, March 23, 1950, in Eisenhower, *Papers* 11:1028–30; DDE to Godfrey Lowell Cabot, November 3, 1950, in ibid., pp. 1400–1401; Eisenhower, *White House Years: Mandate for Change*, p. 196.

Chapter 8

1. *Congressional Record*, 84th Cong., 1st sess., 1955, p. 361.

2. *Public Papers*, 1956, p. 11; ibid., 1958, p. 558; ibid., 1959, p. 557.

3. Johnson, "Eisenhower Personnel Security Program," p. 648.

4. Assistant to the President to J. Edgar Hoover, April 9, 1957, White House Central Files, Official File, Box 482; Belknap, *Cold War Political Justice*, p. 176.

5. *Annual Report of the Attorney General* (1957), p. 73; ibid. (1958), pp. 262, 270; ibid. (1960), p. 275; ibid. (1961), p. 277.

6. Allen interview, COHP, March 1967, p. 89ff; *Public Papers*, 1959, p. 490; *Public Papers*, 1960–61, pp. 189–90. See generally Goodman, *The Committee*, pp. 365–434.

7. O'Reilly, *Hoover and the Un-Americans*, p. 195; Powers, *Secrecy and Power*, pp. 341–43.

8. *Annual Report of the Attorney General* (1960), p. 347. See also ibid. (1956), p. 211; ibid. (1957), p. 198ff; and ibid. (1958), pp. 334–40.

9. *Final Report*, Book II, pp. 43–44; *Church Committee Hearings*, vol. 6, pp. 58–59.

10. *Public Papers*, 1960–61, p. 192.

11. See generally Malcolm Moos, "Election of 1956," in Schlesinger and Israel, *American Presidential Elections* 4:3341–445.

12. Richard Nixon to Jack Beall, July 12, 1956, Nixon Papers, Box 838, NARS. See also material collected in folder marked "McCarthy, Joseph," Nixon Papers, Box 490, NARS.

13. Ambrose, *Nixon*, pp. 421–22.

14. Ambrose, *Eisenhower: The President*, pp. 292–99, 319–22; interview with Eli Ginzberg, DEOHP, May 14, 1975, p. 49.

15. *New York Times*, January 21, 1958, pp. 1, 19; Ambrose, *Eisenhower: The President*, pp. 487–88.

16. Richard Nixon to Jesse Andrews, June 27, 1960, Nixon Papers, Box 40, NARS; Claude Robinson to Richard Nixon, September 9, 1960, Nixon Papers, Box 1, NARS.

17. Theodore Sorenson, "Election of 1960," in Schlesinger and Israel, *American Presidential Elections* 4:3448–562; Parmet, *JFK*, p. 46. See generally White, *Making of the President*.

18. Powers, *Secrecy and Power*, pp. 338–40; Belknap, *Cold War Political Justice*, pp. 184–210; Steinberg, *Great "Red Menace,"* p. 261ff; Starobin, *American Communism in Crisis*, pp. 220–23; Shannon, *Decline of American Communism*, pp. 189, 201–3.

19. Starobin, *American Communism in Crisis*, pp. 224–30; Shannon, *Decline of American Communism*, pp. 272–354 passim; Belknap, *Cold War Political Justice*, p. 184ff; Powers, *Secrecy and Power*, p. 342.

20. *New York Times*, March 5, 1955, pp. 1, 7. See generally *Peters* v. *Hobby*, 349 U.S. 331 (1955).

21. *Pennsylvania* v. *Nelson*, 350 U.S. 497 (1956); *Slochower* v. *Board of Higher Education*, 350 U.S. 551 (1956); *Communist Party* v. *Subversive Activities Control Board*, 351 U.S. 115 (1956); *Watkins* v. *United States*, 354 U.S. 178 (1957); *Service* v. *Dulles*, 354 U.S. 363 (1957). The relevant cases are collected and annotated in Emerson, Haber, and Dorsen, *Political and Civil Rights*, vol. 1, chapter 3. For an excellent and more concise discussion of the Supreme Court and the Communist controversy, see Kelly and Harbison, *American Constitution*, chapter 32. As noted previously, also decided in 1957 was the *Jencks* decision. See Packer, *Ex-Communist Witnesses*, p. 269.

22. *Cole* v. *Young*, 351 U.S. 536 (1956); *Yates* v. *United States*, 355 U.S. 66 (1957); *Kent* v. *Dulles*, 357 U.S. 116 (1958); *Barenblatt* v. *United States*, 360 U.S. 109 (1959); *Greene* v. *McElroy*, 360 U.S. 474 (1959); *Scales* v. *United States*, 367 U.S. 203 (1961). On the percentage of federal employees affected by the *Cole* decision, see Philip Young to Tom Murray, July 5, 1956, White House Central Files, Official File, Box 482. For more on the court and the Communist controversy, see generally Emerson, Haber, and Dorsen, *Political and Civil Rights*, vol. 1, chapter 3, and Kelly and Harbison, *American Constitution*, pp. 884–95, 902–3. In December 1962, President Kennedy granted clemency to Scales, who had been sentenced to six years in prison. Emerson, Haber, and Dorsen, *Political and Civil Rights* 1:153.

23. *New York Times*, April 15, 1957, pp. 1, 12, April 11, 1957, p. 4, April 12, 1957, pp. 1, 4–5, August 16, 1957, pp. 1, 6.

24. L. A. Minnich, Jr., to Rowland B. Hughes, July 26, 1954, Ann Whitman File, Legislative Meetings Series, Box 1; Sherman Adams to Andrew E. Rice, June 15, 1953, Adams Papers, Box 8, Baker Library, Dartmouth; *U.S. News and World Report*, April 29, 1955, p. 62; DDE to Leonard F. Finder, May 2, 1955, in Eisenhower, *Diaries*, ed. Lester, reel 6.

25. Richard Nixon to William Rogers, January 19, 1954, and Richard Nixon to Robert King, January 19, 1954, Nixon Papers, Box 653, NARS; William Rogers to Sherman Adams, March 4, 1955, Rogers Papers, Box 58.

26. Robert Cutler to Sherman Adams, January 15, 1955, and Gordon Gray to Robert Cutler, January 10, 1955, Adams Papers, Box 8, Baker Library, Dartmouth. See also Jacob Blaustein to DDE, May 22, 1954, Ann Whitman File, Ann Whitman Diary Series, Box 2.

27. *New York Times*, June 3, 1955, pp. 1, 14; *Congress and the Nation* 4:1666. See also U.S. Congress, Senate, 84th Cong., 1st sess., *Hearings before a Subcommittee on Reorganization of the Committee on Government Operations on S.J. Resolution 21*.

28. *Public Papers*, 1955, p. 656; DDE to All Department Heads, March 6, 1955, White House Central Files, Official File, Box 482.

29. Hubert H. Humphrey to Richard Nixon, October 18, 1955, Nixon Papers, Box 168, NARS; Theoharis, *Spying on Americans*, pp. 211–13.

30. See *Staff Reports, Commission on Government Security*.

31. See generally *Report of the Commission on Government Security*.

32. *Public Papers*, 1957, pp. 499–500, 506–507.

33. J. Patrick Coyne to Robert Cutler, September 20, 1957, White House Office, OSANSA, Special Asst. Series, Subject Subseries, Box 2.

34. On the Personnel Security Advisory Committee, see William F. Tompkins to All Agency and Department Heads, April 9, 1957, Adams Papers, Box 8, Baker

Library, Dartmouth, and Thomas J. Donegan to Maxwell Rabb, March 23, 1956, White House Central Files, Official File, Box 66.

35. Maxwell Rabb to Sherman Adams, April 4, 1958, White House Office, Cabinet Secretariat Records, Series I, Subseries A, Box 6. See also Maxwell Rabb to Sherman Adams, January 29, 1958, White House Central Files, Official File, Box 17, and William F. Tompkins to Maxwell Rabb, April 4, 1958, White House Office, Cabinet Secretariat Records, Series I, Subseries A, Box 6.

36. Robert Gray to Sherman Adams, July 24, 1958, White House Office, Cabinet Secretariat Records, Series I, Subseries A, Box 6; Robert Gray to Wilton B. Persons, July 6, 1959, in *Minutes and Documents of the Cabinet*, reel 9; ibid., May 16, 1958, reel 7.

37. Robert Gray to Sherman Adams, July 24, 1958, Harvey D. Brown to Mr. Ciciliano, July 16, 1958, White House Office, Cabinet Secretariat Records, Series I, Subseries A, Box 6; *Congress and the Nation* 4:1667.

38. Robert Gray to Sherman Adams, July 24, 1958; Report to the Cabinet from the Interdepartmental Personnel Security Advisory Committee on Recommendations of the Commission on Government Security, August 6, 1958, both in White House Office, Cabinet Secretariat Records, Series I, Subseries A, Box 6.

39. *Minutes and Documents of the Cabinet*, August 8, 1958, reel 8; Cabinet Paper RA-58-114, August 13, 1958, White House Office, Cabinet Secretariat Records, Series I, Subseries A, Box 6.

40. *Congress and the Nation* 4:1667; Roger Jones to Attorney General, March 18, 1959; William Rogers to DDE, March 26, 1959, both in White House Central Files, Official File, Box 482.

41. Action Status Report, August 1, 1960, in *Minutes and Documents of the Cabinet*, reel 10; Cabinet Paper, August 1, 1960, in ibid., reel 1; Loyd Wright to DDE, June 19, 1959, and DDE to Loyd Wright, June 24, 1959, both in White House Central Files, Official File, Box 482.

42. *Public Papers*, 1958, pp. 526–27. Congress did not grant Eisenhower's request. On the passport and visa controversy, see Goodman, *The Committee*, pp. 389–94, 402, and Caute, *Great Fear*, pp. 245–63.

43. Emerson, Haber, and Dorsen, *Political and Civil Rights* 1: 218; Theoharis, *Spying on Americans*, pp. 213–15; Cabinet Notes, June 28, 1957, Adams Papers, Box 8, Baker Library, Dartmouth.

44. *Congressional Record*, 85th Cong., 2d sess., 1958, p. 18511. On the efforts to curb the Court, see generally Murphy, *Congress and the Court*, and Pritchett, *Congress versus the Supreme Court*.

45. *New York Times*, May 1, 1959, p. 9; Charles K. McWhorter to John F. Cushman, May 21, 1959, Nixon Papers, Box 653, NARS.

46. Emerson, Haber, and Dorsen, *Political and Civil Rights* 1:370–76; *Public Papers*, 1959, p. 494.

47. See generally "Industrial Security Program (An Informal Chronology)," undated, Phillip E. Areeda Papers, Box 10.

48. John A. Johnson to Arthur B. Focke, July 13, 1959, Roger W. Jones to Arthur B. Focke, July 16, 1959, Phillip E. Areeda to David W. Kendall, July 23, 1959, John F. Floberg to Arthur B. Focke, July 31, 1959, and William B. MaComber, Jr., to Maurice H. Stans, August 19, 1959, all in Areeda Papers, Box 10.

49. Phillip Areeda to David W. Kendall, September 30, 1959, Areeda Papers, Box 10.

50. Theoharis, *Spying on Americans*, pp. 215–18; *Congress and the Nation* 4:1667; Emerson, Haber, and Dorsen, *Political and Civil Rights* 1:383–84; *New York Times*, February 21, 1960, pp. 1–2.

51. *Public Papers*, 1960–61,, p. 683.

52. On the administration's ambiguous view of Castro, see Ambrose, *Eisenhower: The President*, pp. 504–7, 555–58, 582–84. The United States did not sever diplomatic relations with Cuba until January 3, 1961, only days before Eisenhower left office. *Public Papers*, 1960–61, p. 891.

53. *New York Times*, January 26, 1957, p. 1; August 8, 1957, pp. 1, 10. See also *Annual Report of the Attorney General* (1957), p. 51ff; ibid. (1958), p. 239ff; ibid. (1959), p. 248; and ibid. (1961), p. 254ff.

54. *New York Times*, May 18, 1959, p. 23.

55. Ibid., August 6, 1960, pp. 1–2, and September 8, 1960, pp. 1, 11.

56. On the conservative Republican assessment of the Eisenhower presidency, see Hofstadter, *Paranoid Style*, pp. 93–101. On anti-Communist extremism after Eisenhower, see Bennett, *Party of Fear*, pp. 315–31.

57. Humphrey, *Education of a Public Man*, pp. 142–43.

58. See Goodman, *The Committee*, pp. 407–8.

Chapter 9

1. For representative critical assessments, see Burk, *Eisenhower*, pp. 151–53, and Cook, *Declassified Eisenhower*, pp. 160–64.

2. Drummond interview, COHP, June 21, 1967, pp. 28–30; Milton Eisenhower interview, COHP, June 21, 1967, pp. 65–66. See also Eisenhower, *The President Is Calling*, pp. 316–18.

3. Bradley H. Paterson, Sr., to Christian A. Herter, Jr., August 10, 1954, Nixon Papers, Box 606, NARS; Schrecker, *No Ivory Towers*, p. 251.

4. See generally Lewy, *Federal Employee Loyalty-Security Program*, pp. 7–8. See also Morgenthau, "Loyalty-Security Measures," p. 136.

5. Hagerty, *Diary*, p. 146.

6. Quoted in Keeley, *China Lobby Man*, p. xi.

7. Reinhard, *Republican Right*, p. 157ff; Rae, *Liberal Republicans*, pp. 37–43.

8. Goldwater interview, COHP, June 15, 1967, pp. 3–4. The former Arizona senator repeated his negative assessment of Eisenhower's political skills in *With No Apologies*, pp. 67–76. For a similar view from another Republican insider, see Martin, *My First Fifty Years*, pp. 234–35.

9. Brands, *Cold Warriors*, pp. 189–95; Divine, *Eisenhower*, pp. 234–35.

10. See Wills, *Nixon Agonistes*, pp. 115–38.

11. Alexander, *Holding the Line*.

12. Hughes interview, JFDOHP, April 25, 1965, pp. 43–44. See also Anderson, *Outsider in the Senate*, p. 148, and Hodgson, *America in Our Time*, pp. 44–47.

13. On the growth of executive privilege under Eisenhower, see Theoharis, *Spying on Americans*, pp. 236–49, and Schlesinger, *Imperial Presidency*, pp. 155–59. On the administration's lackluster civil rights record, see generally Burk, *Eisenhower Administration*.

Bibliography

Primary Sources

Manuscripts

Baker Memorial Library, Dartmouth College, Hanover, N.H.
  Sherman Adams Papers
Dwight D. Eisenhower Library, Abilene, Kans.
  Sherman Adams Records
  Phillip E. Areeda Papers
  Stephen Benedict Papers
  John Foster Dulles Papers
  Dwight D. Eisenhower Papers (Ann Whitman File)
    Administration Series
    Ann Whitman Diary Series
    Campaign Series
    Dwight D. Eisenhower Diary Series
    Legislative Meetings Series
    National Security Council Series
  Dwight D. Eisenhower Records (White House Central Files)
    Official File
    Confidential File
    Preinaugural File
  Gordon Gray Papers
  Homer H. Gruenther Records
  Gabriel Hague Papers
  Leonard W. Hall Papers
  John W. Hanes, Jr., Papers
  Bryce N. Harlow Records
  Robert Humphreys Papers
  C. D. Jackson Records
  Carl W. McCardle Papers

Gerald D. Morgan Papers
William E. Robinson Papers
William P. Rogers Papers
Louis S. Rothschild Records
Fred A. Seaton Papers
Bernard M. Shanley Diaries
Thomas E. Stephens Records
Arthur E. Summerfield Papers
White House Office, Cabinet Secretariat Records
White House Office, National Security Council Staff Papers
White House Office, Office of the Special Assistant for National Security Affairs
White House Office, Office of the Special Assistant for Personnel Management
White House Office, Office of the Staff Secretary
Kansas State Historical Society, Topeka, Kans.
Frank Carlson Papers
Massachusetts Historical Society, Boston, Mass.
Henry Cabot Lodge Papers
National Archives and Records Service, Laguna Nigel, Calif.
Richard M. Nixon Vice-Presidential Papers
Sealy G. Mudd Library, Princeton University, Princeton, N.J.
Allen W. Dulles Papers
John Foster Dulles Papers
Emmet J. Hughes Papers
Paul D. Tillet, Jr., Papers

Interviews and Oral Histories

Columbia University Oral History Project
Sherman Adams
George V. Allen
Andrew H. Berding
Charles E. Bohlen
Herbert Brownell
Prescott Bush
Lucius D. Clay
Robert T. Donovan
Roscoe Drummond
Eleanor Lansing Dulles
Dwight D. Eisenhower

Milton Eisenhower
Ralph Flanders
Barry M. Goldwater
Gordon Gray
Homer H. Gruenther
James C. Hagerty
Gabriel Hague
Charles A. Halleck
John W. Hanes, Jr.
Raymond Hare
Bryce N. Harlow
Loy W. Henderson
Robert C. Hill
Roger W. Jones
Walter H. Judd
William F. Knowland
Walter Kohler
Sigurd S. Larmon
Clare Boothe Luce
Gerald D. Morgan
Robert D. Murphy
Wilton B. Persons
Walter S. Robertson
Theodore Streibert
Elbert Tuttle
Arthur Watkins
Sinclair Weeks
Francis O. Wilcox
Dwight D. Eisenhower Oral History Project, Eisenhower Library
Herbert Brownell
Frank G. Carlson
Eli Ginzberg
Charles A. Halleck
Carl McCardle
Robinson McIlvaine
Maxwell Rabb
Bernard M. Shanley
John Foster Dulles Oral History Project, Princeton University
Charles E. Bohlen

Herbert Brownell
Dwight D. Eisenhower
Gabriel Hague
Loy W. Henderson
Emmet J. Hughes
Donald B. Lourie
Robert D. Murphy
Herman Phelger
Charles E. Saltzman

Newspapers and Magazines

Atlanta Constitution, 1945–47
Christian Science Monitor, 1945–47, 1952–53
Foreign Service Journal, 1953–54
Nation, 1953–54
New Republic, 1945–47, 1953–55
Newsweek, 1947, 1952
New York Times, 1948, 1952–60
Time, 1945–47
U.S. News and World Report, 1952–55

Microfilm

Dulles, John Foster. *John Foster Dulles Papers: White House Correspondence and Memoranda Series*. Frederick, Md.: University Publications of America, 1980. 9 reels.

Eisenhower, Dwight D. *The Diaries of Dwight D. Eisenhower, 1953–1961*. Edited by Robert Lester. Frederick, Md.: University Publications of America, 1986. 28 reels.

Kesaris, Paul, and Gibson, Joan, eds. *Minutes of Telephone Conversations of John Foster Dulles and Christian Herter, 1953–1961*. Washington, D.C.: University Publications of America, 1980. 11 reels.

Leuchtenburg, William E., ed. *Papers of the Republican Party, Part II: Reports and Memoranda of the Research Division of the Headquarters of the Republican National Committee, 1938–1980*. Frederick, Md.: University Publications of America, n.d. 15 reels.

Minutes and Documents of the Cabinet Meetings of President Eisenhower, 1953–1961. Washington, D.C.: University Publications of America, 1980. 10 reels.

Government Publications

Annual Reports of the Attorney General, 1953–61.

Annual Reports of the United States Civil Service Commission, 1953–61.

Atomic Energy Commission. *In the Matter of J. Robert Oppenheimer* (1954).

Department of State Bulletin, 1953–61.

Public Papers of the Presidents of the United States: Dwight D. Eisenhower, 1953–61.

Public Papers of the Presidents of the United States: Harry S. Truman, 1952–53.

Report of the Commission on Government Security (1957).

Slany, William Z., ed. *Foreign Relations of the United States, 1952–1954*. Vol. 1, *General Economic and Political Matters* (1983).

———. *Foreign Relations of the United States, 1952–1954*. Vol. 2, *National Security Affairs* (1983).

———. *Foreign Relations of the United States, 1952–1954*. Vol. 3, *United Nations Affairs* (1979).

Staff Reports, Commission on Government Security, 1957.

U.S. Congress. *Congressional Record*, 1946, 1953–58.

U.S. Congress. House. 83d Cong., 1st sess. *Hearings before Subcommittee No. 3 of the Committee on the Judiciary on Wiretapping for National Security* (1953).

U.S. Congress. Senate. 83d Cong., 1st sess. *Hearings before the Committee on Foreign Relations on Nomination of Charles E. Bohlen* (1953).

———. *Hearings before the Committee on Foreign Relations on Nomination of Henry Cabot Lodge to be United States Representative to the United Nations* (1953).

———. *Hearings before the Committee on Foreign Relations on Nomination of John Foster Dulles, Secretary of State-Designate* (1953).

———. *Hearings before the Committee on the Judiciary on Herbert Brownell, Jr.* (1953).

———. *Hearings before the Permanent Subcommittee on Investigations of the Committee on Government Operations on State Department Information Program—Information Centers* (1953).

———. *Hearings before the Permanent Subcommittee on Investigations of the Committee on Government Operations on State Department Information Program—Voice of America* (1953).

———. *Hearings before the Permanent Subcommittee on Investigations of the Committee on Government Operations on the Army Signal Corps—Subversion and Espionage* (1953).

———. *Hearings before the Subcommittee to Investigate the Administration of the*

Internal Security Act and other Internal Security Laws of the Committee on the Judiciary—Interlocking Subversion in Government Departments (1953).

———. Report No. 223. *Preventing Citizens of the United States of Questionable Loyalty to the United States Government from Accepting Any Office or Employment in or under the United Nations.* Presented by Senator Pat McCarran (1953).

U.S. Congress. House. 83d Cong., 2d sess. *Hearings before Subcommittee No. 1 of the Committee on the Judiciary on Internal Security Legislation* (1954).

———. *Hearings before the Subcommittee on International Organizations and Movements of the Committee on Foreign Affairs* (1954).

U.S. Congress. Senate. 83d Cong., 2d sess. *Hearings before the Permanent Subcommittee on Investigations of the Committee on Government Operations— Communist Infiltration in the Army* (1954).

———. *Hearings before the Select Committee to Study Censure Charges Against Senator Joseph R. McCarthy* (1954).

———. *Hearings before the Special Subcommittee on Investigations of the Committee on Government Operations: Special Senate Investigation of Charges Involving Secretary of the Army Robert T. Stevens, John G. Adams, H. Struve Hensel, and Senator Joe McCarthy, Roy M. Cohn, and Francis P. Carr* (1954).

———. *Hearings before the Subcommittee to Investigate the Administration of the Internal Security Act and Other Internal Security Laws of the Committee on the Judiciary—Activities of United States Citizens Employed by the United Nations* (1954).

U.S. Congress. Senate. 84th Cong., 1st sess. *Hearings before a Subcommittee on Reorganization of the Committee on Government Operations on SJ Resolution 21* (1955).

———. *Hearings before a Subcommittee to Investigate the Administration of the Federal Employees' Security Program of the Committee on Post Office and Civil Service* (1955).

U.S. Congress. Senate. 84th Cong., 2d sess. *Hearings before the Subcommittee on Constitutional Rights of the Committee of the Judiciary on S. Res. 94* (1956).

———. Report No. 2118 of the Committee on the Judiciary. *Preventing Citizens of the United States of Questionable Loyalty to the United States Government from Accepting Any Office or Employment in or under the United Nations* (1956).

———. Report No. 2750 of the Committee on Post Office and Civil Service. *Administration of the Federal Employees' Security Program* (1956).

U.S. Congress. Senate. 94th Cong., 1st sess. *Hearings before the Select Committee to Study Government Operations with Respect to Intelligence Activities* (1975).

U.S. Congress. Senate. 94th Cong., 2d sess. *Final Report of the Select Committee to Study Government Operations with Respect to Intelligence Activities* (1976).

U.S. Department of Defense. *Industrial Personnel Security Review Program: First Annual Report* (1956).

U.S. Supreme Court Reports, 1955–61.

Diaries, Memoirs, and Other Published Primary Sources

Acheson, Dean. *Present at the Creation: My Years in the State Department.* New York: W. W. Norton & Co., 1969.

Adams, John G. *Without Precedent: The Story of the Death of McCarthyism.* New York: W. W. Norton & Co., 1983.

Adams, Sherman. *Firsthand Report: The Story of the Eisenhower Administration.* New York: Harper & Brothers, 1961.

Anderson, Clinton P. With Milton Viorst. *Outsider in the Senate: Senator Clinton Anderson's Memoirs.* New York: World Publishing Co., 1970.

Association of the Bar of the City of New York. *Report of the Special Committee on the Federal Loyalty-Security Program.* New York: Dodd Mead & Co., 1956.

Benson, Ezra Taft. *Cross Fire: The Eight Years with Eisenhower.* Westport, Conn.: Greenwood Press, 1962.

Bentley, Elizabeth. *Out of Bondage.* New York: Devin-Adair Co., 1951.

Bentley, Eric, ed. *Thirty Years of Treason: Excerpts from Hearings before the House Committee on Un-American Activities.* New York: Viking Press, 1971.

Bernstein, Barton J., and Matusow, Allen J., eds. *The Truman Administration: A Documentary History.* New York: Harper & Row, 1966.

Bohlen, Charles E. *Witness to History, 1929–1969.* New York: W. W. Norton & Co., 1973.

Branyon, Robert L., and Larsen, Lawrence H., eds. *The Eisenhower Administration, 1953–1961: A Documentary History.* 2 vols. New York: Random House, 1971.

Buckley, William F., Jr. "For the Record." *National Review,* 10 March 1964, p. 188.

Butcher, Harry C. *My Three Years with Eisenhower: The Personal Diary of Captain Harry C. Butcher, USNR.* New York: Simon & Schuster, 1946.

Byrnes, James F. *All in One Lifetime.* New York: Harper & Brothers, 1958.

Chevalier, Haakon. *Oppenheimer: The Story of a Friendship.* New York: George Braziller, 1965.

Cohn, Roy. *McCarthy.* New York: New American Library, 1968.

Cutler, Robert. *No Time for Rest.* Boston: Little, Brown & Co., 1965.

Davies, John Paton. *Foreign and Other Affairs.* New York: W. W. Norton & Co., 1964.

Eisenhower, Dwight D. *At Ease: Stories I Tell to Friends*. Garden City, N.Y.: Doubleday & Co., 1967.

———. *Crusade in Europe*. Garden City, N.Y.: Doubleday & Co., 1967.

———. *The Eisenhower Diaries*. Edited by Robert H. Ferrell. New York: W. W. Norton & Co., 1981.

———. *Ike's Letters to a Friend, 1941–1958*. Edited by Robert Griffith. Lawrence: University Press of Kansas, 1984.

———. *The Papers of Dwight David Eisenhower*. Edited by Alfred D. Chandler et al. 11 vols. Baltimore: Johns Hopkins University Press, 1970–84.

———. *The White House Years*. Vol. 1, *Mandate for Change, 1953–1956*. Garden City, N.Y.: Doubleday & Co., 1963.

———. *The White House Years*. Vol. 2, *Waging Peace, 1956–1961*. Garden City, N.Y.: Doubleday & Co., 1965.

Eisenhower, John S. D. *Strictly Personal*. Garden City, N.Y.: Doubleday & Co., 1974.

Eisenhower, Milton S. *The President Is Calling*. Garden City, N.Y.: Doubleday & Co., 1974.

Flanders, Ralph E. *Senator from Vermont*. Boston: Little, Brown, & Co., 1961.

Friedman, Leon, ed. *United States v. Nixon: The President before the Supreme Court*. New York: Chelsea House Publishers, 1974.

Fund for the Republic. *Digest of the Public Record of Communism in the United States*. New York: Fund for the Republic, 1953.

Gallup, George H., ed. *The Gallup Poll: Public Opinion, 1935–1971*. 3 vols. New York: Random House, 1972.

Goldwater, Barry M. *With No Apologies: The Personal and Political Memoirs of United States Senator Barry M. Goldwater*. New York: William Morrow & Co., 1979.

Gray, Robert Keith. *Eighteen Acres under Glass*. Garden City, N.Y.: Doubleday & Co., 1962.

Green, Harold P. "The Oppenheimer Case: A Study in the Abuse of Law." *Bulletin of Atomic Scientists* 33 (September 1977): 12–16, 56–61.

Hagerty, James C. *The Diary of James C. Hagerty: Eisenhower in Mid-Course, 1954–1955*. Edited by Robert H. Ferrell. Bloomington: Indiana University Press, 1983.

Hiss, Alger. *Recollections of a Life*. New York: Seaver Books, 1988.

Hoover, J. Edgar. *Masters of Deceit: The Story of Communism in America and How to Fight It*. New York: Henry Holt & Co., 1958.

Hughes, Emmet John. *The Ordeal of Power: A Political Memoir of the Eisenhower Years*. New York: Atheneum, 1963.

Humphrey, George M. *The Basic Papers of George M. Humphrey*. Edited by Nathanial R. Howard. Cleveland, Ohio: Western Reserve Historical Society, 1965.

Humphrey, Hubert H. *The Education of a Public Man: My Life and Politics*. Garden City, N.Y.: Doubleday & Co., 1976.

John Birch Society. *The Blue Book of the John Birch Society*. Boston: Western Islands, 1959.

Judd, Walter H. *Walter H. Judd: Chronicles of a Statesman*. Edited by Edward J. Rozek. Denver: Grier & Co., 1980.

Kahn, Albert E. *The Matusow Affair: Memoir of a National Scandal*. Mount Kisco, N.Y.: Moyer Bell, 1983.

Kennan, George F. *Memoirs, 1925–1950*. Boston: Little, Brown & Co., 1967.

———. *Memoirs, 1950–1963*. Boston: Little, Brown & Co., 1972.

Kretzman, Edwin M. J. "McCarthy and the Voice of America." *Foreign Service Journal*, February 1967, pp. 26–27, 44–46.

Larson, Arthur. *Eisenhower: The President Nobody Knew*. New York: Charles Scribner's Sons, 1968.

Lilienthal, David E. *The Journals of David E. Lilienthal*. Vol. 3, *Venturesome Years, 1950–1955*. New York: Harper & Row, 1966.

Lodge, Henry Cabot. *As It Was: An Inside View of Politics and Power in the '50s and '60s*. New York: W. W. Norton & Co., 1976.

McCann, Kevin. *Man from Abilene*. Garden City, N.Y.: Doubleday & Co., 1952.

McCarthy, Joseph R. *America's Retreat from Victory: The Story of George Catlett Marshall*. New York: Devin-Adair Co., 1951.

Martin, Joe. *My First Fifty Years in Politics*. New York: McGraw-Hill Book Co., 1960.

Matusow, Allen J., ed. *Joseph R. McCarthy*. Englewood Cliffs, N.J.: Prentice-Hall, 1970.

Matusow, Harvey M. *False Witness*. New York: Cameron & Kahn, 1955.

Merson, Martin. *The Private Diary of a Public Servant*. New York: Macmillan Co., 1955.

Murphy, Robert. *Diplomat among Warriors*. Garden City, N.Y.: Doubleday & Co., 1964.

Nixon, Richard M. *The Memoirs of Richard Nixon*. New York: Grossett & Dunlap, 1978.

———. *Six Crises*. New York: Doubleday & Co., 1962.

Official Report of the Proceedings of the Twenty-Fifth Republican National Convention. Washington, D.C.: Judd & Detweiler, 1952.

Oppenheimer, Robert. *Robert Oppenheimer: Letters and Recollections*. Edited by

Alice Kimball Smith and Charles Weiner. Cambridge, Mass.: Harvard University Press, 1980.

Pearson, Drew. *Drew Pearson Diaries, 1949–1959*. Edited by Tyler Abell. New York: Holt, Rinehart & Winston, 1974.

Potter, Charles E. *Days of Shame*. New York: Coward-McCann, 1965.

Slater, Ellis D. *The Ike I Knew*. Privately printed, 1980.

Smith, Margaret Chase. *Declaration of Conscience*. Edited by William C. Lewis, Jr. New York: Doubleday & Co., 1972.

Snyder, Marty. *My Friend Ike*. New York: Frederick Fell, 1956.

Stevenson, Adlai. *The Papers of Adlai Stevenson*. Edited by Walter Johnson. 8 vols. Boston: Little, Brown & Co., 1972–79.

Strauss, Lewis L. *Men and Decisions*. Garden City, N.Y.: Doubleday & Co., 1962.

Sullivan, William C. With Bill Brown. *The Bureau: My Thirty Years in Hoover's FBI*. New York: W. W. Norton & Co., 1979.

Sulzberger, C. L. *A Long Row of Candles: Memoirs and Diaries, 1934–1954*. New York: Macmillan Co., 1969.

Truman, Harry S. *Memoirs*. Vol. 1, *Year of Decisions*. Garden City, N.Y.: Doubleday & Co., 1955.

———. *Memoirs*. Vol. 2, *Years of Trial and Hope*. Garden City, N.Y.: Doubleday & Co., 1955.

———. *Off the Record: The Private Papers of Harry S. Truman*. Edited by Robert H. Ferrell. New York: Harper & Row, 1980.

Vandenberg, Arthur H., Jr., ed. *The Private Papers of Senator Vandenberg*. Boston: Houghton Mifflin Co., 1952.

Warren, Earl. *The Memoirs of Earl Warren*. Garden City, N.Y.: Doubleday & Co., 1977.

Watkins, Arthur V. *Enough Rope*. Englewood Cliffs, N.J.: Prentice-Hall, 1969.

Welch, Robert. *The Politician*. Belmont, Mass.: Belmont Publishing Co., 1964.

Williams, Edward Bennett. *One Man's Freedom*. New York: Atheneum, 1962.

Secondary Sources

Books

Alexander, Charles C. *Holding the Line: The Eisenhower Era, 1952–1961*. Bloomington: Indiana University Press, 1975.

Ambrose, Stephen E. *Eisenhower: Soldier, General of the Army, President-Elect, 1890–1952*. New York: Simon & Schuster, 1983.

————. *Eisenhower: The President*. New York: Simon & Schuster, 1984.

————. *Nixon: The Education of a Politician, 1913–1962*. New York: Simon & Schuster, 1987.

Bachrack, Stanley D. *The Committee of One Million: "China Lobby" Politics, 1953–1971*. New York: Columbia University Press, 1976.

Bayley, Edwin R. *Joe McCarthy and the Press*. Madison: University of Wisconsin Press, 1981.

Bean, Louis H. *Influences on the 1954 Mid-Term Elections*. Washington, D.C.: Public Affairs Institute, 1954.

Belknap, Michael R. *Cold War Political Justice: The Smith Act, the Communist Party, and American Civil Liberties*. Westport, Conn.: Greenwood Press, 1977.

Bell, Daniel, ed. *The Radical Right*. Garden City, N.Y.: Doubleday & Co., 1963.

Bennett, David H. *The Party of Fear: From Nativist Movements to the New Right in American History*. Chapel Hill: University of North Carolina Press, 1988.

Berger, Raoul. *Executive Privilege: A Constitutional Myth*. Cambridge, Mass.: Harvard University Press, 1974.

Bontecou, Eleanor. *The Federal Loyalty-Security Program*. Ithaca, N.Y.: Cornell University Press, 1953.

Brands, Henry W. *Cold Warriors: Eisenhower's Generation and American Foreign Policy*. New York: Columbia University Press, 1988.

Brendon, Piers. *Ike: His Life and Times*. New York: Harper & Row, 1986.

Brown, Ralph S., Jr. *Loyalty and Security: Employment Tests in the United States*. New Haven, Conn.: Yale University Press, 1958.

Buckley, William F., Jr., and Bozell, L. Brent. *McCarthy and His Enemies: The Record and Its Meaning*. Chicago: Henry Regnery Co., 1954.

Burk, Robert F. *Dwight D. Eisenhower: Hero and Politician*. Boston: Twayne Publishers, 1986.

————. *The Eisenhower Administration and Black Civil Rights*. Knoxville: University of Tennessee Press, 1984.

Caute, David. *The Great Fear: The Anti-Communist Purge under Truman and Eisenhower*. New York: Simon & Schuster, 1978.

Cochran, Bert. *Harry Truman and the Crisis Presidency*. New York: Funk & Wagnalls, 1973.

Cohen, Warren I. *America's Response to China: An Interpretive History of Sino-American Relations*. 2d ed. New York: John Wiley & Sons, 1980.

Congress and the Nation. 6 vols. Washington, D.C.: Congressional Quarterly Service, 1965–85.

Cook, Blanche Wiessen. *The Declassified Eisenhower: A Divided Legacy*. New York: Doubleday & Co., 1981.

Cook, Fred J. *The FBI Nobody Knows.* New York: MacMillan Co., 1964.

———. *The Nightmare Decade: The Life and Times of Senator Joe McCarthy.* New York: Random House, 1971.

———. *The Unfinished Story of Alger Hiss.* New York: William Morrow Co., 1958.

Davis, Kenneth S. *Soldier of Democracy: A Biography of Dwight Eisenhower.* Garden City, N.Y.: Doubleday & Co., 1952.

Divine, Robert A. *Eisenhower and the Cold War.* New York: Oxford University Press, 1981.

———. *Foreign Policy and U.S. Presidential Elections, 1952–1960.* New York: New Viewpoints, 1974.

Doenecke, Justice D. *Not to the Swift: The Old Isolationists in the Cold War Era.* Lewisburg, Pa.: Bucknell University Press, 1979.

Donner, Frank J. *The Age of Surveillance: The Aims and Methods of America's Political Intelligence System.* New York: Alfred A. Knopf, 1980.

Donovan, Robert J. *Conflict and Crisis: The Presidency of Harry S. Truman, 1945–1948.* New York: W. W. Norton & Co., 1977.

———. *Eisenhower: The Inside Story.* New York: Harper & Brothers, 1956.

———. *Tumultuous Years: The Presidency of Harry S. Truman, 1949–1952.* New York: W. W. Norton & Co., 1982.

Drummond, Roscoe, and Coblentz, Gaston. *Duel at the Brink: John Foster Dulles' Command of American Power.* Garden City, N.Y.: Doubleday & Co., 1960.

Emerson, Thomas I.; Haber, David; and Dorsen, Norman. *Political and Civil Rights in the United States.* 3d ed. 2 vols. Boston: Little, Brown & Co., 1967.

Ewald, William Bragg, Jr. *Eisenhower, the President: Crucial Days, 1951–1960.* Englewood Cliffs, N.J.: Prentice-Hall, 1961.

———. *Who Killed Joe McCarthy?* New York: Simon & Schuster, 1984.

Freeland, Richard M. *The Truman Doctrine and the Origins of McCarthyism: Foreign Policy, Domestic Politics, and Internal Security, 1946–1948.* New York: Alfred A. Knopf, 1972.

Fried, Richard M. *Men against McCarthy.* New York: Columbia University Press, 1976.

———. *Nightmare in Red: The McCarthy Era in Perspective.* New York: Oxford University Press, 1990.

Gaddis, John Lewis. *The United States and the Origins of the Cold War, 1941–1947.* New York: Columbia University Press, 1982.

Goldman, Eric F. *The Crucial Decade: America, 1945–1955.* New York: Alfred A. Knopf, 1956.

Goodchild, Peter. *J. Robert Oppenheimer: Shatterer of Worlds*. Boston: Houghton Mifflin Co., 1981.

Goodman, Walter. *The Committee: The Extraordinary Career of the House Committee on Un-American Activities*. New York: Farrar, Strauss, & Giroux, 1968.

Gosnell, Harold F. *Truman's Crises: A Political Biography of Harry S. Truman*. Westport Conn.: Greenwood Press, 1980.

Greenstein, Fred I. *The Hidden-Hand Presidency: Eisenhower as Leader*. New York: Basic Books, 1982.

Griffith, Robert. *The Politics of Fear: Joseph R. McCarthy and the Senate*. 2d ed. Amherst: University of Massachusetts Press, 1987.

Guhin, Michael A. *John Foster Dulles: A Statesman and His Times*. New York: Columbia University Press, 1972.

Gunther, John. *Eisenhower: The Man and the Symbol*. New York: Harper & Brothers, 1951.

Hamby, Alonzo L. *Beyond the New Deal: Harry S. Truman and American Liberalism*. New York: Columbia University Press, 1973.

———. *Liberalism and Its Challengers: From FDR to Reagan*. New York: Oxford University Press, 1985.

Harper, Alan D. *The Politics of Loyalty: The White House and the Communist Issue, 1946–1952*. Westport, Conn.: Greenwood Publishing Corp., 1969.

Harris, Louis. *Is There a Republican Majority? Political Trends, 1952–1956*. New York: Harper & Brothers, 1954.

Hartmann, Susan M. *Truman and the 80th Congress*. Columbia: University of Missouri Press, 1971.

Henderson, John W. *The United States Information Agency*. New York: Frederick A. Praeger, 1971.

Higham, John. *Strangers in the Land: Patterns of American Nativism, 1860–1925*. New York: Atheneum, 1965.

Hodgson, Godfrey. *America in Our Time*. Garden City, N.Y.: Doubleday & Co., 1976.

Hofstadter, Richard. *The Paranoid Style in American Politics and Other Essays*. New York: Alfred A. Knopf, 1965.

Hoopes, Townsend. *The Devil and John Foster Dulles*. Boston: Little, Brown & Co., 1973.

Huss, Pierre, J., and Carpozi, George, Jr. *Red Spies in the UN*. New York: Coward-McCann, 1965.

Kahn, E. J., Jr. *The China Hands: America's Foreign Service Officers and What Befell Them*. New York: Viking Press, 1972.

Keeley, Joseph. *The China Lobby Man: The Story of Alfred Kohlberg*. New Rochelle, N.Y.: Arlington House, 1969.

Kelly, Alfred H., and Harbison, Winfred A. *The American Constitution: Its Origins and Development*. 3d ed. New York: W. W. Norton & Co., 1963.

Koen, Ross Y. *The China Lobby in American Politics*. Edited by Richard C. Kagan. 1960. Reprint. New York: Octagon Books, 1974.

Kunetka, James W. *Oppenheimer: The Years of Risk*. Englewood Cliffs, N.J.: Prentice-Hall, 1982.

Kutler, Stanley I. *The American Inquisition: Justice and Injustice in the Cold War*. New York: Hill and Wang, 1982.

Latham, Earl. *The Communist Controversy in Washington: From the New Deal to McCarthy*. Cambridge, Mass.: Harvard University Press, 1966.

Lauren, Paul Gordon, ed. *The China Hands' Legacy: Ethics and Diplomacy*. Boulder, Colo.: Westview Press, 1987.

Levering, Ralph B. *The Public and American Foreign Policy, 1918–1978*. New York: William Morrow & Co., 1978.

Lewy, Guenther. *The Federal Employee Loyalty-Security Program: The Need for Reform*. Washington, D.C.: American Enterprise Institute, 1983.

Lubell, Samuel. *Revolt of the Moderates*. New York: Harper & Brothers, 1956.

Lyon, Peter. *Eisenhower: Portrait of the Hero*. Boston: Little, Brown & Co., 1974.

McCloskey, Robert G. *The American Supreme Court*. Chicago: University of Chicago Press, 1960.

McCoy, Donald R. *The Presidency of Harry S. Truman*. Lawrence: University Press of Kansas, 1984.

Martin, John Bartlow. *Adlai Stevenson of Illinois*. Garden City, N.Y.: Anchor Books, 1977.

May, Gary. *China Scapegoat: The Diplomatic Ordeal of John Carter Vincent*. Washington, D.C.: New Republic Books, 1979.

Mazo, Earl, and Hess, Stephen. *Nixon: A Political Portrait*. New York: Harper & Row, 1968.

Miles, Michael W. *The Odyssey of the American Right*. New York: Oxford University Press, 1980.

Mitgang, Herbert. *Dangerous Dossiers: Exposing the Secret War against America's Greatest Authors*. New York: Donald I. Fine, 1988.

Murphy, Paul L. *The Constitution in Crisis Times, 1918–1969*. New York: Harper & Row, 1972.

Murphy, Walter F. *Congress and the Court: A Case Study in the American Political Process*. Chicago: University of Chicago Press, 1962.

O'Reilly, Kenneth. *Hoover and the Un-Americans: The FBI, HUAC, and the Red Menace*. Philadelphia: Temple University Press, 1983.

Oshinsky, David M. *A Conspiracy So Immense: The World of Joe McCarthy*. New York: Free Press, 1983.

Packer, Herbert L. *Ex-Communist Witnesses: Four Studies in Fact Finding*. Stanford, Calif.: Stanford University Press, 1962.

Parmet, Herbert S. *Eisenhower and the American Crusades*. New York: Macmillan, 1972.

————. *JFK: The Presidency of John F. Kennedy*. New York: Dial Press, 1983.

Paterson, Thomas G. *Meeting the Communist Threat: Truman to Reagan*. New York: Oxford University Press, 1988.

Patterson, James T. *Mr. Republican: A Biography of Robert A. Taft*. Boston: Houghton Mifflin Co., 1972.

Powers, Richard Gid. *Secrecy and Power: The Life of J. Edgar Hoover*. New York: Free Press, 1987.

Pritchett, C. Herman. *Congress versus the Supreme Court, 1957–1960*. Minneapolis: University of Minnesota Press, 1961.

Pusey, Merlo J. *Eisenhower: The President*. New York: Macmillan Co., 1956.

Radosh, Ronald. *Prophets on the Right: Profiles of Conservative Critics of American Globalism*. New York: Simon & Schuster, 1975.

Radosh, Ronald, and Milton, Joyce. *The Rosenberg File: A Search for the Truth*. New York: Vintage Books, 1983.

Rae, Nicol C. *The Decline and Fall of the Liberal Republicans from 1952 to the Present*. New York: Oxford University Press, 1989.

Reeves, Thomas C. *The Life and Times of Joe McCarthy: A Biography*. New York: Stein & Day, 1982.

Reichard, Gary W. *The Reaffirmation of Republicanism: Eisenhower and the Eighty-Third Congress*. Knoxville: University of Tennessee Press, 1975.

Reinhard, David D. *The Republican Right Since 1945*. Lexington: University of Kentucky Press, 1983.

Richardson, Elmo. *The Presidency of Dwight D. Eisenhower*. Lawrence: Regents Press of Kansas, 1979.

Rogin, Michael Paul. *The Intellectuals and McCarthy: The Radical Specter*. Cambridge, Mass.: MIT Press, 1967.

Rosenau, James N. *The Nomination of "Chip" Bohlen*. New York: Henry Holt & Co., 1958.

Rosenbloom, David H. *Federal Service and the Constitution: The Development of the Public Employment Relationship*. Ithaca, N.Y.: Cornell University Press, 1971.

Rovere, Richard H. *Senator Joe McCarthy*. New York: Harcourt, Brace & Co., 1959.

Ruddy, T. Michael. *The Cautious Diplomat: Charles E. Bohlen and the Soviet Union, 1929–1969*. Kent, Ohio: Kent State University Press, 1986.

Schlesinger, Arthur M., Jr. *The Cycles of American History*. Boston: Houghton Mifflin, 1986.

———. *The Imperial Presidency*. Boston: Houghton Mifflin, 1973.

Schlesinger, Arthur M., Jr., and Israel, Fred S., eds. *History of American Presidential Elections, 1789–1968*. 4 vols. New York: Chelsea House Publishers, 1971.

Schoenebaum, Eleanor, ed. *Political Profiles: The Eisenhower Years*. New York: Facts on File, 1977.

Schrecker, Ellen W. *No Ivory Towers: McCarthyism and the Universities*. New York: Oxford University Press, 1986.

Shannon, David A. *The Decline of American Communism: A History of the Communist Party Since 1945*. New York: Harcourt, Brace & Co., 1959.

Sievers, Rodney M. *The Last Puritan: Adlai Stevenson in American Politics*. Port Washington, N.Y.: Associated Faculty Press, 1983.

Smith, Harris R. *OSS: The Secret History of America's First Central Intelligence Agency*. Berkeley: University of California Press, 1972.

Smith, John Cabot. *Alger Hiss: The True Story*. New York: Holt, Rinehart & Winston, 1976.

Smith, Richard Norman. *Thomas E. Dewey and His Times*. New York: Simon & Schuster, 1982.

Starobin, Joseph R. *American Communism in Crisis, 1943–1957*. Cambridge, Mass.: Harvard University Press, 1972.

Steinberg, Peter L. *The Great "Red Menace": United States Prosecution of American Communists, 1947–1952*. Westport, Conn.: Greenwood Press, 1984.

Stern, Philip M. With Harold P. Green. *The Oppenheimer Case: Security on Trial*. New York: Harper & Row, 1969.

Stouffer, Samuel A. *Communism, Conformity, and Civil Liberties: A Cross-Section of the Nation Speaks Its Mind*. Garden City, N.Y.: Doubleday & Co., 1955.

Straight, Michael. *Trial by Television*. Boston: Beacon Press, 1954.

Theoharis, Athan G. *Seeds of Repression: Harry S. Truman and the Origins of McCarthyism*. Chicago: Quadrangle Books, 1971.

———. *Spying on Americans: Political Surveillance from Hoover to the Huston Plan*. Philadelphia: Temple University Press, 1978.

Theoharis, Athan G., and Cox, John Stuart. *The Boss: J. Edgar Hoover and the Great American Inquisition*. Philadelphia: Temple University Press, 1988.

Thompson, Francis H. *The Frustration of Politics: Truman, Congress, and the Loyalty Issue, 1945–1953*. Cranbury, N.J.: Associated University Presses, 1979.

Unger, Sanford J. *FBI*. Boston: Little, Brown & Co., 1976.

von Hoffman, Nicholas. *Citizen Cohn*. New York: Doubleday, 1988.

Weinstein, Allen. *Perjury: The Hiss-Chambers Case*. New York: Alfred A. Knopf, 1978.

White, Theodore H. *The Making of the President: 1960*. New York: Atheneum Publishers, 1961.

White, William S. *The Taft Story*. New York: Harper & Brothers, 1954.

Whitehead, Don. *The FBI Story: A Report to the People*. New York: Random House, 1956.

Wills, Garry. *Nixon Agonistes: The Crisis of a Self-Made Man*. Boston: Houghton Mifflin, 1969.

Zion, Sidney. *The Autobiography of Roy Cohn*. Secaucus, N.J.: Lyle Stuart, 1988.

Articles

Anderson, David L. "China Policy and Presidential Politics." *Presidential Studies Quarterly* 10 (Winter 1980): 79–90.

Bontecou, Eleanor. "President Eisenhower's 'Security' Program." *Bulletin of Atomic Scientists* 9 (July 1953): 215–17, 220.

Brands, W. H. "The Age of Vulnerability: Eisenhower and the National Insecurity State." *American Historical Review* 94 (October 1989): 963–89.

Crosby, Donald F. "The Politics of Religion: American Catholics and the Anti-Communist Impulse." In *The Spector: Original Essays on the Cold War and the Origins of McCarthyism*, edited by Robert Griffith and Athan Theoharis, pp. 18–38. New York: New Viewpoints, 1974.

Fedder, Edwin H. "United States Loyalty Procedures and the Recruitment of UN Personnel." *Western Political Quarterly* 15 (December 1962): 705–12.

Gaddis, John Lewis. "The Unexpected John Foster Dulles: Nuclear Weapons, Communism, and the Russians." In *John Foster Dulles and the Diplomacy of the Cold War*, edited by Richard H. Immerman, pp. 47–72. Princeton, N.J.: Princeton University Press, 1990.

Griffith, Robert. "Dwight D. Eisenhower and the Corporate Commonwealth." *American Historical Review* 87 (February 1982): 87–122.

———. "The General and the Senator: Republican Politics and the 1952 Campaign in Wisconsin." *Wisconsin Magazine of History* 54 (Autumn 1970): 23–29.

————. "The Politics of Anti-Communism: A Review Article." *Wisconsin Magazine of History* 54 (Summer 1971): 299–308.

————. "Ralph Flanders and the Censure of Joseph R. McCarthy." *Vermont History* 39 (Winter 1971): 5–20.

Immerman, Richard H. "Confessions of an Eisenhower Revisionist: An Agonizing Reappraisal." *Diplomatic History* 14 (Summer 1990): 319–42.

"Internal Security—Action in the Current Congress." *Congressional Digest* 160 (May 1954): 136–39.

Johnson, Robert N. "The Eisenhower Personnel Security Program." *Journal of Politics* 18 (November 1956): 625–50.

McAuliffe, Mary S. "Liberals and the Communist Control Act of 1954." *Journal of American History* 63 (September 1976): 351–67.

Markowitz, Norman D. "The McCarthy Phenomenon." *Reviews in American History* 5 (March 1977): 112–17.

Morgenthau, Hans J. "Impact of the Loyalty-Security Measures on the State Department." *Bulletin of Atomic Scientists* 11 (April 1955): 134–40.

Parrish, Michael E. "Cold War Justice: The Supreme Court and the Rosenbergs." *American Historical Review* 82 (October 1977): 805–42.

Pearse, Ben. "The Case of the Unexpected Senator." *Saturday Evening Post*, July 31, 1954, pp. 25, 65–68.

Ricks, John. "'Mr. Integrity' and McCarthyism: Robert A. Taft, Jr., and Joseph R. McCarthy." *Cincinnati Historical Society Bulletin* 37 (Fall 1979): 175–90.

Rovere, Richard H. "Boss of the White House." *Saturday Evening Post*, January 25, 1953, pp. 11, 38–40.

Russell, Bertrand. "Looking Backward to the 1950s." *New York Times Magazine*, April 26, 1953, pp. 12, 58.

Sitkoff, Harvard. "Years of the Locust: Interpretations of Truman's Presidency Since 1965." In *The Truman Period as a Research Field: A Reappraisal, 1972*, edited by Richard S. Kirkendall, pp. 75–112. Columbia: University of Missouri Press, 1974.

Strout, Cushing. "The Oppenheimer Case: Melodrama, Tragedy, and Irony." *Virginia Quarterly Review* 40 (Spring 1964): 268–80.

Theoharis, Athan. "The Rhetoric of Politics: Foreign Policy, Internal Security, and Domestic Politics in the Truman Era, 1945–1950." In *Politics and Policies of the Truman Administration*, edited by Barton J. Bernstein, pp. 196–241. Chicago: Quadrangle Books, 1970.

Unna, Warren W. "Dissension in the AEC." *Atlantic Monthly*, May 1957, p. 37.

Yarnell, Allen. "Eisenhower and McCarthy: An Appraisal of Presidential Strategy." *Presidential Studies Quarterly* 10 (Winter 1980): 90–98.

Unpublished Secondary Source

Purdam, Todd S. "The Politics of Security: The Eisenhower State Department and Scott McLeod." Senior thesis, Princeton University, 1982.

Index